Writing Religion

Writing Religion
The Case for the Critical Study of Religion

EDITED BY
Steven W. Ramey

The First Decade of Aronov Lecturers at
the University of Alabama

THE UNIVERSITY OF ALABAMA PRESS
Tuscaloosa

The University of Alabama Press
Tuscaloosa, Alabama 35487-0380
uapress.ua.edu

Inquiries about reproducing material from this work should be addressed to
the University of Alabama Press.

Typeface: Caslon

Manufactured in the United States of America
Cover design: Michele Myatt Quinn

∞

The paper on which this book is printed meets the minimum requirements of
American National Standard for Information Sciences—Permanence of Paper
for Printed Library Materials, ANSI Z39.48-1984.

Library of Congress Cataloging-in-Publication Data

Writing religion : the case for the critical study of religion / edited by Steven
W. Ramey.
    pages cm
  Includes bibliographical references and index.
  ISBN 978-0-8173-1872-7 (cloth : alk. paper) — ISBN 978-0-8173-
8838-6 (e book)
  1. Religions. I. Ramey, Steven Wesley, editor.
  BL74.W75 2015
  200—dc23
                                                              2015000667

For the private donors to the Department of Religious Studies and the people of the University of Alabama who came before us. Their generosity and forethought continue to enliven this department.

Contents

III. Righting the Discipline

Foreword

The Department of Religious Studies at the University of Alabama was established in 1965 under the directive to "avoid every tendency toward confusing the study of religion with the practice of religion."[1] This kind of a distinction had come into general awareness through the recent *Abington v. Schempp* decision, handed down by the US Supreme Court in 1963 (a remarkable year in the history of civil rights in the United States—and at the University of Alabama, too, for that matter). In their decision, the court ruled that by setting aside time at the beginning of the school day to read from the Bible, the Abington Township school district in Pennsylvania fundamentally violated the state's position of neutrality in matters of religion. Ironically, perhaps, the end of Bible reading in public schools also marked the beginning of the study of religion as an academic discipline in many state colleges and universities. Instruction *about*—rather than *in*—religion was deemed key to the purposes of higher education. Those promoting religious studies at Alabama, for example, argued this way: "The primary task of the University is the education of citizens in the self-knowledge and knowledge of the world which will help them to lead their society forward to greater realizations of individual and social well-being."[2] The study of religion offered one route toward gaining knowledge of the world—its many cultures and systems of beliefs. Within a few years, the Department of Religious Studies was firmly established at the university. It offered both a major and a minor and was comprised of four full-time professors including the College of Arts and Sciences' first African American professor, Dorsey Blake.

With emphases upon the varieties of cultures and the complexities of cultural identities, the Department of Religious Studies was deemed the logical place in which to investigate matters of diversity, multiculturalism, and ethnic identity. Thus in the mid-1980s, a campaign involving numerous people from around the state of Alabama elicited contributions from private citizens and received matching funds from the university and the state toward the establishment of an endowed chair in Judaic studies—the only one in the entire state at either a public or a private institution of higher learning. This position came into being in 1989 and since then has been called the Aaron Aronov Chair in Judaic Studies with reference to the prominent landowner and real estate developer from Montgomery, Alabama, whose vision guided the effort to secure the finances required to endow this distinguished post. Each occupant of the Aronov chair (including one of this foreword's coauthors, Steven Leonard Jacobs, who has held the chair since 2001) has contributed significantly to the work of the academy generally and to the field of Judaic studies—both specifically while at Alabama and also since leaving Tuscaloosa for other institutions (in the cases of the Aronov chairs prior to Jacobs).

The first holder of the Aronov chair, Richard Cohen, had studied with cultural theorists Emmanuel Levinas and Jacques Derrida at the Sorbonne in Paris. In addition to writing about Levinas, Cohen was (and remains) a prominent scholar of Franz Rosenzweig, the modern Jewish and existentialist philosopher of religion. Cohen characterized his responsibility as chair "to provide students with an opportunity to learn about Judaism as part of a university that offers multicultural perspectives."[3] After leaving Alabama, Cohen went to the University of North Carolina at Charlotte, becoming a distinguished professor in the Department of Religious Studies (1994–2008) before moving to his present position as professor of philosophy and the first director of the Institute of Jewish Thought and Heritage at the State University at Buffalo (2008–present). A prolific author, editor, and translator, two of Cohen's many books include *Levinasian Meditations: Ethics, Philosophy and Religion* and *Elevations: The Height of the Good in Rosenzweig and Levinas*, as well as more than seventy articles and book chapters covering the wide expanse of philosophy.

As part of Richard Cohen's duties as the first Aronov chair, he regularly invited scholars of national and international repute to the Tuscaloosa campus to deliver lectures primarily focused upon issues in contemporary Judaic studies, as well as the study of religion more broadly conceived. His successors as Aronov chair (described below), in collaboration with their departmental colleagues, continued the tradition of inviting key scholars to the University of Alabama campus to lead workshops and to deliver lectures. Then, in 2002, a single-lecture series was inaugurated by the department under the direction of Russell T. McCutcheon, then serving his first term as department chair, and Steven Leonard Jacobs, the current holder of the Aronov chair. The aim of the annual Aaron Aronov Memorial Lecture is to introduce to the University of Alabama community a nationally or internationally recognized scholar of religion who is capable of reflecting on issues of broad relevance to scholars from across the humanities and social science disciplines. This volume includes contributions from the first ten Aronov lecturers.

Gilya Gerda Schmidt succeeded Cohen as the Aronov chair, holding the position for one year (1993–94), after first having served as a postdoctoral fellow, research associate, and instructor in the Department of Religious Studies at Alabama. She then moved to the University of Tennessee and is today a professor of religious studies and the director of the Fern and Manfred Steinfeld Program in Judaic Studies. Her areas of concentration include European Jewry, gender and cross-cultural studies. Her books include *Suessen Is Now Free of Jews: World War II, the Holocaust, and Rural Judaism* and the Choice Award–winner *National Socialism and Gypsies in Austria*, among others, along with nearly forty book chapters and articles that range from the interest in Judaism within China to Martin Buber. For anyone in Judaic studies, the centrality of the Holocaust/Shoah as a primary focus of all post–World War II intellectual work continues to make Schmidt's work important and well respected all over the world.

From 1994 to 1997 the Aronov chair was empty until Barbara E. Galli occupied it. Galli left in 1999, when she returned to McGill University, from which she is now retired. Her primary focus has been the work of the significant modernist German-Jewish philosopher Franz Rosenzweig (1886–1929) whose own reconceptualization of Judaism remains the intellectual standard for all subsequent reinterpretations and understandings of Judaism. She has written or translated numerous books, including a translation of his magnum opus *The Star of Redemption* and *Franz Rosenzweig's "The New Thinking."*

In spring 2000, the department invited Ilona Rashkow to serve as Visiting Aronov Chair of Judaic Studies for one semester. Then she returned to her present position of associate professor of Judaic studies, women's studies and comparative literature at State University of New York at Stony Brook. Rashkow's primary research interests include psychoanalytic literary theory with a particular focus on the Hebrew Bible as well as ancient social and literary history and sociology. Her books include *Taboo or Not Taboo: The Hebrew Bible and Human Sexuality* and *Upon the Dark Places: Sexism and Anti-Semitism in English Renaissance Biblical Translation*, among others, and she has published numerous academic articles.

In 2001, Steven Leonard Jacobs, the current Aronov chair, returned to the University of Alabama to occupy this position, having been a visiting professor in the Department of Religious Studies from 1988–90. His own research interests have included the problematics of translations of the Hebrew Bible and the New Testament, Jewish-Christian relations, and the Holocaust and historical and contemporary genocides. To date, he has authored, edited, and/or translated twenty volumes including *Lemkin on Genocide, Confronting Genocide: Judaism, Christianity, and Islam, The Jewish Experience: An Introduction to Jewish History and Jewish Life*, and more than fifty articles and reviews in these fields.

On behalf of the Department of Religious Studies, it is our great pleasure to thank the authors for their contributions to our common life— both through the lectures delivered on campus and through these writings. With the assistance of those scholars who have served as Aronov chair, those who have presented the Aronov Lecture, and the visionaries who brought the Aaron Aronov Endowed Chair of Judaic Studies to the University of Alabama, these various successes we have achieved collectively present a consistent pattern of reaching beyond Tuscaloosa and across disciplinary boundaries to demonstrate the value of instruction *about* religion. We also want to express our gratitude to the University of Alabama Press for continuing this outreach, making these writings available to an extended audience through the medium of print.

Theodore Louis Trost
Department Chair (2009–13)

Steven Leonard Jacobs
Aronov Chair

Notes

1. Trawick, "Report on Academic Study of Religion," A1.
2. "Proposal by the University of Alabama to Danforth Foundation, July 12, 1965," 4.
3. R. Cohen, "Faculty Profile."

Acknowledgments

An edited volume like this requires the contributions of many individuals. My colleagues in the Department of Religious Studies at the University of Alabama, both staff and faculty, have been instrumental in shaping and producing this volume. The support and ideas of Theodore Louis Trost and Russell T. McCutcheon, who have served as department chairs since the inception of the annual Aronov Lecture, were especially instrumental, along with the support of Dean Robert Olin of the College of Arts and Sciences. Silverstein Fellows in the Department of Religious Studies, including Hannah Etchison, Tiffany Nguyen, Emily Vork, and Catie Stewart, have also provided assistance with the conversion of texts and references into a consistent format. The assistance of Betty Dickey in the Department of Religious Studies and the permissions staffs of the various presses has also been instrumental in the completion of this volume.

The best aspect of hosting a series such as the Aronov Lecture has been the opportunity to meet and work with distinguished scholars. Their graciousness as guests in Tuscaloosa, including the ways that they engaged both students and faculty outside the formal lectures, is much appreciated. These experiences have helped refine and further shape my own conception of the critical study of religion. The time that contributors have provided to revise these contributions, and in several cases to prepare previously unpublished materials, has enhanced the volume considerably. Only two Aronov lecturers from the first decade were unable to contribute actively to the volume, so their previously published pieces are included here without authorial revisions. Prior publication information and permissions are referenced in each essay as well as at the end of the acknowledgments.

The University of Alabama Press, particularly my editor Dan Waterman and the copyediting, typesetting, permissions, and marketing staffs, have provided much valuable assistance in seeing this volume through publication. The comments of the two anonymous peer reviewers further improved the text, and their generous recognition of the broader value of this collection was particularly heartening.

Any work not only requires the contributions of these (and other) direct contributors but also builds on the work of so many others whose analyses provided a foundation on which each of the Aronov lecturers built. My hope is that this volume honors the contributions of all of those who have come before by enabling other scholars to build further on the critical study of religion.

Jonathan Z. Smith's "God Save This Honorable Court: Religion and Civic Discourse" was published originally, with the same title, in his volume *Relating Religion: Essays in the Study of Religion*, © 2004 by the Unviersity of Chicago, and is republished here (with minor editorial revisions) with permission of the University of Chicago Press and the author.

Bruce Lincoln's "An Early Moment in the Discourse of 'Terrorism:' Reflections on a Tale from Marco Polo" was published originally, with the same title, in *Comparative Studies in Society and History*, © 2006 by the Society for Comparative Study of Society and History. Reprinted here (with minor editorial revisions) with the permission of Cambridge University Press.

Ann Pellegrini's "'A Storm on the Horizon': Discomforting Democracy and the Feeling of Fairness" is a revised version of an essay published in *Secular Discomforts: Religion and Cultural Studies*, a special issue of *Cultural Studies Review*.

Arjun Appadurai's "Fear of Small Numbers" was originally published as chapter 4 in his volume *Fear of Small Numbers*, © 2006, Duke University Press. All rights reserved. Republished here (with minor editorial revisions) by permission of the copyright holder. www.dukeupress.edu.

Nathan Katz's "Religious Practices and Communal Identity of Cochin Jews: Models, Metaphors, and Methods of Diasporic Religious Acculturation" is a revised version of the article "Understanding Religion in Diaspora: The Case of the Jews in Cochin" originally published in *Religious Studies and Theology*. It is published here (with minor editorial revisions) with permission of the copyright holder Equinox Publishing, Ltd.

Tomoko Masuzawa's "Regarding Origin: Beginnings, Foundations, and the Bicameral Formation of the Study of Religion" is a revised version of her essay "Origins" in *The Guide to the Study of Religion*. It is reprinted with the permission of the publisher, Bloomsbury Publishing Plc.

Amy-Jill Levine's "De-Judaizing Jesus: Theological Need and Exegetical Execution" is a revised version of her article "Theory, Apologetic, History: Reviewing Jesus' Jewish Context," which was originally published in *Australian Biblical Review* and is used with permission of the journal.

A portion of Aaron W. Hughes's "How to Theorize with a Hammer, or, On the Destruction and Reconstruction of Islamic Studies" reflects Hughes's reworking of "The Scholarly Dream of Following Muhammad's Footsteps," chapter 1 in Hughes's *Theorizing Islam: Disciplinary Deconstruction and Reconstruction* (London: Acumen, 2012).

Martin Jaffee's "Personal Self-Disclosure, Religious Studies Pedagogy, and the Skeptical Mission of the Public University" originally appeared in *Bulletin of the Council of Societies for the Study of Religion* and is reprinted here (with minor editorial revisions) with permission of Equinox Publishing, Ltd.

A portion of Russell T. McCutcheon's afterword, "Reinventing the Study of Religion in Alabama," originally appeared in an earlier form under the same title in the *Bulletin of the Council of Societies for the Study of Religion.*

Writing Religion

Introduction

Writing, Riting, and Righting in the Critical Study of Religion

Steven W. Ramey

A charismatic leader in Myanmar who identifies as a Buddhist monk encourages violent attacks against those who identify as Muslim.[1] Self-identified Hindu and Satanist organizations apply to place privately funded monuments alongside the Ten Commandments on the grounds of the Oklahoma statehouse.[2] Men who identify as Khalsa Sikhs have often asserted their right to wear a turban rather than a uniform headcovering because they consider the turban a religious requirement.[3] Media frequently write about a range of conflicts and social issues that they connect with the category "religion." As these contests involve competing groups and interests, extending well beyond debates about texts or philosophies, the critical study of religion supports the analysis of such complex issues, thus increasing the contemporary relevance of the academic study of religion.

Critical study does not assume that writing the word "religion" requires special treatment of the subject but applies critical analysis to the use of the label "religion" as well as other aspects of society. Writing "religion" places any author within a series of contentious debates in popular discourse. Beyond disagreements among some adherents about which collection of conceptions and practices is superior, the term can set aside an activity or conception for revered and protected social and legal status, most notably in the contests over freedom of religion. Some people employ the term to designate an aspect of human existence that is inherently good, helping humans reach their highest potential. For others, describing something as religious places it in a problematic category, premodern, irrational, even dangerous (if opposed to science) or rote, institutional, unthinking (if opposed to spirituality).

Within scholarship, the category raises similar disputes. Throughout the shifting trends over several centuries in what we now call the academic study of religion, the critical aspect of that study has served a variety of ends and has faced, and continues to face, significant opposition.[4]

For some scholars, religion designates something sui generis that is unique and cannot be reduced to other factors. Others have employed methods of analysis associated with other elements of society or have focused on the formation of the category and the ends that it serves. This volume provides examples of leading scholars presenting different approaches to critical study that demonstrate its importance as an expression of respect for the agency of people and communities studied and the usefulness of its analysis. Critical study does not reflect a narrow approach but addresses, in a variety of ways, the challenges that writing "religion" entails.

Critical Study and the History of the Field

Scholars debate the origins of the study of religion, with some tracing aspects of the field to Max Müller or European universities and others emphasizing earlier forms in ancient Greece, India, China, and other parts of the world.[5] Wherever a scholar locates the antecedents to the discipline, many of these antecedents derive from philosophical and theological assertions within particular textual and interpretive communities. In the nineteenth century, an opposing trend challenging theological and institutional assertions arose with figures such as Karl Marx (introduction to *A Contribution to the Critique of Hegel's Philosophy of Right*, published in 1844) and Julius Wellhausen (*Prolegomena zur Geschichte Israels*, published in 1883), among others. Such works generated a tension that continues today between those defining religion as having a sacred reality that limits inquiry and those who make no methodological distinction between elements that people have labeled religious and other aspects of human existence.

One commonly highlighted turning point in the field was the development of Max Müller's philological study of texts deemed sacred in other parts of the world. His work provides one example of a shift away from apologetics and overtly theological pursuits, which often emphasized particular assumptions identified with Christianity, to an emphasis on the commonality of practices in different areas of the world. The tensions became a competition between those who saw religion generally as universal and positive, such as William James and Rudolph Otto, and those who understood religion as a social formation, a tool for social cohesion or repression, such as Emile Durkheim and Sigmund Freud.

In the middle of the twentieth century, various developments around the world influenced the field. The US Supreme Court decision in *Abington Township v. Schempp* (1963) is one of a number of important church/

state rulings from this time period. *Schempp* distinguished between teaching about religion, which the court deemed constitutional, and teaching religion, which it prohibited. While some public universities in the United States already had departments emphasizing religious studies prior to this ruling, their numbers quickly increased after the clear assertion of the legality of teaching about religion in public institutions, thus expanding the field with less overtly apologetic emphases.

The legal precedent of *Schempp* and the growth of religious studies programs that followed combined with a growing interest in cultures and conceptions from other parts of the world, in part developing out of US intervention in Vietnam and other parts of Asia. The rise of the Cold War also increased interest in, and at times funding for, the positive study of a broad conception of religion to heighten the contrast between the United States and atheistic Communism.[6] These various historical developments contributed to the significant growth in the academic study of religion. The result, however, was not primarily critical study but an ecumenical approach that emphasized the positive within a range of practices and texts and thus promoted particular ideological interests rather than assuming the primacy of Christianity.[7]

In this context, a particular construction of the academic study of religion known as phenomenology of religion, which differs considerably from phenomenology in philosophical discourse, became especially prominent in the United States.[8] The ostensibly objective method, advocating the bracketing of the researcher's assumptions and the practice of *epoche*, enabled scholars to assert a scientific approach that avoided promoting a particular collection of practices and conceptions while also maintaining the uniqueness of their object of study. A major figure of the field, Mircea Eliade, assumed a commonality in this unique component of human interaction that he labeled religion, even suggesting its necessity for human thriving.

Critiques of Eliade reveal some of the identity crises within the field, as scholars have highlighted the ideological assumptions within his conceptions. Scholarly debate continues between those viewing religion as tangible phenomena that are irreducible and those who critique the conception that religion is sui generis. Even when Eliade's method is not taken up publicly in contemporary academic discourse, some critics detect his continuing influence in the field, including newer approaches that primarily emphasize description and the avoidance of critical analysis.[9]

Developments within the broader academy have contributed to these ongoing debates. The postcolonial critiques of Eurocentric and Christian-centric studies of colonized communities began to be developed and published in this period of expansion following *Schempp*. These studies raised in new ways the issues of ethics and voice in the construction of knowledge, asking whose voice was excluded and whose conceptions were presented, and thus validated.[10] Similarly, postmodern critiques of language and discourse challenged the assumptions about the historicity of the terms that created the field.

The Critical Study of Religion

This narrative that I have constructed emphasizes some of the diversity within the field that generates tensions over appropriate methods.[11] Even among those who do not see themselves as doing theology, the intersection of postcolonial and postmodern theory with these debates within religious studies proceeded on at least two diverging trajectories. Drawing on the question of power in the production of knowledge and the emphasis on the subaltern, some scholars have critiqued critical studies in a manner that differs from the antireductionist, sui generis stance.[12] Rather than setting religion apart as sui generis, this approach, sometimes termed the study of lived religion, emphasizes respecting everyday practitioners and their constructions and describing sympathetically their construction of their world.[13] Combining an aspect of the postcolonial critique of the construction of knowledge with the concept of *epoche* within the phenomenology of religion, these scholars emphasize describing the assertions of the people they study, as opposed to analyzing them. If the people studied understand their practices in religious language (or language that the scholar identifies as religious), then they are obviously religious. Similarly, if the practitioners understand their community in positive terms, the academic representation is also positive.

The acceptance of practitioner statements, however, is selective. Lived religion scholars, as some have noted themselves, seldom accept without qualification the statements of participants in physically violent movements or activities that these scholars consider unacceptable, such as attacks on minorities in Myanmar.[14] The respect for practitioner statements also does not extend to most politicians, especially if their ideology differs from the scholar's. Accepting the statements of practitioners uncritically also overlooks the multiple motivations of those who claim that yoga or a nativity scene is religious (and thus not allowed in particular public institutions) or apply terms like "faith" and "sacred" to the idea that "copying of information is ethically right" to fight antipiracy laws.[15]

The other trajectory develops concepts from postcolonial and post-modern theory differently and enables broader analysis of the uses of the category of religion. Noting that colonizers often imposed the category of religion during their interaction with communities around the world, a number of scholars have analyzed the implications of power within the ways the study of religion has constructed and defined its subject, even as some within colonized communities have adopted the category. Others have analyzed the ways that language promotes ideological positions within the representation of elements described as religious, by scholars, practitioners, and opponents throughout the globe.

The critical study of religion (as described in this volume) interrogates the power inequities in an effort to establish clearly defined boundaries, whether explicit or implicit. Thus, practitioner statements that assert a proper means of following a religion become a topic for critical inquiry. Similarly, scholarly assertions, including the implicit ideas within much of the world religions paradigm, that promote one understanding of a religion over others become objects of study as they impose particular ideologies in the guise of descriptions. Implicit assertions that Sikhs should wear turbans, Buddhists should be nonviolent, or Ahmadiyya and Mormons are outside the mainstream of Islam and Christianity respectively reflect acts of power that need further critical analysis.

This contrast between the two trajectories, of course, is somewhat contrived. Many scholars who attempt to study religion "on its own terms" provide varying degrees of analysis of the statements of practitioners. Similarly, some whose research assumes the constructed and historical nature of a range of categories accept the assertions of some practitioners, and even the existence of particular categories, uncritically. Nevertheless, constructing a distinction between descriptive, sympathetic study and critical study highlights a significant spectrum of differences within the academic study of religion. Critical study as demonstrated in this volume neither describes the variety of expressions commonly labeled religious nor assumes that religion expresses the pinnacle of human existence. Critical study also does not endeavor to eliminate aspects of society or disabuse students and readers of "misguided" commitments.

Critical study, then, emphasizes the analysis of assertions and classifications. The essays in this volume focus on analyzing assumptions and motivations within the discourses that individuals employ, within the societies in which communities operate, and within the field of religious studies itself. Out of respect for the ability of anyone to represent themselves and their communities in the ways that they desire to be seen, scholars employing critical study analyze the assertions of those whom they study in various ways, including the power relations and interests that influence these assertions. Such an approach extends beyond practitioners to include the assertions of scholars as well as other figures involved in constructing representations of the elements that people commonly, or someone particularly, identify as religion.

Analyses that I label critical study of religion employ a variety of approaches and theoretical assumptions, but they are not based on a stringent commitment to any single theorist. Scholars who write critical analyses, including those represented here, often use a multitude of theorists, including theorists outside the academic study of religion. Such interdisciplinarity illustrates the assertion that elements labeled religious do not require a unique approach. The essays from Aronov lecturers collected in this volume illustrate clearly that critical study is not a narrow approach.

In the analysis of the formation of various categories, including religion, critical study generally recognizes those categories as social constructions. Such recognition is not a normative statement about conceptions of the cosmos but recognizes the historically constructed nature of the category itself and the various social formations that people identify as religion. However, critical study does not require scholars to avoid the category "religion" completely, as some scholars advocate.[16] While challenging assumptions such as the transhistorical nature of the category "religion" is an aspect of critical study, the category has analytical value because people actively employ the category, and the essays that follow, while illustrating critical study, generally do not refrain from using the term. The category is not simply the property of scholars to maintain or reject.[17]

The approaches that this volume advocates extend into issues related to history, performance studies, ethnicity, gender, and anthropology, to name a few. Some of the lecturers, in fact, work in other disciplines and reflect the interdisciplinarity of the critical study of ideologies more generally.[18] The diverse essays in this volume demonstrate the ethical basis, benefits, and relevance of critical study that extend beyond issues commonly labeled religious.

Equality and Power in Critical Study

Two central, and sometimes related, ethical criticisms of critical study arise within the narrative of the field that I have constructed. The older critique, that critical approaches erroneously reduce religion (assumed by the older critique to be sui generis) to other factors of society, is less salient with the development of postcolonial thought and the acknowledgment, at least by many, that the concept religion is socially constructed and historically contingent rather than universally present.[19] The second ethical critique concerns the power differential between the researcher and the research subject.

Although being respectful of the research subject is important, refraining from critical analysis is not respect. Even when scholars attempt to give voice to the assertions of the subaltern or the everyday practitioner, the scholars retain the ultimate power to select what elements deserve attention. Considering the current critique of the universality of the category of religion, accepting a practitioner's assertion that a practice is religious cloaks the ideological work that the category is doing for the practitioner and/or the researcher. Analyzing the assumptions inherent in society and the ideological positions that people construct more fully respects the research subject's ability to represent elements strategically.[20] Assuming that a research subject simply tells the researcher everything without self-censoring treats the research subject as intellectually simple. In fact, most people at almost any age shift their self-presentations depending on their audience. Giving voice to someone's ideas does not challenge the status quo and power structures. Thus an initial inquiry into the interests and ideologies informing research subjects' self-presentations is an aspect of critical study.

Scholars who reject critical analysis of practitioner statements generally employ that approach with those they consider to be lacking power, the subaltern, the common participant, or perhaps the leader of a community in another place. Few, in my experience, refrain from analyzing the assertions of people they see as powerful, as Jonathan Z. Smith does in his analysis of the justices of the US Supreme Court. Smith highlights various assertions that the justices presumed to be obvious but that can be construed very differently (chapter 1). Similarly, the analysis of the social dynamics that lead some majority communities to attack minorities, as Arjun Appadurai presents in chapter 4, would be generally acceptable. Critical study applies similar critiques to the assertions of any research subject. When the assertions of certain groups are set aside as beyond analysis, this well-intentioned move reinscribes on those participants their subordinate, marginal status.

Critical study, then, emphasizes efforts to manage relationships and representations, recognizing that neither practices nor representations are fixed elements. Nathan Katz's ethnography of minority Jewish communities in Cochin, India, (chapter 6) does not criticize their creation of community practices but acknowledges their agency in constructing a tradition within a particular context. Applying critical study to historical texts and noting the historical shifts in representations, as in Bruce Lincoln's analysis of descriptions of the "Assassins" in texts from Marco Polo and others (chapter 2), similarly highlight the ways that historical and contemporary sources construct images according to the needs of the moment. Critical study also highlights the ways other scholars construct their own accounts, sometimes to avoid destabilizing particular presumptions (as Tomoko Masuzawa illustrates in chapter 7 in her analysis of discussions of origins within the history of the field), sometimes to validate the value of particular communities (as in Aaron Hughes's chapter 9 critique of the preference for one understanding of Islam within Islamic studies), and sometimes to distance one community from another (as in Amy-Jill Levine's chapter 8 analysis of academic efforts to separate Jesus from Judaism).

Whether a scholar focuses on everyday practitioners or scholars, institutional leaders or public figures, contemporary communities or individuals from earlier centuries, critical study emphasizes everyone's ability to shift their representations and practices. This approach moves the focus of research away from constructing a better description to analyzing the varied interests, whether oriented toward economics, power, social positioning, or philosophical pronouncements, among others, that inform those communities and their representations. Such an approach is ethical, not only recognizing the capabilities of all participants but also applying the critique of the relationship of power and knowledge that the postcolonial and postmodern turns in theory have emphasized.

The Benefits of the Critical Study of Religion

Through this analysis of representations and the underlying ideologies that often go unchallenged, scholars employing critical study can address power inequalities and uneven access to resources that some raising ethical concerns about voice presumably want to address. Analyzing the interests that generate particular representations highlights the underlying ideologies that involve both a variety of interests and significant assumptions about human society. Questioning the constructed nature of categories like religion or the existence of particular identities creates an opening, a mental space, that enables scholars and readers to develop alternative conceptions and new ideas. The ability to recognize social structures and then innovate or imagine alternative constructions is a significant benefit of these approaches to the academic study of religion.

Such analysis of ideological assumptions can highlight underlying, hidden sources of inequality in society, thereby empowering change. Assertions of feeling and fairness in public discourse sometimes serve to reinforce the marginalization of particular communities. Ann Pellegrini in her analysis of recent controversies surrounding communities in the United States identified as Muslim (chapter 3) demonstrates that critical analysis can generate new reflections on what is required for democracy to succeed. Critical analysis of inequality can generate a different type of reflection, as Judith Plaskow outlines in her description of the power of a "critical consciousness" in the formation of feminist studies (chapter 5).

Such critiques and the innovative ideas that they encourage also need to address ideology and power within scholarship. Research that uncovers various assumptions within the field (Katz's critique of models of diaspora in chapter 6, Levine's analysis of studies of Jesus in chapter 8, and Hughes's analysis of Islamic studies in chapter 9) illustrates particular problems inherent in scholarship that marginalize some communities while validating others. Such studies provide benefits for improving the field and the representations that scholars produce, alongside the benefits of critical study within feminist studies and discussions of democracy.

Yet, critical study also extends beyond an effort to replace one particular ideology with another. Too often, scholarship in religious studies, including pedagogy, serves to challenge assumptions in order to replace them with assumptions that scholars deem preferable, such as generating appreciation of other religions in order to replace exclusivist commitments with pluralist ideals. Fully enacting critical study should encourage people to question a range of ideologies and assumptions, their own, those of the authors they read, those of politicians, and those of professors. Martin Jaffee's assertions (chapter 10) illustrate one way of exhibiting this critical study within the classroom to challenge students of any persuasion to question their own preconceived notions, not to replace them with something predetermined but to encourage critical thought.

Broader Relevance of the Critical Study of Religion

While many of the benefits of critical study relate to the academic discipline, including the contributions of Masuzawa, Hughes, Levine, and Jaffee in this volume, critical study has relevance for those uninterested in the disputes and methodologies within the discipline. Through the analysis of the assumptions and ideologies functioning throughout society, critical study can address an expanded audience, including those who are not oriented to ecumenism or liberal Protestantism or the intricacies of rituals or authoritative texts.

Critical study can expose particular aspects of the formation of society and general practices. Bruce Lincoln's analysis of medieval accounts of the "Assassins" (chapter 2) does not construct a better image of those assumed to be in that community but illustrates the ways narratives shift to address particular issues within the presenter's immediate context. Lincoln, then, relates his analysis to the category of "terrorist" in contemporary society. Similarly, Appadurai's essay (chapter 4) analyzes the ways relations between majorities and minorities can generate dehumanization and violence. Katz's essay focusing on Jews in Cochin adapting to the larger society (chapter 6) also highlights both the power of dominant models of social formation and the issues that minority communities face, whether they form their group around a religious, ethnic, national, or other identification. While Plaskow's examples focus largely on issues of gender within communities commonly understood as religious (chapter 5), the value of "critical consciousness" and an approach that reveals systemic inequality is not limited to communities identified as religious or issues related to gender.

Critical study also intersects directly with legal and political controversies. Smith's analysis of Supreme Court decisions (chapter 1) is as much about the power of discourse to construct general assumptions and influence court rulings as it is about what we commonly term religion. Democracy and the political and social philosophy supporting it are central to Pellegrini's analysis of contemporary controversies in the United States much more than particularities surrounding mosque construction and anti-Shariah laws (chapter 3).

With these examples, the critical study of religion enacts a rejection of the distinctiveness of the category "religion" and any subsequent separation from other aspects of human society. This interdisciplinary nature of the critical study of religion enables a fuller analysis of a range of contemporary expressions and conflicts commonly associated with "religion," as these conflicts and expressions involve a range of interests and ideologies well beyond what is commonly defined as religion. These approaches expand the relevance of the field and analyze the connections enveloping elements that people identify as religious and nonreligious.

The Structure of This Volume

Although the critical study of religion remains contested, the following essays illustrate how critical study produces a range of intriguing and relevant analyses when applied to practices and conceptions commonly understood to relate to religion. While this volume celebrates ten years of Aronov lecturers and the variations on critical study that the lecturers demonstrate, the following essays are not transcripts of the lectures that they gave at the University of Alabama. Rather, they reflect significant examples of each lecturer's work that demonstrates this critical study in its varied forms. Some of the essays are revised versions of the actual lecture, including the contributions of Smith, Pellegrini, Plaskow, Katz, Hughes, and Jaffee. The others are drawn from other work by the lecturer.

The volume could be organized in many ways, as the preceding pages demonstrate. I have organized these essays thematically, according to three, somewhat arbitrary sections illustrating three general types of critique that arise within the critical study of religion. These sections are arbitrary in the sense that each essay could fit two or three of these divisions, and certainly other divisions are possible.

Since organizing is necessary, a word of explanation about the themes may help. The first section, "Writing Discourses," includes three essays that illustrate ways that critical study enables the analysis of discourses in society and history. First, Smith analyzes the discourse that Supreme Court majority opinions develop in cases defining the separation of church and state. Second, Lincoln compares the shifting representations of "Assassins" in medieval European literature, particularly the shifts in Marco Polo's representations, and the ways those shifts intersect with different discursive interests. Third, Pellegrini critiques the discourse that surrounds both democracy and particular controversies related to minority rights in a democracy, noting contradictions between the two democratic discourses. Of course, writing an analysis of discourses also involves each author constructing or writing their own discourse.

"Riting Social Formations," the title of the second section, refers to both the power of rites to construct society and the act of "riting" as a form of disciplining or controlling action (as in rites that both prescribe and proscribe actions). Appadurai analyzes the proscribed and prescribed factors in the construction of majorities over minorities, whom the majorities come to fear, and the ways that understanding those constructions can assist in addressing potentially violent social relations. Plaskow addresses the ways feminist consciousness, as a "critical consciousness," critiques both rites and textual interpretations within some communities and works to discipline those rites and interpretations to foster gender equality. Katz discusses the rites that the Jews of Cochin developed within the context of a Hindu majority area. He argues that conceptions of diaspora, with prescribed notions of the ways communities develop, fail to acknowledge

and legitimize their rites and decisions. Thus, critical study, while analyzing ideological positions and their promotion of power, can also advocate a change or adjustment in society.

The third section, "Righting the Discipline," emphasizes the correction
of movements within the academic study of religion, in essence disciplining the discipline. Masuzawa provides a broad historical analysis of particular attitudes toward origins within the field and the ways that competing assumptions about origins relate to ongoing divisions. Levine critiques
particular movements within the study of the person of Jesus that subtly,
and not so subtly, distance Jesus from one understanding of Judaism, suggesting that such moves reflect contemporary threads of anti-Semitism.
Hughes concludes his analysis of the apologetic nature of much of Islamic
studies with suggestions—in fact, ten theses—for creating a new Islamic
studies. The final essay in this section presents the text of the first Aronov
Lecture, in which Jaffee argued for the value of self-disclosure, in its often conflicted and shifting nature, to challenge the assumptions of a range
of students, not just those who either reject the value of what they identify as religion or maintain a strong commitment to those elements. In this
final essay, the value of critical study to challenge a wide range of assumptions and ideological positions, thus enabling critical analysis and creative
and innovative thought, is apparent. Whatever form of critical study that
a scholar employs when writing religion, it can produce analysis of significant relevance to both the academy and the broader society.

Notes

1. Beech, "The Face of Buddhist Terror."
2. Horton, "Hindu Group Wants Monument."
3. Sinha, "Irish Court Sikhs Can't Wear Turban."
4. Bruce Lincoln asserts that the minority of scholars who employ critical
approaches often face opposition from others who "remain committed to a validating, feel-good perspective, and do not welcome interventions that disrupt the
serene, benign, and eirenic ethos they have fostered," *Gods and Demons*, 135.
5. King, "Copernican Turn," 147.
6. Arnal and McCutcheon, *Sacred Is the Profane*, 72–90.
7. Lincoln, *Gods and Demons*, 133–34.
8. Penner, *Impasse and Resolution*, 50–51.
9. Many of the essays in Bryan Rennie's edited volume *Changing Religious
Worlds* reference the ongoing influence of Eliade's approach, including those who
criticize this influence and those defending it.
10. See, for example, Asad, *Genealogies of Religion*.

11. Other scholars emphasizing critical study have constructed narratives of the history of the field that reach similar conclusions. See, for example, Lincoln, *Gods and Demons*, 131–36; and Arnal and McCutcheon, *Sacred Is the Profane*, 72–90.

12. Orsi, "Everyday Miracles," 7.

13. See, for example, Gunn, "'On Thursdays We Worship,'" 46. Dialogue, in Gunn's description, which draws on Bakhtin, creates an impression of attempting to understand the subject's position sympathetically. For a more general example of the lived religion approach, see McGuire, *Lived Religion*.

14. McGuire, *Lived Religion*, 91, 118; Orsi, *Between Heaven and Earth*.

15. First Church of Kopimism for the USA, "What Is Kopimism?"

16. For one example of an assertion that the critical study of religion emphasizes critiquing the category of religion, see Fitzgerald, *Discourse on Civility and Barbarity*, 5–6. For arguments concerning the avoidance of the term "religion," see Fitzgerald, *Ideology of Religions Studies*, and Dubuisson, *Western Construction of Religion*.

17. Schilbrack has defended the analytical usefulness of the term "religion" in a manner that has similarities to what I am arguing. See, for example, "Social Construction of 'Religion,'" 97–117.

18. For example, Arjun Appadurai holds a position in a Department of Media, Culture, and Communication, and Tomoko Masuzawa holds affiliations with Departments of Comparative Literature and History. Ann Pellegrini holds a dual appointment in performance studies and religious studies.

19. The instability of the term within European Christian contexts further illustrates the problem of assuming its universality. See, for example, Smith, "Religion, Religions, Religious."

20. I have argued for this assertion more fully in "When Acceptance Reflects Disrespect."

I
Writing Discourses

1

God Save This Honorable Court

Religion and Civic Discourse

Jonathan Z. Smith

Jonathan Z. Smith visited the University of Alabama as the second
Aronov lecturer. On September 23, 2003, he presented a version of the
following essay.

My friend and sometime colleague Professor William Scott Green at
the University of Rochester has established, with epigrammatic precision,
the contours of this essay when he observed that the study of religion is
the only humanistic field in the American academy whose subject matter
is explicitly governed by the US Constitution. On another occasion, ar-
ticulating one aspect of the commonsense sort of distinction between religion and the study of religion, Green noted, with no small bitterness, that
in preparation for Easter news reporters always contact the local bishop
to inquire about the significance of the holiday, while they call the local
college's Department of Religion to find out why there are Easter bun-
nies and Easter eggs. The first observation suggests the gravity of the enterprise, the second, its simultaneous marginalization. Whatever religion
"is," its definition seems to be thought to lie with others—with courts and
practitioners—and not with the academic field charged with its study. This
odd displacement is only encouraged when scholars of religion at times
assume the stance that their subject matter is by nature undefinable. But
this latter is not the issue of this essay.[1] Rather, I wish to look at the consequences of some legal understandings of religion from the point of view
of a student of religion.

Let me begin with some items many will have encountered on the
instructions for filing Internal Revenue Service schedule SE, the form
for figuring self-employment Social Security tax. Nearly three-quarters
of the instruction page is taken up with matters organized under headings
such as "Employees of Churches and Church Organizations," "Ministers
and Members of Religious Orders," and "Members of Certain Religious

Sects." The second of these topics contains a new provision from the 2000 tax law: "If you are a minister, a member of a religious order not under a vow of poverty, or a Christian Science practitioner who previously elected exemption from social security coverage and self-employment tax, you can now revoke that exemption." The section called "Members of Certain Religious Sects" begins: "If you have conscientious objections to social security insurance because of your membership in and belief in the teachings of a religious sect recognized as being in existence at all times since December 31, 1950, and which has provided a reasonable level of living for its dependent members, you are exempt from SE [self-employment] tax if you received IRS approval by filing *Form 4029*."[2] The Internal Revenue Service is, both de facto and de jure, America's primary definer and classifier of religion. It reproduces the imperial Roman government's efforts at distinguishing licit and illicit religions as subtypes of a wider legal concern for distinctions between licit and illicit associations.

How does the Internal Revenue Service fulfill these defining and classifying functions? We see this most clearly in the regulations governing the tax-exempt status of religious organizations in section 50l(c)(3) of the Internal Revenue Code, a subset of provisions for the larger tax-exempt category of "nonprofit" organizations. (The same criteria likewise govern the tax-deductible status of contributions to such organizations [section 170]). The main criterion is that a religious organization "must be organized and operated exclusively for religious purposes," with exclusivity and purpose specified in the same general terms that apply to all tax-exempt organizations: no individual financial benefit and no substantial political lobbying or participation in political campaigns. However, there is one important difference. All other sorts of tax-exempt groups file annually both a statement of activities and an informational tax return; however, "churches, their integrated activities, and conventions or associations of churches, and organizations claiming to be churches" do not have to submit these documents. In Department of the Treasury Regulation 1.511-2(a)(3)(ii), "church" for the purpose of this rule, is defined as the following: "The term 'church' includes a religious order or a religious organization if such order or organization is (a) an internal part of a church, and (b) is engaged in carrying out the functions of a church." The regulation continues but scarcely clarifies: "A religious order or organization shall be considered to be engaged in carrying out the functions of a church if its duties include the ministration of sacerdotal functions and the conduct of religious worship. What constitutes the conduct of religious worship or the ministration of sacerdotal functions depends on the tenets and practices of a particular religious body constituting a church."[3]

In this passage, as elsewhere in government documents, legal discourse appears to stammer in a setting that, at least putatively, recognizes religious pluralism and remains antiestablishmentarian. At first glance, what we read appears to be a set of tautologies masked as definitions in violation of the first rule of lexicography, "a word may not be defined in terms of itself." Surely, it is singularly uninformative to assert with the Internal Revenue Service that a religious organization must be organized for religious purposes or that a church must be a part of a church or engaged in carrying out the functions of a church! The circularity of these definitions suggests, at the practical level, that the Internal Revenue Service is reluctant, in most cases, to adjudicate the claims of religious organizations, except those it judges to be extraordinarily or patently fraudulent (for example, mail-order ministries such as the Universal Life Church founded in 1962).

For the student of religion, something more fundamental is at work: a notion of self-evidence derived from using lay understandings of varied forms of Christianities to serve as what cognitive scientists term a "prototype." A prototype functions in classification by providing an image of a commonplace example that then serves as an ideal or typical exemplar of a category with decisions as to whether another object is a member of the same category being based on matching it against features of the prototype (for example, employing a robin as the prototype for "bird"). While matters are no longer quite so blunt as Justice Gilbert's statement, writing for the Georgia Supreme Court in 1922 in *Wilkerson v. Rome*, that "Christianity is the only religion known to American law," or Thomas MacIntyre Cooley's observation in his influential handbook on constitutional law, "The Christian religion was always recognized in the administration of the common law,"[4] the unproblematized use in tax law of terms such as "church," "sect," "religious organization," "religious orders," "ministers," "sacerdotal," and so forth suggests that the features of other religions are routinely being matched against some Christian prototype.

Matters are more complex at the level of the US Supreme Court, which will be my focus for the remainder of this essay—not on the court as the ultimate authority on the US Constitution, most especially the First Amendment's negative guarantee with respect to religion and Article VI's prohibition of religious tests as a qualification for federal office (initially designed to protect Christians from Christians), but rather on the court as the legally authorized interpreter of religion. For this reason I shall draw, in what follows, on the opening narrative statements as to the facts of the case in the majority's decision rather than on the legal reasonings of the decision itself.

For the Supreme Court, classification by prototype continues to be common. Let me give as an example the 1993 case of the *Church of the Lukumi Babalu Aye, Inc., and Ernesto Pichado v. City of Hialeah.*[5] This is a case that should never have come before the court but rather should have been settled in the lower courts in the petitioner's favor. The issue was one of "free exercise," a matter less frequently litigated than "establishment" cases before the court. A Cuban American Santeria church leased property and planned to construct a religious complex in which, among other things, animal sacrifice would be performed. The Hialeah City Council subsequently issued a set of resolutions prohibiting animal sacrifice and the possession of animals intended for ritual killing. The Supreme Court unanimously declared these resolutions to be in violation of the Constitution's free exercise clause.

There are many interesting features specific to this decision that would well repay discussion, including the multiple concurrent opinions and the court's clear consciousness of the contemporary 1993 congressional debates concerning the Religious Freedom Restoration Act, which sought to set aside the implications of an earlier, 1990, free exercise decision.[6] The court subsequently invalidated the act in a 1997 decision.[7]

From a different perspective, the student of religion might note, as the court need not, that the court's deliberative processes evidence little interest in the divisive sociopolitical environment that resulted in the city council's actions, in particular, the racial and economic class distinctions between the two Cuban immigrant groups, the upper- and middle-class Hispanic Catholic opponents and the working-class black Santerians. This division made all the more remarkable the opponents' odd argument that Santeria ought to be dismissed as a religion because it was illegal in Castro's Cuba—perhaps the only occasion at which this group of Cuban Americans have cited Castro's perspicacity in religious questions! Indeed, there is no sign of the justices' awareness of the massive influence of Santeria in Cuba (one of the reasons, after all, for the papal visit, in the late 1990s, to the island) nor of its historical and structural relations to other Afro-Caribbean religions. However, for the purposes of this essay, I want to focus only on the court's familiarizing attempts to "place" Santeria in relation to the Christian prototype and to "place" animal sacrifice with respect to that prototype of religion on the basis of information the court

cites from both the Florida District Court records of the case and standard reference works, including, most prominently, Mircea Eliade's *Encyclopedia of Religion*.[8]

Let me quote, with only occasional abridgement, the first three framing
paragraphs of Justice Kennedy's majority opinion, commenting on each in
turn. The decision begins:

> This case involves practices of the Santeria religion, which origi-
> nated in the 19th century. When hundreds of thousands of mem-
> bers of the Yoruba people were brought as slaves from western Af-
> rica to Cuba, their traditional African religion absorbed significant
> elements of Roman Catholicism. The resulting syncretism, or fu-
> sion, is Santeria, "the way of the saints." The Cuban Yoruba express
> their devotion to spirits, called *orishas*, through the iconography of
> Catholic saints, Catholic symbols are often present at Santeria rites,
> and Santeria devotees attend the Catholic sacraments. 723 F. Supp.
> 1467, 1469–1470 (SD Fla. 1989); 13 The Encyclopedia of Religion
> 66 (M. Eliade ed. 1987); 1 Encyclopedia of the American Religious
> Experience 183 (C. Lippy & P. Williams eds. 1988).[9]

Kennedy's first domesticating paragraph is preeminently genealogical.
While measured on the time scale of familiar Western religions, Santeria
is relatively new; Justice Kennedy portrays it as being a combination of two
more archaic elements, "traditional African religion" and "Roman Catholicism." While its devotion to "spirits" (*orishas* in Yoruba) clearly mark it as
"African" (indeed, Justice Kennedy employs the curious locution "the Cuban Yoruba" as if the tribal identification remained intact), Catholic elements, in Justice Kennedy's domesticating representation, clearly prevail.
As this paragraph is largely composed of paraphrases and unmarked direct quotations from Joseph M. Murphy's article on Santeria in the Eliade
Encyclopedia, it is significant that the last sentence by Kennedy, "Catholic
symbols are often present at Santeria rites, and Santeria devotees attend
Catholic sacraments," carries the reverse implication in Murphy, "Despite
the frequent presence of Catholic symbols in Santeria rites and the atten-
dance of santeros at Catholic sacraments Santeria is essentially an African
way of worship drawn into a symbiotic relationship with Catholicism."[10]

The second paragraph faces up to the difficulty caused by Kennedy's familiarizing interpretation. If Santeria is but an ethnically colored Catholicism, in principle no different than Justice Kennedy's Irish Catholicism,
what about animal sacrifice? "The Santeria faith teaches that every indi-

vidual has a destiny from God, a destiny fulfilled with the aid and energy of the *orishas*. The basis of the Santeria religion is the nurture of a personal relation with the *orishas*, and one of the principal forms of devotion is an animal sacrifice. 13 The Encyclopedia of Religion, *supra*, at 66."[11]

Let me interrupt Kennedy at this point to note further elements of domestication. He now uses Protestant nomenclature, thoroughly assimilated in American discourse, of "the Santeria faith" along with "the Santerian religion" and emphasizes that the presupposition of this faith is "that every individual has a destiny from God." Again reverting to American Protestant language, Kennedy asserts that the "basis of the Santerian religion is the nurture of a personal relation with the *orishas*," without a hint that this evangelical-sounding "personal relation" is one of spirit possession. Kennedy's sources, strategically not quoted at this point in his decision, state that this relation culminates in a lengthy initiation in which the "*orisha* is 'enthroned' in the head of the devotee and is 'sealed' as a permanent part of the devotee's personality." Furthermore, again unnoted by Kennedy, this "personal relation with the *orishas*" is regularly effected, in Santeria, through divinatory procedures, spirit mediumship, and spirit possession, as well as by sacrifice, understood, in native practice, as an intimate, divine/human sharing of food. Kennedy prefers a blander understanding of the latter, interpreting sacrifice as a mode of worship, a form of personal "devotion." Despite this attempt at familiarization, animal sacrifice remains stubbornly alien, and thus requires further efforts at placement. "The sacrifice of animals as part of religious rituals has ancient roots. See generally 12 *id.*, at 554–556. Animal sacrifices are mentioned throughout the Old Testament, see 14 Encyclopaedia Judaica 600, 600–606 (1971), and it played an important role in the practice of Judaism before the destruction of the second Temple in Jerusalem, see *id.*, at 605–612. In modern Islam, there is an annual sacrifice commemorating Abraham's sacrifice of a ram in the stead of his son, See C. Glassé, Concise Encyclopedia of Islam 178 (1989); 7 Encyclopedia of Religion, *supra*, at 456."[12]

Note that, despite Justice Kennedy's citation here of the article on sacrifice by Joseph Henninger in the Eliade *Encyclopedia*, the justice's illustrations of sacrifice contain no allusion to its role in traditional religions, including those of Africa. "Ancient roots," antiquity, is normatively represented, in his account, by the religion of Israel as described in the "Old Testament." As Kennedy continues his history, he clearly has in mind some version of the triple formulation of the "Abrahamic tradition" encapsulated in President Bush's reiterated phrase "churches, synagogues, or mosques" (the order is not without significance), a formation as problematic as its predecessor, "the Judeo-Christian tradition," which first came to prominence at the 1939–40 New York World's Fair in Flushing, New York. The "Abrahamic tradition" maps Christianity as the center, Judaism the near neighbor, and Islam the far. In Kennedy's account, animal sacrifice is on the map of recognizable religious practice because Jews once practiced it, and Muslims still do, but only once a year. These two traditions are linked as the Islamic practice is held to commemorate an event in biblical tradition, although Kennedy does not note that Abraham's son who was spared by the substitution of a ram is frequently held to be Ishmael and not Isaac. Kennedy need not speak the obvious exception: Christianity, as he thinks of it, did not and does not perform animal sacrifice. (Kennedy does not record the ambivalence in Islam to sacrifice. For the student of religion, it is notable that metaphorical sacrificial language dominates most Christianities, which lack rituals of sacrifice, while it is distinctly muted in both Judaism and Islam, which have real histories of animal sacrifice.)

Almost in passing, Kennedy announces in the first sentence of his third framing paragraph the logic of Santerian sacrifice: "The *orishas* are powerful bur not immortal. They depend for survival on the sacrifice." That is to say, as in Numbers 28, sacrifice provides superhuman beings with their necessary food, but this rationale—apparently as estranging to Kennedy as it is correct—is quickly overcome by a flood of (largely irrelevant) information in the rest of the paragraph, which enumerates, in considerable detail, the occasions for sacrifice, the sorts of animals commonly sacrificed, and the procedures for killing, cooking, and eating the animal. "Sacrifices are performed at birth, marriage, and death rites, for the cure of the sick, for the initiation of new members and priests, and during an annual celebration. Animals sacrificed in Santeria rituals include chickens, pigeons, doves, ducks, guinea pigs, goats, sheep, and turtles. The animals are killed by the cutting of the carotid arteries in the neck. The sacrificed animal is cooked and eaten, except after healing and death rituals. See 723 E Supp., at 1471–1472; 13 Encyclopedia of Religion, *supra*, at 66; M. Gonzalez-Wippler, The Santeria Experience 105 (1982)."[13]

What Justice Kennedy has undertaken in this initial statement of fact, or more properly, of data, that is to say, facts accepted for purposes of the argument, is an essay in familiarization, largely enabled by the deployment of a Christian prototype. That which initially appeared strange—Santerian animal sacrifice—has been reduced to an instance of the known. In favor of Kennedy's procedure, the heavy social and political cost of leaving the practice in the realm of the exotic is indicated by the comments of Hialeah officials cited in the body of the court's opinion.

Councilman Mejides indicated that he was "totally against the sacri-
ficing of animals" and distinguished [the Jewish practice of] kosher
slaughter because it had a "real purpose." The "Bible says we are allowed to sacrifice an animal for consumption," he continued, "but for
any other purpose, I don't believe that the Bible allows that." . . . The
chaplain of the Hialeah Police Department told the city council that
Santeria was a sin, "foolishness," and the worship of "demons." He
advised the city council: "We need to be helping people and sharing
with them the truth that is found in Jesus Christ"; He concluded: "I
would exhort you . . . not to permit this Church to exist."[14]

Kennedy's redescription of Santeria is an effort, at one and the same time,
both similar to and different from that familiarizing project undertaken
by the study of religion as it works through the necessary tension between
the near and the far.

The relations between the near and the far, the familiar and the exotic,
have been a preoccupation of western students of religion ever since the
Ionian ethnographers. Although the presuppositions and techniques have
altered over time, the fundamental devices have remained the same: comparison, translation, and redescription. These projects work with difference,
relaxing it but never overcoming it. Because nothing is ever quite the same
as another, these efforts require judgment and criticism.

Translation and difference and criticism challenge, each in their own
way, the confidence attendant on the deployment of some form of Christianity as a prototype, whether practiced by the Internal Revenue Service,
the US Supreme Court, a scholar of religion, the daily press, or ourselves
as citizens.

What is more, in the three paragraphs cited from Justice Kennedy,
terms such as "religion," "syncretism," and "sacrifice" are employed as if
they were self-evident. In his decision, they are innocent of either controversy or entailments; they have no history. There is no hint of the problematics of redescription, of translation, here, at the level of a second-order
theoretical language.

I contrast this to the strongest example of these processes in the study
of religion that I know: Durkheim's translation in *Elementary Forms of Religious Life* (1912) of the language appropriate to religion (for him, in this
work, functioning as the unknown) into the language appropriate to society (for him, the known). From the precising definitions on the very first
page to the redescription of aboriginal rituals in the final part, Durkheim
has taken care.

For the purposes of this essay, this is not the aspect of Durkheim I need to stress.[15] Rather, I want to use his work to illustrate the contrary impulse to familiarization, one that is equally imperative in the human sciences in general, and the study of religion in particular, namely, defamiliarization. This is a process of making the familiar seem strange in order to enhance our perception of the familiar—equally a matter of redescription. For it is the aforementioned requirements of difference and criticism, as well as the process of defamiliarization, that prevent the study of religion from being an exercise in the transmission of a religious tradition.

To illustrate defamiliarization, allow me to introduce a second Supreme Court case, *Lynch v. Donnelly*, decided in 1984.[16] The case concerns a Christmas nativity display (a crèche) erected by the city of Pawtucket, Rhode Island, at their downtown shopping center. By a narrow margin, 5–4, the court ruled in favor of the city that the exhibit was not primarily religious in that (1) it contained secular as well as religious symbols—for example, a talking wishing well along with the infant Jesus, and (2) that it was erected for a secular, commercial purpose. The first criterion was thought crucial, inasmuch as five years later, in 1989, in *Allegheny County v. ACLU*, the court found the erection of a crèche in the county's courthouse square, accompanied by a banner proclaiming "Gloria in excelsis Deo," to be an illicit entanglement of religion and state but found permissible a second civic display, one block away, likewise on government property, containing a Christmas tree, a menorah, and a banner reading "During this holiday season the city . . . salutes liberty. Let these festive lights remind us that we are keepers of the flame of liberty and our legacy of freedom."[17] This second display was judged proper in that, unlike the first, it contained a mixture of sacred and secular objects (the Christmas tree and the menorah on the one hand, the banner on the other) and was erected, at least in part, for the secular purpose of fostering patriotism. (I leave aside the additional issue of the possible ameliorating effects of displaying, together, symbols from two religions.)

I quote, without intervening comment, two extracts from the majority opinion in *Lynch v. Donnelly*, written by Chief Justice Burger. The first may be taken as an ethnographic description, the second as a statement by native informants. The first, descriptive statement is based on a summary by Judge Pettine when the case was decided, previously, by the US District Court of Rhode Island.

Each year, in cooperation with the downtown retail merchants association, the city of Pawtucket, RI . . . erects a Christmas display as part of its observance of the Christmas holiday season. The display is situated in a park owned by a non-profit organization and located in the heart of the shopping district. The display comprises many figures and decorations traditionally associated with Christmas, including, among other things, a Santa Claus house, reindeer pulling Santa's sleigh, candy striped poles, a Christmas tree, carolers, cut out figures representing such characters as a clown, an elephant, a teddy bear, a talking wishing well, hundreds of colored lights, a large banner that reads "Seasons Greetings," and a crèche. The crèche has been on display for forty or more years. It consists of the traditional figures including the Infant Jesus, Mary and Joseph, angels, shepherds, kings and animals, all ranging in height from five inches to five feet. The crèche is positioned in a central and highly visible location, an almost life sized tableau marked off by a white picket fence.[18]

As part of the argument for the propriety of the exhibit, that it was not an unconstitutional mingling of state and church, the city had argued that it was not erected for religious purposes. As I have indicated, this statement may be taken as if it were one by native informants. It was offered by David Freeman, professor of philosophy at the University of Rhode Island, who had appeared as an expert witness for the city in the US District Court hearing of the case. "The display engenders a friendly community spirit of goodwill in keeping with the season. The display brings into the central city shoppers and serves commercial interests and benefits merchants and their employees. It promotes pre-Christmas retail sales and helps engender goodwill and neighborliness commonly associated with the Christmas season. It invites people to participate in the Christmas spirit, brotherhood, peace, and to let loose with their money."[19]

I propose we undertake a thought experiment in the service of defamiliarization in which we replace one of the members of the Supreme Court with Emile Durkheim. We will instruct him to ignore the constitutional question of government and religion (inasmuch as Durkheim's translation language of "church" and "society" is not equivalent to the American vocabulary of "church and state"), asking him only to argue the question whether, from the point of view of his redescriptive theory and solely on the basis of the two extracts I have quoted, the *totality* of the Pawtucket display constitutes a religion. A number of Durkheimian interpretative possibilities present themselves—I shall offer ten—no one of which is necessarily correct. Interpretation, whether in the human sciences or in a court of law, is a matter of persuasion not of truth. Persuasion depends on the power of the relations argued between the stipulated data (in this instance, the two reports) and the rhetorical-interpretative frame placed upon them (in the present experiment, that of Durkheim).

Let us begin by granting for purposes of argument the finding of fact by the court: that the display consists of the copresence of sacred and secular items. In the court's reasoning, religion would be present only if the exhibit consisted entirely of sacred symbols; that is to say, for the court, following some generalized Christian prototype, religion is the sacred. Durkheim might reject both the court's premise and its conclusion, while accepting its finding of fact. For Durkheim, religion is the oppositional relationship of sacred to profane. The presence of both are required for there to be religion. I assume, in arguing this understanding, that he might accept the court's categorization of the nativity scene as sacred, what the court termed "the traditional figures," and note their separation from the other items in the display by the "picket fence" as guarding it against profanation. But I doubt Durkheim would remain content with this initial move.

Durkheim would surely go on to argue that, conceptually, one must start an interpretation of any group's religion with their beliefs rather than with their rites or symbols. Here, as Durkheim does persistently with respect to Australian data, the scholar must reject the native's claimed pragmatic results in favor of a social scientific interpretation; an interpretation from the outside, dependent on the scientist's theories and comparative knowledge. That is to say, translation is required.

In the case at hand, the native informant predictably stressed the economic and pragmatic consequences of the display. This understanding was, from Durkheim's view, erroneously accepted as true by the court. The informant claimed that the exhibit "benefits merchants and their employees," it "serves commercial interests," it "promotes retail sales," it causes folk to "let loose with their money." Durkheim might remark that embedded in this economic discourse is a second language of sociality, specifically tied to a particular season. Rather than holding this to be a secondary effect of the economic initiatives, he would hold it to be the primary cause for the display. The scene "engenders a friendly community spirit of goodwill in keeping with the season," it brings members of the society "into the central city," it "helps engender goodwill and neighborliness commonly associated with the Christmas season," "it invites people to participate in the Christmas spirit, brotherhood [and] peace." As translated by Durkheim, members of the Pawtucket society usually live dispersed in their separate homes, following individual biological and economic pursuits. For Durkheim, this is the fundamental, social translation of the profane. By

contrast, in the shopping center, these same folk come together to "participate" in what Durkheim would define as a "moral community," his translation of the sacred. For Durkheim, the alternation between these two types
of time, one individual, the other collective, is in fact the social origin of
the distinction between the profane and the sacred. It is this temporal opposition that marks the two qualities; it is never an inherent distinction
between objects. This collectivity needs to be periodically refreshed and
renewed. (Durkheim may be credited with introducing the potent prefix,
re-, as a centrally important element in the understanding of religion.) The
coming together "into the central city" is a ritual that resignifies the sacred. In Durkheim's sense of the term, this coming together in the shopping center constitutes Pawtucket's "church."

From this perspective, Durkheim might go on to argue two reinterpretations of the native informant's account. Both would reject the court's understanding that Pawtucket's beliefs are secular. On the one hand, Durkheim might argue that, in religion, the experience of the collectivity is
objectified, often as an impersonal force, sometimes as a supernatural being. In the native's erroneous understanding, it is this force (or being)
rather than the coming together that is thought to "engender" the power-
fully experienced sentiments of collective life. In Pawtucket, this objectification is variously named the "Season," the "Christmas Season," or the
"Christmas Spirit." This is a sacred power in that it can be profaned. Think
of the canonical example of Scrooge.

Alternatively, Durkheim might argue that as these sentiments are "en-
gendered" by this periodic coming together, seasonal shopping in Pawtucket constitutes that society's religious ritual. Taking a different tack,
Durkheim might question the court's literal acceptance of the native informant's claim of commercial motivation. He might note that, unlike what
occurs in profane time, where money is spent shopping largely to meet
the needs of sustenance, whether individual or those of a biological family,
here, in this season, money is being spent on gifts for family, for a socially
constructed extended family, and for others. This recognition of nonutili-
tarian mutual obligations between social actors who are not biologically
related marks for Durkheim a moral community, which, when named in
religious idiom, is what he calls a "Church." (Note that the French *l'Église*
from the Greek *ekklesia* carries a social, associative sense not found in the
English "church," which refers to divine ownership of a building.)[20]

Given this translated understanding of Pawtucket's religious beliefs,
Durkheim might next turn his attention to a revaluation of the description
of the display, bearing in mind, again, his injunction that the scientist must

know how to "get beneath" the symbols to the social realities they represent, while rejecting the interpretations offered by their believers, which are "almost always false."

The ritual nature of the entire display is signaled by the notice that the display is erected "each year," some items for "forty years." It is repetitive and periodic. This said, Durkheim might remind the court that such objects are best understood as collective representations; that, if religious, they will exhibit an opposition between sacred and profane; and that, rather than being inherent in the object, sacrality is arbitrarily "superadded" by society. Durkheim might recognize, as did the court, an apparent distinction between two groups of representations: the nativity scene and everything else. But as a first move he might reverse the court's evaluation of the nativity scene as self-evidently sacred.

Within the group of "everything else" classified as secular by the court, Durkheim might note three central objects: the banner "Seasons Greetings," the Christmas tree, and the figure of Santa Claus. For Durkheim, as already suggested, the banner marks both sacred time (i.e., collective time) and the objectification, as the "Season," of the power of socially renewed collectivity. Both the Christmas tree and Santa Claus are collective representations of gift giving, that mutual, moral obligation within the framework of a socially constructed community which marks, for Durkheim, a "Church." The other representations are all associated with these three.

Each of these three primary representations can be profaned, a sign of their sacrality. For a familiar example, in the case of Santa Claus, despite his present iconic origins in a Coca-Cola ad campaign, think of the drunk Santa Claus in the opening scene of *Miracle on 34th Street*. For a more complex example, one of deliberate profanation, I refer to the French incident on Christmas Eve 1951, when a figure of Santa Claus was hung by the neck from the railing of the Dijon Cathedral, followed by the burning of the effigy in the cathedral square. These acts were undertaken with the prior agreement of the clergy in front of several hundred Sunday school children as a protest against the "Americanization" of Christmas.[21]

With these various "other" objects established as the collective representations of the Church of Pawtucket, Durkheim can turn to the nativity scene. Anticipating a possible objection—the "white picket fence"—Durkheim might here argue that the Christian scene is profane relative to the collective representations of the Church of Pawtucket and is therefore being separated from them. After all, divisiveness, as opposed to collectivity, is, for Durkheim, the hallmark of the profane. The very fact that there is a lawsuit concerning the nativity scene is, in itself, sufficient demonstration of its profanity. Besides, remember the alternation of times. From the coming together at the shopping center, the members of the Church of Pawtucket disperse to their individual homes and denominational houses of worship, a dispersal that likewise marks the profane.

Alternatively, Durkheim might again invoke the requirement to "get beneath" the symbols while rejecting the interpretations of believers. If so, the nativity scene might be reinterpreted as a collective representation of Pawtucket's religion as understood by Durkheim. In Joseph, Mary, and Jesus we are presented with an ideal extended family, one surely not bound together by blood. Jesus and the kings are presented as an ideal of mutual gift giving and so on.

This sort of interpretation might lead Durkheim to suggest, consistent with his understanding of Australian aboriginal organizations, that there are, in fact, two religions in Pawtucket. The first, which is a relatively more inclusive "tribal" or "pan tribal" one, is that objectified as the "Season." The second, that of a relatively more limited "clan," is represented by the Christian figures as Durkheim might redescribe them. Both, properly translated and explained, complement each other. Both are representations of the Church of Pawtucket.

I have undertaken this exercise in Durkheimian translation in order to make a simple point. The disciplined study of any subject is, among other things, an assault on self-evidence, on matters taken for granted, nowhere more so than in the study of religion. The future of our increasingly diverse societies will call on all our skills at critical translation; all our abilities to occupy the contested space between the near and the far; all our capacities for the dual project of making familiar what, at first encounter, seems strange, and making strange what we have come to think of as all-too-familiar. Each of these endeavors needs to be practiced and refined in the service of an urgent civic and academic agendum: that difference be negotiated but never overcome.

Notes

This chapter was published in Smith's volume *Relating Religion: Essays in the Study of Religion* (Chicago: University of Chicago Press, 2004), © 2004 by the Unviersity of Chicago. It is republished here with permission of the University of Chicago Press and the author with minor editorial changes to correspond to the style of this volume.

1. See, especially, Smith, "Religion, Religions, Religious."
2. See Internal Revenue Service, "Social Security for Clergy."

3. I am indebted to the discussion of the Internal Revenue Code in Evans, *Interpreting Free Exercise of Religion*, 139–43.

4. Wilkerson v. City of Rome, 152 Ga. 762, 110 S.E. 895 (1922); Cooley, *General Principles of Constitutional Law*, 206.

5. Church of the Lukumi Babalu Aye, Inc., and Ernesto Pichado v. City of Hialeah, 508 US 520 (1993).

6. Employment Division, Department of Human Resources of Oregon v. Smith, 494 US 872 (1990).

7. City of Boerne v. Flores, 521 US 519 (1997).

8. Church of the Lukumi Babalu Aye, Inc., and Ernesto Pichado v. City of Hialeah, 723 F. Supp SD Fla. (1989). Eliade and Adams, eds., *Encyclopedia of Religion*.

9. Lukumi Bablu Aye v. Hialeah, 508 US 520, citations in original.

10. Eliade and Adams, *Encyclopedia of Religion*, 13:66.

11. Lukumi Bablu Aye v. Hialeah, 508 US 520, citations in original.

12. Ibid.

13. Ibid.

14. Ibid.

15. See especially Smith, "Topography of the Sacred," and "Mana, Mana, Everywhere," in *Relating Religion*. All Durkheim quotations and references, below, are from Durkheim, *Elementary Forms of Religious Life*.

16. Lynch v. Donnelly, 465 US 668 (1984). While I have a different set of interests, see the important monograph on *Lynch v. Donnelly* by Sullivan in *Paying the Words Extra*. Professor Sullivan has a law degree as well as a PhD in the history of religions.

17. County of Allegheny v. ACLU, 492 US 573 (1989).

18. Lynch v. Donnelly.

19. Ibid.

20. Compare this understanding with several recent (critical) studies of Christmas and consumerism, including Schmidt, *Consumer Rites*; Nissenbaum, *Battle for Christmas*; and the collection coedited by Horsley and Tracy, *Christmas Unwrapped*. From a quite different perspective, I much appreciate the analyses and comparisons of Christmas and Easter in Caplow, Bahr, and Chadwick, *All Faithful People*, 182–98; cf. Caplow and Williamson, "Decoding Middletown's Easter Bunny."

21. Lévi-Strauss, "Le Pere Noël supplicié."

2

An Early Moment in the Discourse of "Terrorism"

Reflections on a Tale from Marco Polo

Bruce Lincoln

In fall 2008, Bruce Lincoln presented "In Praise of Things Chaotic: Politics in Creation Mythology" as the seventh Aronov Lecture. His original lecture was published in Danish translation in *Chaos* and republished in English in Lincoln's *Gods and Demons, Priests and Scholars: Critical Explorations in the History of Religions*. The chapter published here is a different essay from Lincoln's Aronov Lecture; this chapter presents his analysis of historical and contemporary discourses.

I

My goal in this chapter is to revisit a classic text that raises the most contemporary of issues: Marco Polo's stereotyped, highly influential, and highly prejudicial description of the "Old Man of the Mountain," a text of virtually mythic status and power. Having invoked the category of "myth," however, in a context where it is not commonly applied, it is useful to indicate how I use this term and why it seems appropriate. To begin, I would reject three widely accepted notions. First, myths are not sacred narratives. Although many myths claim sacred status, in this they misrecognize their own nature, for they are human stories like any other. They simply make more exaggerated claims to a more elevated kind of authority. Second, myths are not collective narratives or the speech of any group as a whole. Rather, they are stories that are told and retold in countless variants. Often the authorship of these variants is unacknowledged, forgotten, or deliberately hidden, but in its details each variant advances the specific interests of those responsible for its production, revision, and circulation. These anonymous agents and absent authors misrepresent themselves— and those for whom they speak—as the group as a whole. Third, myths are neither false stories nor true, but simply stories that claim to speak with authority about issues of deep importance. Sometimes these claims succeed and sometimes they fail, and the same story can change its status over time from myth to fable and back again, since such status is a function of reception.

If myths are not sacred, not collective, not true or false, what distinguishes them from other narratives? My best attempt at definition runs as follows. Myth is ideology in narrative form. More precisely, mythic discourse deals in master categories that have multiple referents: levels of the cosmos, terrestrial geographies, plant and animal species, logical categories, and the like. Their plots serve to organize the relations among these categories and to justify a hierarchy among them, establishing the rightness (or at least the necessity) of a world in which heaven is above earth, the lion the king of beasts, the cooked more pleasing than the raw. Sometimes issues of human society are given explicit attention—in stories that treat the relations of men and women, uncles and nephews, our tribe and its neighbors, etcetera—and sometimes these are left implicit, as when stories about lions serve to make points about royalty. But always this concern to rank (or to recalibrate the ranking of) human groups is present, and this is the most consequential aspect of any mythic story.[1]

Scholars have long recognized Polo's description of the "Old Man of the Mountain" as a text that raises the most contemporary of themes: the conjunction of religion, politics, violence, and fear. Beyond this, as I hope to show, it also takes pains to ponder the relations of three populations—Christians, Muslims, and Mongols—that encountered one another in the Middle East and Central Asia of the thirteenth century. Certain events disrupted what Polo's Christian audience considered the normative hierarchic ranking of these peoples, and his text responded to this situation in an extremely creative, and hitherto unappreciated, way. But we are getting ahead of our story.

II

After twenty-four years of travels in Asia (1271–95), Messer Marco Polo returned to Venice, only to be captured by the Genoese shortly thereafter, following which he was put in prison, where he remained from 1298 until July 1299.[2] There, he encountered a certain Rustichello da Pisa, an author of chivalric romances.[3] Apparently a friendship developed and the two men coauthored a text that combined the literary genres Rustichello controlled and the content Polo gathered in Asia. The latter included memories of his own experience and the hearsay testimony of others, as their prologue acknowledges:

> Those who will find all the greatest marvels and the great diversities of Greater Armenia and Persia, of the Tartars and of India, and many other territories, our book will relate them to you openly, in the order that Messer Marco Polo, a wise and noble citizen of Venice, recounted them, just as he saw them with his own eyes. There are also things that he did not see, but heard from reliable and truthful men.
>
> Therefore, we will set down the things that were seen as seen, and those heard as heard, so that our book may be true and dependable, without any lies. And those who read or hear this book can believe it, for all these things are true.[4]

The chance encounter of a Venetian merchant and a Pisan author in a Genoese jail thus made possible the production of a text that rapidly diffused throughout Europe.[5] It was not random fortune, however, that prompted the merchant's travels.[6] Rather, this came in response to large historic forces: specifically, the way the Crusader beachhead in the Levant (1100–1291), coupled with Mongol conquests further east (1206–1260), conspired to permit the resumption of trade in silk, spices, and other precious goods, which had been disrupted since the rise of Islam in the seventh century.

Vatican diplomats were the first to investigate the new opportunities.[7] In their immediate wake followed merchants, led by Niccolò and Maffeo Polo, who in 1260 set out from Constantinople and made their way to Sudak, Bukhara, and Beijing (Khan-balik) before returning home. In Beijing, they met with Kubilai Khan (whose reign spanned 1259–94) and when they made ready to depart, he sent an ambassador with them, bearing a letter for the Pope. In addition, he asked the brothers to return with holy oil from Jerusalem and a hundred Christian missionaries.[8] Falling ill, the Mongol ambassador abandoned the journey, and the Vatican has no record of receiving his letter. Other correspondence between Mongol rulers and the papacy is preserved, however, dating as early as 1246.[9] For their part, the Polos returned to Venice in 1269. After some unanticipated delays, they set out on a second voyage in 1271, this time as personal emissaries of Pope Gregory X. As requested, they took with them holy oil, also papal letters and sumptuous gifts for the Great Khan. In place of the requested hundred missionaries, however, the Pope could spare only two Dominican friars, who quickly turned back. More determined was Niccolò's seventeen-year-old son Marco (1254–1323), who accompanied his father and uncle on the journey.[10]

Part travelogue, part merchants' manual, part geographic treatise, Messer Marco's book describes countless regions and cities, from Armenia in the west to Cathay in the east, and southward to Sri Lanka. Typically, it recounts the customs and mores, religion and politics, remarkable sights, natural resources, and outstanding industries of each locale.

To organize the myriad peoples it describes, the text employs three master categories based on considerations of religion: Christians in the first place, Muslims or "Saracens" in the second, and Buddhists or "idolaters" in the third. (This last term may also encompass Confucians, Taoists, Manicheans, and Hindus, all of whom otherwise go unmentioned.)[11] The text also provides three figures, who serve as the paradigmatic leaders of each community. The Great Khan played this role for the idolaters, as did the legendary Prester John for the Christians.[12] For the Saracens, it fell to the so-called Old Man of the Mountain.[13]

Although the "Old Man" is the only Muslim leader mentioned in Messer Marco's account, the title encompassed a number of individuals, all of whom served as the heads of various Nizari Isma'ili communities.[14] The Nizaris were a radical Shiite sect, which is to say a minority within a minority. Full consideration of their beliefs and practice lies beyond the scope of this chapter, but several excellent accounts are available.[15] Like other Shi'is, they maintained that spiritual authority rightly belongs to the Prophet's direct descendants and that such leaders—whom they call imams—are desperately needed, for they alone possess the charisma and esoteric knowledge on which humanity depends. And like other Isma'ilis, the Nizaris believe that upon the death of the sixth Imam in 765, his successor withdrew from this troubled world and went into occultation. Until the return of the hidden imam as a triumphant savior (*Mahdi*), the community stands in wait.

Unlike other Isma'ili factions, however, the Nizaris adopted a less pacific and patient attitude toward their adversaries, who arrogated authority for themselves on very different principles. Beginning in the 1090s, the Nizaris waged active struggle against their Sunni enemies, above all the sultanate of the Saljuq Turks, who held paramount military, political, and religious power.

Nizari strategy involved seizing mountain fortresses and using them to stage subsequent operations. The first and most important was at Alamut, in the Alburz range of northern Iran. Others followed in Persia, Khurasan, Syria, and Lebanon. Young men fiercely committed to this movement and its leaders held the title of *fida-'i* (plural *fedayeen*): "devotee, self-sacrificer." On occasion, they were charged with the murder of the movement's opponents and a small number of spectacular killings provoked widespread discussion. Most victims were high-ranking Saljuq officials, but the Syrian and Lebanese branches, which confronted Crusaders as well as Sunnis, were responsible for the deaths of several European nobles, beginning in the latter half of the twelfth century.[16]

"Old Man of the Mountain" is the title Christian authors used for Nizari leaders, mistranslating Arabic *Shaykh* as "old man" rather than "lord," and associating Nizaris everywhere with Alamut.[17] Similarly, Europeans generally referred to the *Nizari fedayeen* as "Assassins," after the Arabic *hashishiyan*. Most literally, this word denotes "hashish-users," but it was also employed as a term of opprobrium for lowlives and scoundrels in general. The Sunnis seem to have used the less restrictive sense in their anti-Nizari invective, since none of the surviving Islamic sources ever charge the group with drug use.[18]

III

If the Sunnis gave the name "Assassins" to Nizari *fedayeen*, they called the community in general *malāhida*, "heretics" (singular *mulhid).* This term—and its construction of the Nizaris as outside Islam proper—were taken over by Western authors who obtained their information about the sect from its Sunni adversaries. The earliest of these was Benjamin of Tudela, a Jewish traveler who visited the Holy Land in 1167. Taking the term of disparagement "*mulahid*" ("heretic") for the name of a territory, he located it in Lebanon, where one finds "a people who do not believe in the religion of the Ishmaelite [Islam] and they settle in the high mountains. They answer to an elder, who is in the land of al-Hashishim."[19]

Benjamin's account is the earliest Western description of the Assassins, although his use of the derogatory terms Mulahid and Hashishim reveals his dependence on Sunni polemic, as does his judgment that the Nizaris were not really Muslims. He wrote of them as follows: "Near Gebala is a people called al-Hashishim and they do not believe in the religion of the Ishmaelite [Islam], but in one of their number whom they think to be a prophet, and everything he says to them they will do, whether for death or for life. They call him Shaykh-al-Hashishim. He is their Elder, and upon his command all of the men of the mountain come out or go in. The place where they settle is in the city of Kadmus, which is Kadmot in the land of Sihon. And they are believers of the word of their elder and everyone everywhere fears them, because they even kill kings."[20]

Six points are noteworthy in Benjamin's account and will recur in others that follow it: (1) the name of the group ("Assassins"); (2) its heretical nature ("they do not believe in the religion of the Ishmaelite"); (3) identification of its leader as the Old Man ("Elder," also "Shaykh"); (4) the absolute obedience of the Old Man's followers; (5) the Old Man's status as a prophet (a charge of scandalous heresy according to the normative tenets of Islam, and one that badly distorts the Nizaris' position); and (6) the Old Man's use of the *jedayeen* to murder—"assassinate"—his adversaries.

Farhad Daftary has carefully studied the way subsequent Christian authors reproduced these points and added to them. Gradually, several other stereotyped items accumulated around the picture of the Assassins, including (7) residence in a mountain stronghold, with castles and gardens reminiscent of paradise; (8) rigorous training of devotees in many languages, which knowledge they used to infiltrate their enemies' camps; (9) the devotees' practice of prostrating themselves before the Old Man; (10) the Old Man's promise of heavenly reward to those who carried out his bidding, whether they lived or died in the attempt; (11) the gift of a consecrated dagger; and (12) the use of drugs. The distribution of these motifs over the relevant Western texts of the twelfth and thirteenth centuries is detailed in table 1. In other ways, the authors responsible for these accounts differed from one another, often quite markedly. The extent to which they agreed regarding the Old Man, about whom they told much the same story, with much the same terminology and details, recounted in much the same order—suggests that they participated in a common discourse, drawing on the same sources and, in some cases at least, quoting from one another.

Although Messer Marco explicitly states that his account of the Old Man and Assassins was based on oral testimony gathered in situ,[21] the pattern evident in table 1 suggests that he, too, recycled conventional motifs drawn from earlier written sources. Working these into a single coherent narrative, he and Rustichello produced what subsequently became the definitive version of the legend.[22] Two motifs that figured in earlier variants were dropped by the coauthors. One of these—the dagger—has no great significance. The other is enormously important: all other Western authors took their lead from Sunni sources and treated the Assassins as heretics,

Table 1. Motif Analysis of Western Descriptions of the Nizaris, 1167–1299.

	Benjamin of Tudela (1167)	Burchard of Strassburg (1175)	William of Tyre (1180)	Arnold of Lübeck (before 1210)	James of Vitry (c. 1216–1228)	Marco Polo (1299)
1) Name "Assassins"	X	X	X		X	X
2) Heretics	X	**X**		X	**X**	
3) Leader "Old Man"	X	(X)	X	X	X	X
4) Absolute obedience	X	X	X	X	X	X
5) Leader regarded as prophet	X			(X)		X
6) Murder of high-ranking enemies	X	X	X	X	X	X
7) Mountain fortress and gardens		X			X	X
8) Rigorous training of devotees		X			X	X
9) Self-prostration		X		**X**		X
10) Promise of paradisal reward		X		X	X	**X**
11) Consecrated dagger		X	X	X	X	
12) Drug use				X		**X**

Boldface type indicates a particular exaggeration of the motif; parentheses mark a subtler or less emphasized version than usual.

construing the sect as outside the pale of Islamic orthodoxy and in active opposition to it. Polo's text, in the strongest possible contrast, treated the Old Man and his minions as an emblematic part of the Saracen world, which revealed with exceptional clarity the dangerous, threatening nature of Mohammed's religion. For example, in describing the details of the paradise garden, Messer Marco noted that the Old Man had it built "in the same fashion that Mohammed had made the Saracens understand."[23] Such an assertion occurs in no other Western account, and the same is true of Polo's observation that *fedayeen* placed in the garden recognized where they were because they had "heard it said that according to their prophet Mohammed, paradise was made in such a manner."[24]

More telling still, the Venetian offered an interpretation of the imaginary place-name "Mulecte" (Arabic *malāhida*) that transformed its original sense ("heretics") into the very opposite: "Mulecte means 'of the Saracens.'"[25] So shocking a transformation was this that the editor of the critical edition felt obliged to imagine the text was defective. Although the vast majority of manuscripts make no explicit mention of heresy, he relied on a late, atypical Latin version (MS. Z) and emended the text in a way that undoes Messer Marco's attempt to represent the Assassins as good Muslims.[26] That the Latin text restores the older view of the group as heretical is interesting in itself, and a point to which we will return.

In two other motifs, one also notes significant change from earlier to later variants, as discourse about the Old Man became more fabulous and lurid with repetition. Thus, Burchard of Strassburg's account of the Assassins was quoted by Arnold of Lübeck and survives in the latter's *Chronicle of the Slavs*. In his own account, Arnold generally followed Burchard's lead, but when Burchard described the Nizari practice of prostrating themselves to signify submission, Arnold either misunderstood or wanted to tell a more dramatic story.[27] In his version, the Assassins did not just bow to the Old Man *(predibus suis provoluti)*, but leapt to their death *(se precipitaverunt)* on his command. The two variants are contrasted in table 2.

Arnold also went beyond his sources on another point. Thus, where earlier authors used the name Assassins in its nonrestrictive sense, he alone heard a reference to drug use.[28] In his version, when the Old Man dispatched the *fedayeen* on a mission, "he intoxicates them with a drink that carries them off to ecstasy or madness. By his magic he shows them fantastic dreams full of pleasures and delights—no, full of foolishness—and he asserts they will have these eternally in return for such deeds."[29]

All prior authors treat the promise of paradise in terms consistent with Islamic doctrine, as the reward extended to martyrs. Insofar as they offered

Table 2. The Incident of Throwing One's Self Down in Two Western Sources.

Burchard of Strassburg (1175)	Arnold of Lübeck (before 1210)
1 When they are set in the presence of the Prince, he asks if they wish to obey his commands	
2 In order that he might confer paradise on them.	He also offers them a certain hope and certain pleasures of eternal prodigious enjoyment so that they are better able to die than to live.
3 And as they have been instructed, without contradiction or ambiguity, all respond, **throwing themselves at his feet.**	Many of them at his nod or command, when standing on a high wall **will throw themselves down**
4 Fervent in soul, they will obey in all that he has commanded them.*	
5	so that they die in a miserable death with a broken neck.†

*Burchard of Strassburg, quoted in Arnold of Lübeck, *Chronicle of the Slavs*, bk. 7, ch. 8; text in Pertz, ed., *Arnoldi Chronica Slavorum*, 275: Tunc in presentia principis contituti, querit ab eis, si preceptis suis velint obedire, ut eis conferat paradisum. Qui ut instructi sunt, omni contradictione et amiguitate remota, predibus suis provoluti ferventi animo respondent, se fore obedientes in omnibus, que preceperit eis.

†Arnold of Lübeck, *Chronicle of the Slavs*, bk. 4, ch. 16; text in Pertz, *Arnoldi Chronica Slavorum*, 145–46: Qui etiam quondam spem et quedam gaudia eterne iocunditatis monstruose eis pollicetur, ut potent magis mori quam vivere. Sepe enim multi eorum at nutum vel imperium suum stantes in muro excelso se precipitaverunt, ita ut cervicibus fractis miserabili morte interirent.

any critique, it was to suggest, if only subtly, that the Old Man's promises may have been self-serving.[30] Arnold, however, was more aggressive in his diction and, more importantly, in his story of drug use.[31] The Polo text took this further still. Here, the Old Man is said to have built splendid gardens in his mountain redoubt and filled them with beautiful maidens. After giving his *fedayeen* a drink that rendered them unconscious, he had them carried into his garden. When they awoke, they believed they were in paradise and as long as they remained there, the women—favored Orientalist trope of Muslim concupiscence—were constantly at their service.[32] When the Old Man wanted to send a *fida-'i* on a mission, however, the lad was drugged once more and carried out.

> When these youths awoke and found themselves in the castle and palace, which were great marvels, they were not happy with it, for they would never have left the paradise from which they came by their own will. Now they went before the Old Man and they bowed deeply before him, as if they believed he was a great prophet. The Old Man asked them where they came from and they said that they came from paradise. And they said that truly this was the same paradise that Mohammed described to our ancestors. They told all the things that they found there. And the others who heard this and had not been there, had great desire to go to paradise and wished to die, because they would be able to go there and they greatly desired to go there that day. And when the Old Man wanted to have a great lord killed, he assigned it to the one of his assassins who was best. He sent many very far from him to other countries and ordered them to kill these men. Now they went and obeyed the order of their lord, then they returned to his court—those who escaped, since some were taken prisoner and died—when they had killed the man.[33]

In varying degrees, earlier accounts of the Assassins permitted one to regard the Old Man as a religious leader, albeit dangerously misguided. Committed to a cause he regarded as sacred, he recruited and trained other believers, to whom he promised—in good, if mistaken, faith—a heavenly reward. In contrast, Polo's text introduced sex, drugs, and illusion to the myth of the Assassins' paradise, thereby reconstituting the Old Man as a cynical, deceptive cult leader, a fiend worthy of Orientalist romance, and a murderer devoid of scruples. At the same time, it transformed those who constructed themselves as *fedayeen, mujahedeen,* and *shahideen—self-sacrificers* struggling on behalf of their faith and courting martyrdom—into drug-addled dupes and "terrorists" or, as the recent commander of the War on Terror has defined this term, "barbaric criminals who profane a great religion by committing murder in its name."[34]

There is one last place where the Polo text was innovative, partly because its authors had different purposes than did their predecessors and partly because new information was available to them. While earlier works treated the Assassins as an ongoing problem, Messer Marco and Rustichello spoke of them in the past tense, for they wrote after the Nizari community had been destroyed, first at Alamut by the Mongols in 1256, then in Syria and Lebanon by the Mamluks in 1273. Conflating these two defeats, misdating them, and giving all credit to the Mongols, the Italians provided a satisfying closure for the story.

> It was about the year 1262 after Christ had been born, that Alau, the lord of the Tartars of the Levant, who knew all the evil things that the Old Man did, said to himself that he was going to destroy him. He took some of his barons and sent them against that castle with a great many men. They besieged the castle a full three years without being able to take it. And they would never have taken it, had those inside been able to eat. But after three years, they had nothing more to eat. Thus the Old Man was taken and killed, the one named Alaodin, with all his men. And from that Old Man up to now, there has been no other Old Man and no Assassins, and with him all the lordship ended, as did the evils that the Old Men of the Mountain had done in the past.[35]

In truth, the battle was much less fierce and the siege much less long, but the text is concerned to exaggerate both the formidable nature of the Assassins and the admirable nature of the Mongols' victory. Its last sentence passes final judgment, construing the whole as a morality play, with Alaü—that is, Hulagu, younger brother to both Möngke (who reigned from 1248 to 1259) and Kubilai Khan (whose reign was from 1259 to 1294)—as the instrument through whom sinners were punished and righteousness secured.

IV

The Polo text makes clear that people and goods were in global circulation long before the modern or postmodern eras and further that the circulation of people and goods then, as now, stimulates and yields material for the circulation of narratives. In the thirteenth century, we observe a dense network of interaction, leading from Constantinople to Persia and Cathay; France, England, and Egypt to Acre; Alamut to Lebanon and Baghdad; Mongolia to Alamut; Beijing to Venice, and to a Genoese prison. The traffic involved diplomats, merchants, missionaries, soldiers, *fedayeen*, and authors of romances.

Circulation of goods and people often produces conflict, be it of a mercantile, martial, or religio-ideological sort. And conflict often conditions

Table 3. Recalibration of Hierarchic Relations in Asia, as Advanced in
Variants of the Assassin Myth

Rank	Sunni propaganda	European confidence pre-1291	European fears post-1291	Polo reminder	Polo's implicit suggestion
1	Sunni	Christians	Saracens [= Sunni]	Mongols	Mongol-Christian Alliance
2	Assassins [= Heretics]	Saracens [= Sunni]	Christians	Assassins [= Saracens]	Saracens [= Sunni]
3		Assassins [= Heretics]			

the circulation of narratives and signs, for the myths people tell about the
others they encounter are instruments for mediating and theorizing their
relations, but also instruments of struggle. Always, they reflect the perspective and advance the interests of those who tell them.

As such myths diffuse, their variants ramify, for every telling is a retelling that spawns others in its wake. Every variant, moreover, draws on earlier versions but revises their details to pointed purpose, as struggles are
waged through the introduction, elimination, or modification of motifs,
episodes, and characters in a widely circulating narrative. The goal of such
interventions is to reposition the story's master categories to the benefit of
some and the detriment of others.

In the preceding discussion, I have tried to trace changes in the way the
Assassins were narrated over numerous texts that culminate in the book
of Marco Polo (table 3 illustrates the shifting hierarchy through multiple
variants). The trajectory begins with Sunni propaganda, the purpose of
which was to establish the superiority of the orthodox Sunnis to the heretic Nizaris (and to the Shi'is in general). All Western authors before Polo
adopted this position but added a third category—Christians—which they
set in the paramount position, higher than Muslims of whatever sort.

To appreciate the force of Messer Marco's retelling, one must understand that he wrote in the immediate aftermath of 1291, when Acre—
the last Crusader stronghold in the Levant—fell to the Egyptian Mamluks, who were fast replacing the Saljuq Turks as the chief Muslim power.
After two centuries of crusading, Christendom had nothing to show for
its efforts. The trade routes, briefly opened, were now closing down and

the Saracens seemed triumphant once more. Inter alia, Polo's book addressed Europeans' fears at this reversal of fortunes, reminding them that beyond their Muslim enemies lay a greater power still, and a potential ally. This was the Mongols and their Khan, who had proven their superiority when they crushed the Old Man and his Assassins, whose representation was revised so that he might appear as the most terrifying Muslim of all.

Making common cause with the Mongols offered a solution to the problem of Islamic power, for which Polo's narrative offered a precedent in its account of how the descendants of Prester John and Chingiz Khan forged an alliance to vanquish common enemies.[36] Many in Europe were urging a new Crusade in the 1290s, and Venetians were prominent among them. In support of this venture, they actively explored the possibility of a Mongol alliance, particularly after the Mongols won several victories over the Mamluks in 1299–1300.[37] Along these lines, it has been plausibly suggested that Messer Marco meant to advertise himself as a potential ambassador to Ghazan Khan (who reigned between 1295–1304), Mongol ruler of Persia, who was responsible for those victories and whom Polo knew well, having delivered a bride to him as the agent of Kubilai Khan.[38]

Neither the personal nor the international ambitions came to pass, however. European negotiations with the Mongols continued until 1307 but ultimately went nowhere, and such enthusiasm as there was for a Ninth Crusade gradually waned. Released from prison when Genoa and Venice made peace in 1299, Messer Marco returned home and lived out his life without further adventure. Many years later, when the worries of the 1290s were long past, he prepared a revision of his book for his own private use and for circulation among a small circle of trusted friends.[39] There, when he was no longer agitating for another Crusade, Mongol alliance, or diplomatic employment, he revised his text to make it less aggressive, restoring the notion that the Assassins were heretics and deleting all mention of their drug use (Table 4).

Regardless of whether Polo accomplished his immediate objectives, his version of the Assassin myth had considerable effect and its influence was of an enduring nature. His portrait of the Old Man has become a stock item of the Western imaginary, its elements continually reproduced in variants that range from Sax Rohmer's Fu Manchu to George W. Bush's Osama bin Laden. As implied in this last example, the simplistic fantasy of East and West united in a "coalition of the willing" against the Islamic middle remains current in certain circles. Nor should we forget that Polo's description of Cathay's wealth stimulated a Genoese sailor to imagine a westward passage by sea that would avoid the unfortunate obstacle

Table 4. Revision of Polo's Text Late in Life to Restore the Charge of Heresy (Items 2 and 7) and Remove the Charge of Drugs (Items 4 and 6)

	Marco Polo, Manuscript F (written with Rustichello for a broad public, circa 1299)	Marco Polo, Manuscript Z (private text, revised late in life)
1	Mulecte is a country where the Old Man of the Mountain used to live in the past	Mulhec is that country in which the Old Man of the Mountain was accustomed to live in ancient time.
2	Mulecte means "of the Saracens. . . . ."*	**In that country lived those who were heretics according to Saracen laws. . . .†**
3	He had a castle at the entrance of the garden, so strong that no man of the world could take it; on the other hand, one could only enter by that way.	At the entrance was an extremely strong fortress.
4	The Old Man took into his court all the youths of that country between twelve and twenty years old: it was these who seemed to be men of arms. They knew well, having heard it said, that according to their prophet Mohammed, paradise was made in such a manner as I have told you, and thus they truly believed it. And what should I tell you about it? The Old Man had these youths put in this paradise in groups of four, ten, or twenty, as he liked in this fashion. **For he had them given drinks that made them fall asleep right away.** Then he had them taken and placed in this garden and had them awakened. When the youths were awakened and found themselves inside and they saw all the things I have described to you, they believed themselves truly to be in paradise. And the ladies and maidens stayed with them constantly, playing music and dancing and soothing them greatly and doing their every wish. It was as if these youths had all they wanted and never would they willingly leave there. And the Old Man held his court, very beautiful and grand, and he lived very nobly and made the simple people of the mountains around him believe that he was a prophet.	
5	And when the Old Man wanted to send someone in some place and have him kill some man.	The Old Man sent those attendants to commit many bad deeds.

Continued on the next page

Table 4. *Continued*

Marco Polo, Manuscript F (written with Rustichello for a broad public, circa 1299)	Marco Polo, Manuscript Z (private text, revised late in life)
6 **He had him given the drink, as much as he liked.** And when he was asleep, he had him taken to his palace. And when these youths awoke and found themselves in the castle and palace, which were great marvels, they were not happy with it, for the would never have left the paradise from which they came by their own will.	
7 Now they went before the Old Man and they bowed deeply before him, as if they believed that he were a great prophet.	**He made simple people believe him a prophet,** and they truly believed.
8 The Old Man asked them where they came from and they said that they came from paradise. And they said that truly this was the same paradise that Mohammed described to our ancestors. They told all the things that they found there. And the others who heard this and had not been there, had great desire to go to paradise and wished to die, because they would be able to go there and they greatly desired to go there that day. . . .‡	
9 And when the Old Man wanted to have some lord killed, or some other man, he took some of his assassins and sent them where he wanted and he told them that he wanted to send them to paradise and that they should go kill these men and, if they died, they would all go to paradise.	Thus, he promised them paradise if they would kill certain magnates,
10 Those who were thus ordered by the Old Man, they gladly did more things than they thought to do and they went and did all that the Old Man ordered them. And in this way, no man escaped being killed when the Old Man of the Mountain wanted it.§	and in this way he had many killed.‖

*Benedetto, *Il Milione,* 32: Mulecte est une contree la ou le Viel de la montagne soloit demorer ansienemant. Mulecte vaut a dire de Sarain. Note Benedetto's attempt to emend this passage, discussed earlier in the text, and in note 26.

†Barbieri, ed., *Marco Polo, Milione,* 57; Mulhec est quedam patria in qua Veglus de Montanea manere consuevit antiquitus; in qua patria habitabant heretici secundum legem sarracenam.

‡ Benedetto, *Il Milione,* 33–34: Il avoit un castiaus a l'entreee de cel jardin si fort ne doutroit home dou monde, et por autre part ne i se pooit entrer que por iluec. Les Vielz tenoit o lui, en sa cort, tult les jovenes de doç anz en vint de la contree, ce estoient celz que senbleient estre homes d'armes: les quelz savoient bien por oir dir, solonc que Maomet lor profete dist elz, que le parais estoit fait en tel maner com je vos ai contés: et ensi croient il voiramant. E que vos en diroie? Li Vieilz en fasoit metre de cesti jeune en cel parais a quatre et a X et a XX, selonc que il voloit, en cest mainere: car il faisoit elz doner bevrajes por lo quel il s'adormoit mantinant; puis les faisoit prendre et metre en cel jardin et les faisoit desveiller. Et quant les jeunes estoient desvoillés, et il se trovent laiens et il voient toutes cestes couses que je vos ai dit, il croient estre en parais voiramant. Et les dames et les dameseles demoroient tout jor con elz sonant et cantant et faisant grant soulas; et en fasoient a lor voluntés. Si que cisti jeune avoient tout ce que il voloient et jamés por lor voluntés ne istront de laiens. Et le Viel tient sa corte mout belle et grant et demore mout noblemant et fait creere a cel senple jens des montagnes que entor lui sunt qu'il est profete: et ensi croient il voiramant. Et quant le Vel en vult aucun por envoier en aucun leu e faire occire aucun home, il fait doner le be[v]raje a tant come il li plet; et quant il sunt endormia il fait prendre [et porter] en son palasio. Et quant cesti jeune sunt desveillés, et il se trovent en cel caustiaus el palais, il s'en font grant meraveie et nen sunt pas lies, car del parais dont il venoient por lor voluntés nen s'en fuissent il jamés partis. Il alent mantinant devant li Vieus et se humelient mout ver lui, come celz que croient que soit grant profete. Le Vielz le demande dont il viennent et celz dient qu'il viennent dou parais. Et disoient que voiramant est cel le meme parais come Maomet dist a nostri ancesor. Lor content toutes les couses qu'il hi trovent. Et le autre que ce ocut et ne avoient esté, avoient grant volunté d'aler el parais et avoient volunté de morir porcoi il hi posent aler et mout desiroient cel jor qu'il hi aillent.

§ The Franco-Italian contains two variants of this passage, one given in chapter 42 and the other in chapter 43 (both in Benedetto, *Il Milione,* 34). The latter is the more polished of the two and is the one quoted here. The earlier version follows immediately on the passage cited in cells 3–8 of this table. The two variants read as follows.

	Chapter 42	Chapter 43
1	Et quant le Vielz vuelt faire occir un grant sire,	Et quant le Vielz voloit fair occir aucun segnor ou aucu[n] aotro homo,
2	Il fait aprover de sien asciscin celz que meior estoient.	Il prennoit de cesti sien asciscin
3	Il envoie plosors ne grantment logne environ soi por les contrees,	Et les envoie la ou il voloit,
4	Et lor comandent qu'il ocient cel homes.	Et lor disoit qu'il les voloit mandere en parais et qu'il alasent occire le tiel homes et, se il morisen, que tant tosto ira en parais.

Continued on the next page

	Chapter 42	Chapter 43
5	Celz vont mantinant et font le comanda- mant lor segnor,	Celz, que cest estoit lor comandés por le Vielz, le fasoient mout volunter plus que couse que il penssent faire et aloient et fasoient tout ce que le Viel lor comandoit.
6	Puis retornent a cort—celz que escanpent, car de telz hi a que sunt pris et morti— puis qu'il ont occis le home.	Et en ceste mainere ne escanpoit nul home que ne fust occis, quant le Vielz de la montagne voust.

||Barbieri, *Marco Polo, Milione*, 58: In introitu erat quidem quoddam castrum fortissimum. Qui Veglus mitebat istos satellites ad multa mala commitendo; qui faciebat gentes simplices credere quod esset propheta, et vere credeba (n) t; et sic promitebat eis paradisum si velent occidere aliquos magnates, et sic multos fecit occidi.

of Muslim power. On Columbus's first voyage, he constantly consulted Messer Marco's book, but to consider that moment of circulating bodies, goods, and narratives would open another chapter in the history of myth and globalization.[40]

Notes

This essay is reprinted from *Comparative Studies in Society and History* (2006): 242–59, © 2006 by Society for Comparative Study of Society and History. Reprinted with the permission of Cambridge University Press, with minor editorial adjustments.

1. I have treated these issues most extensively in *Discourse and the Construction of Society* and *Theorizing Myth*.

2. Unless otherwise cited, I have followed the critical edition of the earliest Franco-Italian text: Benedetto, ed., *Il Milione, prima edizione integrale*. The information regarding the circumstances of the text's writing is found in its first chapter (pp. 3–4).

3. Rustichello, who is sometimes referred to as Rusticiano da Pisa, is best known for a "Romance of Palamedes" that makes use of Arthurian materials. The text is available in Löseth, ed., *Le Roman en prose de Tristan*. See further del Guerra, *Rustichello da Pisa*.

4. Benedetto, *Il Milione*, 3: "Et qui trouverés toutes les grandismes mervoilles et les grant diversités de la grant Harminie et de Persie et des Taqrtars et [de] Indie, et de maintes autres provinces, sicom notre livre vos contera por ordre apertemant, sicome meisser Marc Pol, sajes et noble citaiens de Venece, raconte por ce que a sez iaus meisme il le voit. Mes auques hi n'i a qu'il ne vit pas, mes il l'entendi da homes citables et de verité. Et por ce metreron les chouse veue por veue et

l'entendue por entandue, por ce que notre livre soit droit et vertables sanz nulle na[n]sogne. Et chascuns que cest livre liroie ou oiront le doient croire, por ce que toutes sunt chouses vertables."

5. More than 150 medieval and renaissance manuscripts of the Polo text survive in a dozen different languages. Regarding the relations among these, see Benedetto, *Il Milione*, xi–ccxxi; Moule and Pelliot, *Marco Polo*, I:40–52; or Lamer, *Marco Polo and Discovery*, 46–58,105–15.

6. On the ancient trade between Mediterranean Europe and China, its disruption by the rise of Islam, and medieval attempts at its reestablishment, see Curtin, *Cross-Cultural Trade*, 90–135. Regarding the role played by Venetians, see R. Lopez, "Venezia e le grandi linee," 37–82; and Renouard, "Mercati e mercanti veneziani," 83–108.

7. The first were Giovanni di Piano Carpini, sent to the Mongols in Karakorum by Pope Innocent IV in 1245, and William of Rubruck, sent by Louis IX of France (St. Louis) in 1253.

8. Benedetto, *Il Milione*, 6.

9. See Mosstaert and Woodman, "Trois documents Mongols" and *I tesori dell'Archivio segreto vaticano*, 104, and plate XXXVII. Philippe Ménard, ed., *Le devisement du monde*, 179, also mentions correspondence between Mongol rulers and Philip the Fair of France that is preserved in the French national archives, dating from 1289 and 1305.

10. Benedetto, *Il Milione*, 8–9.

11. Those referred to as *sensin* in Benedetto, *Il Milione*, 65, may be Taoists. If so, they are treated respectfully. In some manuscripts, Jews appear in a few formulaic phrases, but they play no part in the action.

12. A great deal has been written of late on the place of Prester John in early Orientalism. See Rachewiltz, *Prester John and Europe's Discovery*; Gumilev, *Searches for Imaginary Kingdom*; Hamilton and Beckingham, eds., *Prester John, Mongols, and Ten Lost Tribes*; and Baum, *Die Verwandlungen des Mythos vom Reich des Priesterkönigs Johannes*.

13. The "Old Man" appears in chapters 41–43 (Benedetto, *Il Milione*, 32–35). Useful secondary literature includes: Nowell, "Old Man of the Mountain"; Olschki, *L'Asia di Marco Polo*; Gabriel, *Marco Polo in Persien*; Daftary, *Assassin Legends*; and Bartlett, *Assassins*.

14. The most important of these figures were Hasan-i Sabbah (d. 1124), Rashid aI-Din Sinan (d. 1192 or 1193), who led the Syrian community at the height of their power, and 'Ala-al-Din Muhammad III (1221–55), penultimate ruler of the Persian Nizaris.

15. The modern discussion begins with Hodgson, *Order of Assassins*. Subsequent contributions include Lewis, *Assassins*; Filippani-Ronconi, *Ismaeliti ed 'Assassini'*; and Bartlett, *Assassins*.

16. Hodgson, *Order of Assassins*, facing p. 88, lists the following assassinations by the Nizaris: Sâwa muezzin (1082), Nizâm al-Mulk (1092), Jahâh ad-Dawla

(1102), Mutarshid (1135), Râshid (1138), Raymond of Tripoli (1152), and Conrad of Montferrat (1192). Unsuccessful attempts were also made on Saladin and Prince (later King) Edward of England in 1272.

17. An Arabic equivalent, *Shaykh al Jabal* ("Old Man of the Mountain"), is not attested in any extant source. Regarding the terminology and its implications, see Daftary, *Assassin Legends*, 114–17, passim.

18. The etymology and significance of the term was established by Sylvestre de Sacy, "Mémoire sur la dynastie des Assassins," an expanded version of which was published in the *Mémoires de l'Institut Royal de France*, 4. An English translation of the latter is included in Daftary, *Assassin Legends*, 136–88. For more recent discussions, see ibid., 89–92; or Bartlett, *Assassins*, 213–16.

19. Translation by Maria Rethelyi. The text is found in M. Adler, ed., *Itinerary of Benjamin of Tudela*, 53–54. Cf. William of Rubruck's report to Louis IX (*Itinerary* 18.4): "To the south are the Caspian mountains and Persia; to the east, the mountains are Muliech [variant: Mulihet], that is, the mountains of the Assassins." (Habet enim montes Caspios et Persidem a meridie, montes vero Muliech, hoc est Haxasinorum.) Text in van den Wyngaert, ed., *Sinica Franciscana*, I:210.

20. Translation by Maria Rethelyi. The text is in Adler, *Itinerary of Benjamin of Tudela*, 16–17.

21. Benedetto, *Il Milione*, 32: "I will tell you all his story just as I, Messer Marco, *heard it told* by many men." (Or vos conterai tout son afer solonc que je meser Marc *oi la conter* a plusors homes.)

22. See, for instance, John Critchley's pronouncement: "The well-informed among Polo's fourteenth-century readers would have found his book a mixture of the familiar and the incredible. And the incredible stories were ones they had heard before. . . . The most over-ripe chestnut among Polo's near-eastern anecdotes was the story of the Old Man of the Mountains." *Marco Polo's Book*, 83–84.

23. Benedetto, *Il Milione*, 33: "Et por ce l'avoit faite en tel mainere que Maomet ne fist entendre a les Sarain."

24. Benedetto, *Il Milione*, 33: ". . . les quelz savoient bien por oir dir, solonc que Maomet lor profete dist elç, que le parais estoit fait en tel maner com je vos ai contés."

25. Benedetto, *Il Milione*, 32: "Mulecte vaut a dire de Sarain."

26. Benedetto, *Il Milione*, 32, emended as follows: "Mulecte vaut a dire (*heretiques selon la loy*) de Sarain." Not only is this contrary to the clear wording and sense of the Franco-Italian text, of the 130 manuscripts he consulted it finds support in only two: the late MS. Z, discussed below, and the Tuscan of MS. R, which includes a learned interpolation: "Mulehet is a country, in which the Old Man called 'of the Mountain,' used to live in the past, because this name 'Mulehet' means 'place where there are heretics' in the Saracen language, and the men of that place are called 'Mulehetics,' that is heretics under their law, as the Patarine Christians learned." (Mulehet è una contrada, nella quale anticamente soleva stare il vecchio detto della montagna, perchè questo nome di Mulehet è come a dire luogo dove

stanno li heretici nella lingua saracena e da detto luogo gli huomini si chiamano Mulehetici, cioè heretici della sua legge, si come appresso li Christiani Patarini.) Unnecessary and unwarranted, the emendation has regrettably obscured one of the most original, important, and intriguing features of the Polo text.

27. The motif of self-prostration recurs in the same position in the Polo text, but there is no question of self-immolation (Benedetto, *Il Milone*, 33): "They now went before the Old Man, *and they bowed deeply before him*, as if they believed that he were a great prophet." (Il alent mantinant devant li Vieus et *se humelient mout ver lui*, come celz que croient que soit grant profete.) The Tuscan version of the text states that the fedayeen kneeled (*inginocchiandosi*).

28. Here, William of Tyre's testimony is of interest (*Chronicle*, bk. 20, ch. 29): "Neither our people, nor the Saracens know from what the name Assassins was taken." (Hos tam nostri quam Sarraceni, nescimus unde nomine deducto, Assissinos vocant.) Huygens, ed., *Guillaume de Tyr*, 953.

29. Arnold of Lübeck, *Chronicle of the Slavs*, bk. 4, ch. 16, text in Pertz, ed., *Arnoldi Chronica Slavorum*, 146: "tunc poculo eos quodam, quo extasim vel amentiam rapiantur, inebriat, et eis magicis suis quedam sompnia in fantastica, gaudiis et deliciis, immo nugis plena, ostendit, et hec eternaliter pro tali opere eos habere contendit."

30. Thus, William of Tyre omits the promise of paradisal reward from his account, while Burchard of Strassburg has no unfavorable comment on it. Only James of Vitry shows hesitation when he describes the *fedayeen*, inflamed by this promise, as "wretched and misguided youths" *(miseri et seducti adolescentes)*. Text in de Sandoli, *Itinera Hierosolymitana Crucesignatorum*, 3:304.

31. In contrast to all earlier authors, Arnold speaks of the Old Man as having used "tricks" or "illusions" *(prestigiis)* to deceive his Assassins.

32. This motif is taken from Sûras 52, 55, and 56 of the Qurân, which were notorious in medieval Europe. Compare, for instance, the testimony given by Burchard of Strassburg: "The Saracens also believe one can obtain paradise in the land to which one is transferred after this life, where they believe there are four rivers: one of wine, the second of milk, the third of honey, the fourth of water, and they say that every species of fruit is born, and they feast and drink there. Every one of them, every day sleeps with nine virgins for the satisfaction of his sensuality *(pro voluptatis explemento)*, and if he should die in battle with a Christian, in paradise he sleeps with ten virgins daily." (Item credunt Sarraceni, se habere paradisum in terra, in quem post hanc vitam sint transituri, in quo credunt esse quatuor flumina, unum scilicet de vino, secundum de lacte, tertium de melle, et quartum de aqua, et omne genus fructuum ibidem dicunt nasci, et ibi pro velle comedent et bibent; unusquisque eorum omni die pro voluptatis explemento nove virgini commiscetur, et si quis in prelio a christiano moritur, cottidie in paradiso decem virginibus utitur.) Text quoted in Arnold of Lübeck's *Chronicle of the Slavs*, bk. 7, ch. 8, in Pertz, *Arnoldi Chronica Slavorum*, 271. See further, Southern, *Western Views of Islam*.

33. Benedetto, *Il Milione*, 33–34: "Et quant cesti jeune sunt desveillés, et il se

trovent en cel caustiaus el palais, il s'en font grant meraveie et nen sunt pas lies, car del parais dont il venoient por lor voluntés nen s'en fuissent il jamés partis Ils alent maintenant devant li Vieus et se humelient mout ver lui, come celz que croient que soit grant profete. Le Vielz le demande dont il viennent et celz dient qu'il viennent dou parais. Et disoient bien que voiramant est cel le parais come Maomet dist a nostri ancesor. Lor content toutes les couses qu'il hi trovent. Et le autre que ce oent et ne avoient esté, avoient grant volunté d'aler el parais et avoient volunté de morir porcoi il hi posent aler et mout desiroient cel jor qu'il hi aillent. Et quant le Vielz vuelt faire occir un grant sire, il fait approver de sien asciscin celz que melor estoient. Il envoie plosors ne grantment logne environ soi par les contrees, et lor comandent qu'il ocient cel homes. Celz vont mantinant et font le comandamant lor segnor, puis retornent a cort-celz que escanpent, car de telz hi a que sunt pris et morti-puis qu'il ont occis le home."

34. Bush, "Presidential Address," 33.

35. Benedetto, *Il Milione*, 34–35: "Il fu voir que, entor a les MCCLXII anz que avoit que Crist avoit nasqui, Alaü, les sire des Tartars dou levant, que soit toutes cestes mauveis chouse que cest Vielz faisoit, il dit a soi meesme qu'il le fara destruere. Adonc prist de sez baro[n]s e les envoie a cest castiaus con grant gens. Et asejent le caustaus bien trois anz que ne le postrent prendre. Et ne l'ausent jamés pris tant com il aussent en que mangier; mes a chief de trois anz il ne ont plus que mangier. Adonc furent pris et fu ocis le Vielz, que avoit a nom Alaodin, con tute sez homes. Et de cestui Viel jusque a cestui point ne i ot Viel ne nul asescin et en lui se fenist toute le segnorie et les maus que les Vielz de la montagne avoient fait jadis ansi[e]nemant." William of Rubruck, the French ambassador who was at the court of Möngke Khan in 1255, reported back to Louis IX concerning the Assassins' fate (Itinerary 32.4): "This Möngke has eight brothers: three full brothers and five half-brothers on his father's side. He sent one of the full brothers to the land of the Assassins, which is called Mulibet after them, and he commanded that all of them be killed." (Ipse Manguchan habet octo fraters: tres uterinos et quinque de patre. Unum ex uterinis misit in terram Hasasinorum, qui dicuntur Mulibet ab eis, et precepit quod omnes interficiantur.) Text in van den Wyngaert, *Sinica Franciscana*, I:287. On the considerations that prompted the Mongol assault, see Allsen, *Mongol Imperialism*.

36. Prester John's rivalry with the Mongols and his defeat by Chingiz Khan are narrated in chapters 64–68 of the Polo text (Benedetto, *Il Milione*, 50–52). The story of how his descendants and those of the Khan cooperated to defeat the Kaidu appears at chapter 200 (Benedetto, *Il Milione*, 218–20).

37. Diplomatic exchanges between the Mongol rulers of Persia (the Il-khans, descended from Hulagu) and European powers, seeking to make common cause against the Mamluks, dated back to 1262, when Hulagu made overtures to Louis IX, and continued until 1307. See further, Sinon, "Les relations entre les Mongols et l'Europe"; Boyle, "Il-khans of Persia"; Schein, "Gesta Dei per Mongolos"; Meyvaert, "Unknown Letter of Hulagu"; Tyerman, "Marino Sanudo Torsello and Lost

Crusade"; Richard, "Chrétiens et Mongols au concile"; Morgan, *Mongols*, 183–87; and Critchley, *Marco Polo's Book, 68–70.*

38. In *Benedetto, Il Milione*, 11–13, chapters 18–19 tell how the Polos were charged by Kubilai Khan to escort a bride to his great-nephew Arghun (whose reign lasted from 1284–1291; Arghun was the grandson of Hulagu). After a long and difficult journey, however, they arrived shortly after Arghun's death and, following some consultation, conferred her on his son, Ghazan (variant: Taxan). The idea that Messer Marco's book was motivated, in part, by a desire to advertise his potential utility as an ambassador is explored by Critchley, *Marco Polo's Book,* 68–76.

39. On the nature and significance of Manuscript Z, see Lamer, *Marco Polo and Discovery*, 46–58.

40. Regarding the extent to which Columbus was inspired by reading Marco Polo and perceived the Americas through the mediation of his text, see Reichert, "Columbus und Marco Polo."

3

"A Storm on the Horizon"

Discomforting Democracy and the Feeling of Fairness

Ann Pellegrini

Ann Pellegrini presented to the University of Alabama community a version of the following essay for the tenth Aronov Lecture in February 2012. An earlier version of this essay has been published in *Secular Discomforts: Religion and Cultural Studies*, edited by Holly Randell-Moon and Sophie Sunderland, a special issue of *Cultural Studies Review*.

Overture

"There's a bright golden haze on the meadow, there's a bright golden haze on the meadow." So begin the opening lines of *Oklahoma*, the 1943 Richard Rodgers and Oscar Hammerstein musical that is widely credited as one of the first full-blown "book musicals." The original Broadway production ran for an astonishing 2,212 performances, and the play was adapted into an Academy Award–winning film in 1955, during the height of the Cold War.[1] The Oklahoma Territory portrayed in the Rodgers and Hammerstein musical was riven by conflicts between farmer and cowman. Could these rivals become friends? Yes! They can! Peace and social harmony win out, and the community forged by play's end shines as golden-bright as the Oklahoma sun. And yet, the histories of so many are left offstage, out of view. *Oklahoma* sanitizes the story of American expansion, presenting a liberal fable of democratic harmony bursting forth amid social difference.[2] The violent death of "Pore Jud Fry" is but an afterthought, the man who killed him quickly acquitted so that he can enjoy his honeymoon with his new bride. As for the violent displacement of Native Americans into and from the "unassigned lands" that became Oklahoma? Within the musical world of *Oklahoma*, it is no thought at all. Ultimately, the beautiful American morning the show celebrates requires setting some others beyond the pale.

Although *Oklahoma* may not be accurate as history, its exclusions, the stories it does not or cannot tell, nonetheless testify to the failures of liberal tolerance to make room for wider forms of social difference. Making social space for difference does not mean that everyone has to be friends. Indeed, the widening I will argue for in this essay both requires and produces an agonistic public square that exceeds its own parameters. This is democracy as discomfort. Democracy does not require that we agree with each other, let alone like each other. In a democracy, social cohesion is built by interaction among those who disagree with each other, not by setting some viewpoints and some people outside the frame of possibility from the start.[3] As recent events in the real-life Oklahoma suggest, agonistic democratic pluralism is an unfinished project.

*   *   *

In November 2010, Oklahoma voters overwhelmingly approved a ballot measure that bans judges from "considering or using Shariah Law" when making a ruling. State Question 755—also known as SQ 755, the Shariah Amendment, the Oklahoma International Law Amendment, and, most apocalyptically, the "Save Our State" Amendment—garnered the support of 70 percent of voters. In addition to amending the state constitution to ban judicial consideration of Shariah law, the measure also more broadly forbids courts from "considering or using international law."

This coupling of Shariah law and international law requires some preliminary explanation and conceptual untangling. The section of SQ 755 that forbids a state court from "considering or using international law" reflects a broader conservative distrust of any citation of international law as amounting to a violation of American sovereignty. This hostility is seen even among some jurists themselves. For example, Supreme Court justice Antonin Scalia has been a very public critic of reference to foreign law in US courts. One notable case in point is his withering dissent in *Lawrence v. Texas*, the 2003 Supreme Court case that found laws against consensual "homosexual sodomy" to be unconstitutional. The vote in that landmark case was 6–3. Justice Scalia voted in the minority to uphold antisodomy statutes. His dissent was wide ranging, but he was particularly exercised by the majority opinion's approving reference to a 1981 holding by the European Court of Human Rights that "laws proscribing [consensual homosexual conduct] were invalid under the European Convention on Human Rights."[4]

This hostility to international law is hardly some quirk of Justice Scalia, as can be seen in the US Congress's unwillingness to ratify any number of international treaties. Moreover, such opposition cuts across simplistic partisan political distinctions and extends a long tradition of American exceptionalism, whose shadow gives cover to nativist suspicions of "foreigners." A state amendment to ban a court's consideration of foreign laws could probably survive constitutional scrutiny and be upheld by the courts. It is the singling out of a *specific religion*—Islam—that poses constitutional issues, a point I will come back to below. In fact, two other US states, Tennessee and Louisiana, both passed more neutrally worded "anti-foreign law" bills, in 2010, which made no reference to any religion, precisely in order to avoid this legal problem.

Legalisms aside, however, we should not lose sight of the ugly challenge to democratic values posed by these carefully worded bans on foreign law. The contemporary organized movement to pass such bans is in fact the "polite" face of what is, at its foundation, an anti-Muslim campaign.[5] Moreover, whether or not a law passes constitutional muster does not tell us the whole story. Thus, even as I am concerned by the constitutional dilemmas posed by anti-Shariah laws, the larger concern of my analysis is the extralegal effects of such bans, how they simultaneously illuminate and animate anti-Muslim bias, as well as reveal broader problems raised by the US discourse of tolerance.

As of this writing, Oklahoma's ban on the consideration of Shariah law and any foreign law has not gone into effect. Within days of the measure's passage, US district judge Vicki Miles-LaGrange granted a preliminary injunction against State Question 755. She was responding to a lawsuit filed by Muneer Awad, executive director of the Oklahoma chapter of the Council on American-Islamic Relations (CAIR). In issuing the injunction, Judge Miles-LaGrange determined that Awad had made a "preliminary showing" that the Oklahoma amendment violated the First Amendment to the US Constitution.

The First Amendment begins, "Congress shall make no law respecting an establishment of religion, or prohibiting the free exercise thereof." Religious freedom has two components: disestablishment and free exercise, and a lot of ink has been spilled over the relation between these two aspects of religious freedom, how they are related, whether one is more important than the other, and how to balance their principles when they seem to conflict. These are not just academic questions. In *Love the Sin: Sexual Regulation and the Limits of Religious Tolerance*, Janet R. Jakobsen and I argue that it matters a great deal for the practice of democratic social relations whether one sees these two principles as separable or interstructuring.[6] Public political debates over the meaning of religious freedom in the United States all too often produce the following balkanization: proponents of more religion (really, more Christianity) in US public life and in government lean heavily on the free exercise component and underplay disestablishment. Conversely, many secularists—not all secularists, to be sure, but many—stress the absolute separation of church and state and minimize free exercise. In contrast, Jakobsen and I see disestablishment as the structuring condition for free exercise. Otherwise, those who are religiously different or not religious at all may well find their lives not simply less admired and valued than those who belong to the dominant religion; they may find they have diminished legal status.

Jakobsen and I are sympathetic to those who are nervous about an overpresence of religion in American public life; however, we do not think the problem is religion per se, with the banishment of religion from public life as the only remedy. Rather, the problem is one of social dominance.[7] Currently, the religion that enjoys the most room for "free exercise" in the United States is Christianity. Christianity offers the model for what other religions are supposed to look and feel like, such that even the Supreme Court, the very body charged with interpreting the meaning of disestablishment and free exercise, defaults to Christian—more accurately, to Reformed Protestant—notions of what religion "is" when deciding whether or not particular religious rights have been violated.[8] This can work out well if the claimants belong to mainline Protestant denominations, but not so well, if they do not. As conservative legal scholar Frederick Mark Gedicks reports, "No Jewish, Muslim, or Native American plaintiff has ever prevailed on a free exercise claim before the Supreme Court. Fundamentalist Christians and sects outside so-called mainline Protestantism have had only mixed success in seeking exemptions."[9]

One of the ways Christian dominance works is that particular Christian practices and ideals can "float," sometimes being overtly marked as religious, at other times passing as secular, something Jakobsen and I have referred to as "Christo-normativity." Stephen M. Feldman examines this phenomenon as it has played out in a string of Supreme Court cases concerning religious freedom. Because "Christian domination is so deeply rooted in American history," he argues, "any judicial reliance on tradition or history likely will result in the constitutional approval of Christian practices and values."[10] This is not a matter of bad faith (pun intended). The court does not operate in a vacuum but is itself embedded in the symbols, structures, and context of Christian dominance.[11] Nor should we necessarily expect this situation to change radically now that there are three

Jewish justices and six Catholic justices on the Roberts Court—the first time that there have been no Protestant members of the Supreme Court.[12]

This is because the court's historic Christian bias is not due to any one individual justice's or particular group of justices' blind spots. The problem arises out of institutional practices, interpretive assumptions, and structuring conditions, which reproduce Christian domination. One effect of this persistent Christian bias in judicial decisions—and in legislative policies, as well—is that, as Feldman concludes, "outgroup religions are more likely to be protected [from discrimination] when their practices and tenets resemble those of Christianity."[13] But democratic freedom should not require that those who are religiously different be or become the same as the dominant norm in order to be treated as equals before the law. Such a requirement—to become like or like *enough*—significantly reduces democratic social space not just for being different but for performing—practicing—one's difference in public.

The ongoing dominance of Christianity and its default status as the measure of "the religious" have produced a situation where religious difference is at best seen as at odds with American identity. At worst, it is imagined to be an actual threat to "traditional" American values, where "traditional" means Christian but can be stretched to the hyphenated Judeo-Christian under certain circumstances. This is precisely the dynamic playing out in the Oklahoma amendment. If enacted, the amendment would establish a class of religious outsiders, whose religious practices and social identities are afforded lesser legal protections and public status than their religiously orthodox neighbors. In its preliminary injunction, the district court found that the amendment "does not have a secular purpose, that its primary purpose inhibits religion, and that it fosters an excessive government entanglement with religion."[14] No compelling state interest was advanced to justify these linked violations of the establishment clause. Quite the contrary: despite claims that Question 755 was necessary to "save our state," proponents of the law could not point to any concrete instances where Shariah law actually had been imposed on Oklahoma citizens. In the preliminary hearing conducted by the district court immediately after voter passage of the amendment, Scott Boughton, an assistant attorney general for the state, conceded that he knew of no case in which an Oklahoma court had in fact invoked Shariah law. And yet, facts were apparently no obstacle, for he persisted in defending the law on behalf of the state.

Muslims are a slim minority in Oklahoma: 30,000 out of a total state population of 3.7 million. However, who needs actual Muslims when you have the potent figure of "the Muslim," an all-purpose bogeyman for the American twenty-first century.[15] Moreover, the dangerous Muslim conjured by the US political imaginary is almost always male; when Muslim women do appear, they do so veiled and victimized—by Muslim men and Shariah law.

Fear-mongering rhetoric notwithstanding, the caliphate is not coming to Oklahoma any time soon, nor anywhere else in the United States for that matter. Nevertheless, the Oklahoma amendment, which was blocked by the courts before being enacted, would have had a chilling effect on the free exercise rights of Muslims in that state. As law professor Aziz Huq explained in the *New York Times*, "A butcher would no longer be able to enforce his contract for halal meat—contracts that, like deals for kosher or other faith-sanctioned foods, are regularly enforced around the country. Nor could a Muslim banker seek damages for violations of a financial instrument certified as 'Sharia compliant' since it pays no interest."[16] This burden on free exercise thus violates the second component of First Amendment religious freedom. To its credit, the Oklahoma district court did not pull its punches in identifying the anti-Muslim bias animating the amendment: the "amendment is not facially neutral, discriminates against a specific religious belief, and prohibits conduct because it is undertaken for religious reasons."[17]

The district court's injunction survived legal appeal and has become permanent. Consequently, the anti-Shariah amendment is dead, for now, in the state of Oklahoma. More than legal prohibitions were—and remain—at stake, however. A law does not have to be enacted and enforced to have profound effects on public debates over insiders and outsiders to the nation. Legislators in six other states are considering similarly worded bans on Shariah law, and, as Huq reports, many more (fourteen at this counting) are considering wider bans on the use of "foreign laws." The public language used in these debates contributes to an atmosphere in which "Muslim Oklahoman" or, simply, "Muslim American" is an impossible identity. For example, in a June 2010 interview with ABC News, state representative Rex Duncan, chair of Oklahoma's House Judiciary Committee and an author of the anti-Shariah amendment, used a meteorological metaphor to explain the vital need for the law: "It's not an imminent threat in Oklahoma yet, but it's a storm on the horizon in other states."[18] Subsequently, in an interview with MSNBC, he turned to military metaphors to describe the amendment as a "a war for the survival of America" and "a pre-emptive strike" against Islamic law and against "liberal judges" who want to undermine America's "founding principles."[19] By *founding prin-*

ciples, though, Duncan did not mean the Constitution. "Oklahomans," he continued, "recognize that America was founded on Judeo-Christian principles." It is these values the amendment defends, to ensure "that our courts are not used to undermine those founding principles, and turn Oklahoma into something that our founding fathers and our great grandparents wouldn't recognize."

In this rhetorical circuit, Duncan ties a knot between America and particular religious values ("Judeo-Christian") and links social recognition to a matter of family resemblance: what "our founding fathers and our great grandparents" would or would not recognize. The conjoined language of family and of self-defense—*Save Our State*—recodes the amendment. To its legislative backers, like Duncan, and to the overwhelming number of Oklahomans who voted for it, State Question 755 was not about discrimination against Muslims.[20] It was about defending core American principles. And who would be against that, except those who are un- or anti-American?

The dense network of ties spun by Duncan—he equates *nation* with *Judeo-Christian* and *family*—produces powerful affective resonances across ideological and creedal affiliations.[21] The addition of "Judeo" is important here, as it further cements the notion that State Question 755 is not religiously discriminatory. First, the hyphenate Judeo-Christian posits a false identity and equality between Judaism and Christianity.[22] Second, in the specific context of public debates over the place of Muslims in American life, Judeo-Christian effectively triangulates two groups of religious outsiders—American Jews and American Muslims—identifying the former as manifesting an acceptable form of religious difference and setting the latter outside the boundaries of national belonging.

Such acts of naming are part of the process by which the lines between who belongs and who does not are drawn and reinforced.[23] Public discourse, how we talk about and frame debates over difference, matters; it materializes. Indeed, how we talk about and name "others" can turn social difference, which is not or need not be a problem, into social division, which is. This is not a recent dilemma, and tolerance is not the solution. Robust democratic engagement that widens the space for difference, rather than requiring those who are different to become more of the same, is.

In *The Citizen Machine: Governing by Television in 1950s America*, Anna McCarthy analyzes the emergence of television as a technology of national belonging, tracing how corporations, nonprofit foundations, intellectuals, and politicians variously sought to use the new medium to teach citizens how to properly engage in democratic life in the United States during the Cold War.[24] One of the things McCarthy illuminates is how a centrist language of balance and moderation was deployed by both conservatives and liberals to discredit opposing positions as "extremist" and over the line. Of course, not every individual or group was equally positioned to have its appeals to centrism credited. In practice, the language of the center was also a vocabulary of marginalization that secured the boundaries of the general public by relegating some subjects to its outside.

In one especially telling incident, McCarthy recounts President Dwight D. Eisenhower's refusal to meet with civil rights leaders after *Brown v. Board of Education*. In that landmark 1954 case, the Supreme Court held that the racial segregation of public schools was unconstitutional, effectively ending separate but equal as a matter of law.[25] How well this mandate was carried out in practice is a separate issue, especially in light of the court's language in a follow-up hearing, in 1955, to determine how desegregation should be achieved: namely, "with all deliberate speed." This ambiguous language was used by opponents of desegregation to delay implementation of the new policy.

For his part, Eisenhower justified his refusal to meet with civil rights leaders on the grounds that if he met with them he would also have to meet with the Ku Klux Klan, a logic that effectively equated peaceful activists for racial equality with an organization dedicated to the violent suppression of racial and religious minorities. This equation was utterly of its moment, however. As McCarthy underlines, Eisenhower's appeals to balance and moderation were of a piece with broader Cold War attempts to cultivate a democratic citizenry that was engaged, but not "extremist." (Cue *Oklahoma*'s "Oh, the farmer and the cowman should be friends . . . territory folks should stick together, territory folks should all be pals.") Within this logic, "extremist" meant "activist," a logic of equivalence that actually promoted inequality. How so? This equation made it impossible to make important moral and political distinctions between advocates of freedom and equality and advocates of hateful violence.

In *Love the Sin*, Jakobsen and I discuss this reductionist logic in relation to the structure of tolerance. To be tolerant is to be "fair and balanced"—and that sounds pretty good, right? Nevertheless, we have to ask, fair and balanced as seen from where or from whose point of view? Although American common sense prizes and seeks to cultivate tolerance as a response to violence and social division, in practice, tolerance works to affirm existing social hierarchies by establishing an us–them relationship between a dominant center and those on the margins. Us-them commonly triangulates, as when a dominant center (also known as the phantom "general public") distinguishes itself from—and morally elevates itself above—two equally "extremist" others. This is the dynamic at work in Eisenhower's "inertial stance on racial equality."[26] This stance stakes out a middle ground in which a dominant white majority need not move the boundaries of national belonging at all or, at least, can cede as little ground as slowly as possible. When the rhetoric of "fair and balanced" meets "with all deliberate speed," expect a stall.

"Fair and balanced" is also the self-serving (and trademarked) slogan of Fox News, which is part of Rupert Murdoch's News Corporation. Fox's claims to be "fair and balanced" have been extensively challenged by media watchdogs like Fairness and Accuracy in Reporting, but without seeming to dent the news network's popularity. If anything, attacks from the left only embolden Fox's claims to be speaking for "real" American values. And real American values continue to speak from and to an imagined center, from President Barack Obama's much-repeated hopes of rising above partisanship, to comedian Jon Stewart's "call-to-reasonableness" via his October 2010 national "Rally to Restore Sanity," to the American media's two sides to every story approach to complex social controversies. I want to be clear that I am not against "reasonableness" per se. My concern here is with the way such appeals actually function in the storm of public debates over the boundaries of US public life. This is a rather different "storm" than the one Duncan worries over. Reasonableness or rationality can also work hand in hand with its ostensible opposite: namely, a mobilization of public feelings.

Feelings do not occur in a vacuum. They have a political and social history as well as a psychic life. Too often, calls to mollify, repair, or just plain avoid hurt feelings come to function as a kind of institutionalized forgetting of the social structures and histories of inequality within which feelings circulate and "attach" to people and particular hot-button topics. As a consequence, the need to repair the hurt feelings of *some* becomes an end unto itself, elevated above the promotion of substantive equality and social justice for some *others*. This is a long-standing issue in American life. We can hear its strains in the majority opinion in *Plessy v. Ferguson*, the infamous 1896 Supreme Court case that held that separate was equal. Justice Henry Brown, toward the end of his majority opinion, offered an answer to the question of how to tell the difference between a law that promotes the "public good" and one that was enacted for the "annoyance or oppression of a particular class." The short answer was "reasonableness." The somewhat more elaborated one continues to haunt contemporary US debates over "fairness": "In determining the question of reasonableness," Justice Brown wrote for the court's 8–1 majority, "[the state] is at liberty to act with reference to the established usages, customs, and traditions of the people, and with a view to the promotion of their comfort and the preservation of the public peace and good order."[27] This appeal to the established "traditions of the people" and the majority's ongoing "comfort" is crucial here, especially as it is used to explain the difference between reasonable laws and unreasonable discrimination. The legal logic of separate but equal would at last be overturned in *Brown v. Board of Education*, in 1954. Nevertheless, the cultural logics through which the feelings of the majority and the preservation of their established traditions must be protected and "comforted" persist—in ways that are deeply disabling for a vibrant democracy and social justice for all.

We can see this dynamic at work in so many facets of contemporary US public life, both in civil society (to use an old term) and the state. Consider in this regard the intensely mediatized political tempest over Cordoba House, the proposed Islamic center in downtown Manhattan.[28] This project has become (un)popularly known as the "Ground Zero Mosque"— an act of misnaming that stuck and has powered much of the controversy over the proposed building. The language of reasonableness may sound softer and kinder than the blatant Islamaphobia of many of the project's opponents, but it amounts to much the same thing: narrowing the social space available to be different and "do" difference in public. Wading into the controversy, President Obama spoke the language of reason and constitutional history when he declared that "Muslims have the same right to practice their religion as anyone else in this country. That includes the right to build a place of worship and a community center on private property in lower Manhattan, in accordance with local laws and ordinances. This is America, and our commitment to religious freedom must be unshakeable. The principle that people of all faiths are welcome in this country, and will not be treated differently by their government, is essential to who we are. The writ of our Founders must endure."[29]

Obama made these comments in August 2010, at an official White House event celebrating Ramadan, a White House tradition of hosting an Iftar meal that goes back several years and is akin to the White House–hosted "Christmas parties, seders, and Diwali celebrations." In what may at first seem like an aside, in his prepared remarks the president mentioned that he was not the first US president to host a dinner celebrating a Muslim holiday. However, this is more than a historical footnote, given the significant percentage of Americans who suspect that President Barack

Hussein Obama is himself a secret Muslim. Indeed, that very month, August 2010, the Pew Research Center released a new report titled: "Growing Number of Americans Say Obama Is a Muslim."[30]

Neither Obama's remarks nor its careful packaging did anything to tamp down the controversy over the Cordoba House project. Just the opposite: his remarks immediately drew fire from opponents of Cordoba House. The comments of Congressman Peter T. King, a Republican from the state of New York, were typical of the more "moderate" criticisms the president received: "President Obama is wrong. It is insensitive and uncaring for the Muslim community to build a mosque in the shadow of Ground Zero. While the Muslim community has the right to build the mosque they are abusing that right by needlessly offending so many people who have suffered so much. The right and moral thing for President Obama to have done was to urge Muslim leaders to respect the families of those who died and move their mosque away from Ground Zero. Unfortunately the President caved into political correctness."[31] In response to such criticisms—and worrying about anticipated Democratic party losses in the November 2010 midterm elections, in which they lost big, the same elections in which Oklahoma voters passed the ban on Shariah—on August 14, just a day after Obama's rousing remarks at the White House event, he clarified his meaning: "My intention was simply to let people know what I thought, which was that in this country, we treat everybody equally and in accordance with the law, regardless of race, regardless of religion. I was not commenting and I will not comment on the wisdom of making the decision to put a mosque there."[32]

In both King's criticism and Obama's dancing-on-a-pin response, we see what happens when a call to reasonableness meets up with appeals to public feelings: the feelings of some people must be protected, even if that means running roughshod over the *rights* of some others. This is so because such debates are conducted under conditions of dominance in which some positions are staked out from the beginning as the mark and measure of both reason and reasonable emotional response. If some Muslims come away with hurt feelings, or even limited free exercise rights (as would be the result if Oklahoma's anti-Shariah amendment were enacted), that is just the price they must pay for (eventual?) acceptance.

Tolerance in this context supports anti-Muslim bias and "Christonormativity" in the public square. Tolerance, as Jakobsen and I argue at length in *Love the Sin*, is in many respects a secular version of religious toleration in which an established church allows dissenters the right to worship without fear of persecution, but at the same time withholds from them equivalent public or civic rights and privileges. Although the United States is formally secular—again, the First Amendment promises disestablishment and free exercise of religion—Christianity (Reformed Protestantism) has long functioned as the backdrop against which claims of being a moral person or having values achieve cultural legibility. To put this another way: the Christian assumptions underlying tolerance may also help to make sense of why the anti-Muslim feelings animating public debates over Cordoba House are not seen or experienced as prejudice, at least not from the standpoint of the tolerant center. Indeed, the opponents of Cordoba House see themselves as defending a wounded post–9/11 America.

Freud's framework of mourning and melancholia is here helpful. In an essay written during the early years of World War I, Freud traces an analogy between mourning (which he considers a normal psychological response to loss) and melancholia (which he describes as a pathological response). He seeks to show what mourning and melancholia have in common and, especially, where they differ. The array of objects that may be lost in grief includes not just loved persons but also abstractions like patriotism, liberty, and other cherished ideals. For Freud melancholia—as opposed to mourning—involves an object loss that has been withdrawn from consciousness and *absorbed into the ego*. All unknowing, Freud observes, "The shadow of the object fell upon the ego." [33] Significantly, by the time he came to write *The Ego and the Id* (1923), Freud had revised his views on melancholia. No longer does melancholia constitute a "pathological" turning away from the world. Instead, "normal" processes of identification come more and more to resemble the melancholic model of object identification he had diagnosed as pathological in "Mourning and Melancholia." *The Ego and the Id* offers a picture of a body self-forged in the wake of loss: "The character of the ego is a precipitate of abandoned object-cathexes . . . and contains the history of those object-choices." [34]

The depathologization of melancholia is important for a number of reasons. It takes melancholia, and conversations about it, out of a narrowly clinical and individualizing frame and invites us to think about the larger social and political contexts in which loss is lived and negotiated. Where the *psychic* life of tolerance is concerned, we can, with Kathleen Roberts Skerrett, reconceptualize tolerance as a kind of melancholic reaction, or defense, that protects the agents of tolerance from knowing just how far short they have fallen from their own professed commitments to being fair and doing good. [35] This is not about the "hypocrisy," "bad faith," "false consciousness," or "social pathology" of some individuals or groups. Being and feeling "tolerant" are more than an individual's defense against feeling "bad" about himself. These individual acts of "forgetting" connect to a larger national imaginary in which the sometimes violent exclusions at the heart of American democracy are recast and misremembered as inclusiveness.[36]

Tolerance is a wedge against recognizing and grappling with loss. As long as "we" conduct our antidemocratic politics with "kindness and good will and decency," "we" need not grieve, nor fight to restore, the lost objects of democracy, freedom, justice. The moralizing strains of tolerance are here conceivable as self-reproach turned *outward*—a projection of unbearable aspects of oneself—onto those others whose ongoing inequality (and the irksome noisiness with which "they" proclaim it) threatens to bring lost ideals back into view. Recall my earlier point about the specifically Christian history of tolerance in the United States and the fact that the constitutional promises of religious freedom were supposed to redress the inequalities built into tolerance. In its flag-waving, finger-pointing moralism, perhaps tolerance betrays the trace of this specifically religious lineage.

This often high-decibel moralism connects to another crucial moment in Freud's analysis of mourning and melancholia, namely, the manic phase of melancholia. Mania, Freud suggests, is the voluble side of foreclosed mourning; it is how melancholia speaks and acts out—unthinkingly, often violently—when it stops berating itself and turns its force instead on the world outside.[37] The often vituperative verbal attacks on the Cordoba House project thus function as a kind of warding off after the fact and bespeak a kind of manic defense against mourning. Given this, opponents of the "Ground Zero Mosque" may even experience themselves as "morally glamorous," to use Skerrett's resonant phrase.[38] For those on the margins of US national belonging, the receiving end of such tolerance probably feels neither good nor glamorous.

In the controversy over the "Ground Zero Mosque," Muslim Americans are not being formally excluded by a democratic majority, as they were by Oklahoma voters. Rather, they are being asked (albeit not so politely) to subordinate their free exercise rights, guaranteed under the First Amendment, to the hurt feelings of the rest of America; they are also being called upon to identify with the dominant center—to feel its pain as their own. This set of substitutions assumes that Muslim Americans are not already part of the United States and also reveals just how limited are the boundaries of moderation, fairness, and tolerance.

The frame of tolerance—the way it legitimates some actors and their public feelings—even as it delegitimates some others can also help make sense of the morally stupefying equivalence some political pundits and media outlets in the United States made between Evangelical pastor Terry Jones's announced "International Burn a Koran Day," which was timed to coincide with the ninth anniversary of 9/11, and the planned Cordoba Center. Both came to be represented as actions that were within the First Amendment rights of the groups proposing them but that would be "hurtful." As with Eisenhower's refusal to meet with civil rights leaders more than sixty years ago, once again we see how inadequate "moderating" notions like fair and balanced are to making crucial moral distinctions and creating more democratic social space for being different and "doing" difference.

In the song with which I launched this essay, the hero of *Oklahoma* proclaims his "beautiful feelin' that everything's goin' my way." Democracy, however, is not only about beautiful feelings and having things your way. This is among the reasons we need courts to protect the rights of unpopular minorities from the sentiments of majority rules. However, law is not the only forum, and certainly not the most common one, for democratic engagement with difference. In everyday life, we bump up against each other and may well be discomforted by differences we cannot assimilate or will not understand. But difference is not a problem or "the" problem to get over. It is rather the very material of our lives with others and the democratic worlds we may yet make.

Coda

In September 2011, amid numerous national and local commemorations of the tenth anniversary of the 9/11 attacks, Pennsylvania's Richland School District provided a haunting coda. The district is located in western Pennsylvania, not far from United Airlines Flight 93's crash site, which is now a national memorial.[39] Planning for that annual ritual of public and private schools across the country—the high school musical—was already underway at Richland, which had selected *Kismet* for its 2011–12 production. More Orientalism than deep ethnography, this "musical Arabian night,"[40] as the original 1953 program described it, won the Tony Award for best musical in 1954. Its plot centers on a Muslim street poet in old Baghdad. Apparently, old Baghdad was not old enough for the citizens of Richland. Facing community criticism for "insensitivity" after some residents complained it was not the right time to do a play that (sympathetically?) portrayed Muslims and Islam, the superintendent of schools,

Thomas Fleming, canceled the planned production. The district's performing arts committee chose *Oklahoma* as its replacement.[41]

Notes

1. The film was nominated for four Academy Awards: cinematography, film editing, sound recording, and scoring of a musical picture. It won in the latter two categories.

2. For a trenchant analysis of liberalism and the religious and racial politics of *Oklahoma*, see Most, "'We Know We Belong to the Land.'"

3. Let me here mark my indebtedness to my long collaboration with Janet R. Jakobsen, whose own work on the ethics of democratic social relations continues to inspire me.

4. See Lawrence et al. v. Texas, 539 US 558 (2003), p. 573.

5. See Elliott, "The Man behind the Anti-Shariah Movement."

6. Jakobsen and Pellegrini, *Love the Sin*. My discussion of the false opposition between disestablishment and free exercise and how this false opposition actually reinforces Christian dominance draws heavily on chapter four of *Love the Sin*, "The Free Exercise of Sex," 103–26.

7. Jakobsen and Pellegrini, *Love the Sin*, 111–12.

8. For an astute discussion of this issue, see Feldman, "Christian America and the Separation of Church and State."

9. Gedicks, *Rhetoric of Church and State*, 116. Jakobsen and I invoke Gedicks in our discussion of the meaning of government neutrality in the face of religious difference in *Love the Sin*, 110. See chapter 1 for an important Supreme Court case in which religious practices on the frontiers of Christianity were accorded free exercise protections, Church of the Lukumi Babalu Aye, Inc., and Ernesto Pichado v. City of Hialeah, 508 US 520 (1993), which concerned Santeria, a syncretic Afro-Caribbean religion.

10. Feldman, "Christian America and the Separation of Church and State," 262.

11. Feldman, "Christian America and the Separation of Church and State," 261; Jakobsen and Pellegrini, *Love the Sin*, 3–4.

12. The Supreme Court's finding in Hosanna-Tabor v. EEOC 565 US ____ (2012) Docket 10-553 that a ministerial exception trumped otherwise applicable state and federal antidiscrimination laws might suggest that a "Catholic" view of "religion" and "religious freedom" is emerging on the court over and against an earlier Supreme Court focus on individual religious freedom. Moreover, as Winnifred Fallers Sullivan has shown, during the oral arguments in Hosanna-Tabor several of the justices worried that not granting a ministerial exception would open the Catholic Church to sex discrimination lawsuits for not ordaining women as priests—and this despite the fact that the case at hand concerned the legality, under the Americans with Disabilities Act, of a Lutheran School's termination of an employee whom it defined as a "called minister." In my view, the una-

nimity of the finding in Hosanna-Tabor argues against interpreting the majority's decision, which was written by Chief Justice Roberts, as forwarding a Catholic understanding of "religion." Rather, in line with Sullivan, I see the 9–0 decision in this case as endorsing a disturbing conception of religious freedom as held, first and foremost, by hierarchically organized "corporate" church bodies, whose freedom consists in large measure by the freedom to enforce discipline and form conscience. In this respect, then, the decision in Hosanna-Tabor in favor of corporate rights over and against an individual's forms a kind of sequel to the contested finding—by a highly divided court—for a corporation's First Amendment free speech rights in Citizens United v. FEC just two years earlier 558 US 310 (2010). As this book goes to press, the court recently announced its finding in another case—Hobby-Lobby v. Sebelius—that ruled that for-profit private corporations can claim some protections based on the First Amendment free exercise rights. For Sullivan's discussions of Hosanna-Tabor, see: "Going to Law," and "'The Church.'"

13. Feldman, "Christian America and the Separation of Church and State," 266.

14. Muneer Awad v. Paul Ziriax et al., Case No. CIV-10-1186-M, US District Court for the Western District of Oklahoma (November 9, 2010), p. 6.

15. See Puar and Rai, "Monster, Terrorist, Fag."

16. Huq, "Defend Muslims, Defend America."

17. Muneer Awad v. Paul Ziriax et al., p. 7.

18. Siegel, "Islamic Sharia Law to Be Banned."

19. Qtd. in Rayfield, "Rep. Aims To Stop 'Liberal Judges.'"

20. As we have seen, a US district court judge thought otherwise, and she was instantly attacked by supporters of the amendment as a "liberal" Clinton appointee.

21. See Kintz, *Between Jesus and the Market.*

22. For a discussion of the rhetorical work "Judeo-Christian" has done in US debates and even in judicial decisions concerning homosexuality, see Jakobsen and Pellegrini, *Love the Sin*, 31.

23. For a parallel case, see Jakobsen's and my discussion of the Defense of Marriage Act, or DOMA, which President Bill Clinton signed into law in 1996 and which was struck down by the Supreme Court in 2013. DOMA forbade federal recognition of same-sex marriage. Supporters of this antigay law disclaimed homophobia as a motive; instead, they framed their support as a matter of defending traditional marriage and "the" American family. See *Love the Sin*, 63. In arguing against difference as a problem and against tolerance as a solution to social division, I am condensing a much longer argument developed in my joint work with Jakobsen in *Love the Sin*. See especially chapter 3, "What's Wrong with Tolerance?," 45–73.

24. McCarthy, *The Citizen Machine.*

25. See Brown v. Board of Education, 349 US 294 (1955).

26. McCarthy, *Citizen Machine*, 13.

27. I am grateful to Karen Shimakawa for drawing my attention to this key section of *Plessy*.

28. My discussion of hurt feelings and the melancholic politics surrounding the so-called Ground Zero Mosque are condensed from "Protesting Death: *Snyder v. Phelps* and the Space of Mourning," *Law and Mourning*, ed. Austin Sarat and Martha Umphrey (Stanford: Stanford University Press, in press).

29. Qtd. in Sorensen, "Obama Breaks His Silence."

30. The report found that nearly one in five Americans (18 percent) believes the president is Muslim, up from 11 percent in a March 2009 survey. Just as strikingly, the August 2010 survey indicated that the number of Americans who correctly identified Obama's religion as Christian had declined to 34 percent from 48 percent in 2009. Pew Forum on Religion and Public Life, "Growing Number of Americans."

31. Wyatt, "3 Republicans Criticize Obama's Endorsement."

32. Tumulty and Shear, "Obama."

33. Freud, "Mourning and Melancholia," 249.

34. Freud, "The Ego and the Id," 29.

35. Skerrett, "Homosexuals, Heretics, and the Practice of Freedom."

36. Eng and Han, "A Dialogue on Racial Melancholia," 347.

37. Freud, "Mourning and Melancholia," 253–58. In an essay that has been very helpful for my own thinking about melancholia's manic turn, David L. Eng underscores the "value of silence" as a counter to the violent mania of US nationalism post–9/11and proposes silence not as the opposite of speech, but rather as a precondition for the transformation of loss into meaning. See Eng, "The Value of Silence." I have also benefitted from the important prompts offered in Douglas Crimp's *Melancholia and Moralism*.

38. Skerrett, "Homosexuals, Heretics, and the Practice of Freedom," 392.

39. National Park Service, "Flight 93 National Memorial."

40. Qtd. in "The Theatre: Lavish Musical."

41. See MSNBC.com, "School Pulls Musical 'Kismet.'"

II
Riting Social Formations

4
Fear of Small Numbers

Arjun Appadurai

Arjun Appadurai was the sixth Aronov lecturer to visit the University
of Alabama. On March 11, 2008, he presented "The Offending Part:
Sacrifice and Ethnocide in the Era of Globalization." The essay
published here addresses a similar concern for contemporary violence.

There is a basic puzzle surrounding rage about minorities in a globalizing
world. The puzzle is about why the relatively small numbers that give the
word "minority" its most simple meaning and usually imply political and
military weakness do not prevent minorities from being objects of fear and
of rage. Why kill, torture, or ghettoize the weak? This may be a relevant
question for ethnic violence against small groups at any time in history.[1]
Here, I seek to engage this puzzle with special reference to the era of globalization, especially from the late 1980s until the present.

Fear of the Weak

The comparative historical question does not, in any case, apply to all of
human history, since minorities and majorities are recent historical inven-
tions, essentially tied up with ideas about nations, populations, representation, and enumeration that are no more than a few centuries old. They are
also today *universal* ideas, since the techniques of counting, classification,
and political participation that underlie the ideas of majority and minority
are everywhere associated with the modern nation-state.

The idea of a majority is not prior to or independent from that of a minority, especially in the discourses of modern politics. Majorities are as
much the product of enumeration and political nomination as are minorities. Indeed, majorities need minorities in order to exist, even more than
the reverse.

Hence, the first step toward addressing why the weak are feared in so many ethnonationalist settings is to go back to the "we/they" question in elementary sociological theory. In this theory, the creation of collective others, or *them*s, is a requirement, through the dynamics of stereotyping and identity contrast, for helping to set boundaries and mark off the dynamics of the we. This aspect of the theory of the scapegoat, the stereotype, and the other grows out of that brand of symbolic interactionism that was made explicit in the works of Cooley and Mead, but it is also entirely central to the core of Freud's understanding of group dynamics, including his classic essay on the narcissism of minor differences (which I discuss later in the chapter).

In this sociological tradition, the understanding of the process of we-making is limited, since it is seen as a mechanical by-product of the process by which theys are created. The process requires simple contrasts and sharp boundaries that help to consolidate "we" identities. The making of *we*s, of collective selves, is given short shrift in this tradition, since it is regarded as sociologically natural and unrequiring of deeper thought. Mainstream sociological theory, especially in regard to group formation, does explore the role of conflict (as in the tradition of Simmel) or of religion (in the tradition of Durkheim) or of antagonistic interest (as in the tradition of Marx) in the building of collective identities. But even though these traditions do cast some light on the formation of we identities as a partially independent process, without reference to the we/they dialectic, they do not tend to be deeply reflective about the formation of what I have elsewhere called "predatory identities."[2]

Predatory Identities

I define as predatory those identities whose social construction and mobilization require the extinction of other proximate social categories, defined as threats to the very existence of some group, defined as a we. Predatory identities emerge, periodically, out of pairs of identities, sometimes sets that are larger than two and have long histories of close contact, mixture, and some degree of mutual stereotyping. Occasional violence may or may not be part of these histories, but some degree of contrastive identification is always involved. One of these pairs or sets of identities often turns predatory by mobilizing an understanding of itself as a threatened majority. This kind of mobilization is the key step in turning a benign social identity into a predatory identity.

The formation of an ethnos into a modern nation often provides the basis for the emergence of predatory identities, identities that claim to require the extinction of another collectivity for their own survival. Predatory identities are almost always majoritarian identities. That is, they are based on claims about, and on behalf of, a threatened majority. In fact, in many instances, they are claims about cultural majorities that seek to be exclusively or exhaustively linked with the identity of the nation. Sometimes these claims are made in terms of religious majorities, such as Hindus, Christians, or Jews, and at other times in terms of linguistic, racial, or other sorts of majorities, such as Germans, Indians, or Serbs. The discourse of these mobilized majorities often has within it the idea that it could be itself turned into a minority unless another minority disappears, and for this reason, predatory groups often use pseudodemographic arguments about rising birthrates among their targeted minority enemies. Thus, predatory identities arise in those circumstances in which majorities and minorities can plausibly be seen as being in danger of trading places. This inner reciprocity is a central feature of this analysis and will be revisited below in this chapter.

Predatory identities emerge in the tension between majority identities and national identities. Identities may be described as "majoritarian" not simply when they are invoked by objectively larger groups in a national polity but when they strive to close the gap between the majority and the purity of the national whole. This is a key point about the conditions under which identities turn predatory. Majority identities that successfully mobilize what I earlier defined as the *anxiety of incompleteness* (as minorities represent the inability of majorities to unite a nation as a single whole, fear and violence develop against the source of that incompleteness[3]) about their sovereignty can turn predatory. Incompleteness, in this sense, is not only about effective control or practical sovereignty but more importantly about purity and its relationship to identity.

Mary Douglas's contributions to the subject of purity and categorical identity can be extended to note that predatory identities, especially when they are associated with majoritarianism, thrive in the gap between the sense of numerical majority and the fantasy of national purity and wholeness. Predatory identities, in other words, are products of situations in which the idea of a national peoplehood is successfully reduced to the principle of ethnic singularity, so that the existence of even the smallest minority within national boundaries is seen as an intolerable deficit in the purity of the national whole. In such circumstances, the very idea of being a majority is a frustration, since it implies some sort of ethnic diffusion of the national peoplehood. Minorities, being a reminder of this small but frustrating deficit, thus unleash the urge to purify. This is one basic element of an answer to the question: Why can small numbers excite rage? Small numbers represent a tiny obstacle between majority and totality or total purity. In a sense, the smaller the number and the weaker the minority, the deeper the rage about its capacity to make a majority feel like a mere majority rather than like a whole and uncontested ethnos.

The most remarked twentieth-century example of this sense of frustrated purity is, of course, the mobilization of "Germanness" as a predatory identity by the Nazis, directed especially but not exclusively against the Jews. Many scholars have forcefully argued that especially for the assimilated Jewish members of the German bourgeoisie, it was possible even well into the period of Nazi power, to believe that they were Jewish in an entirely secondary sense and that they were in every important regard fully German. Conversely, it is possible to argue that far from being a successful mobilization of a continuous, unchanging, nationally coded feature of the German people, anti-Semitism had to be regularly mobilized and reawakened through powerful campaigns of racial and political propaganda, through which Jews could be seen as non-Germans and anti-Germans. The special contribution of Nazis to the complex traditions of European anti-Semitism has been identified by some important scholars to be the infusion of scientific racism and its accompanying eugenic and demographic ideas to earlier forms of religious and social stereotyping.

Even Daniel Goldhagen,[4] who otherwise creates a remarkably racialized picture of the identities of "ordinary Germans," concedes that the Nazis made critical new contributions to the definition and mobilization of Germanness as the identity of a threatened majority, threatened especially by the racial cancer (also a Nazi trope) of the Jews. Whatever the status of Goldhagen's arguments about what he called "eliminationist anti-Semitism" and its mobilization among the vast majority of ordinary Germans, the major weakness of the hook is its refusal to recognize its own massive evidence, not so much of a deep, primordial, and hardwired form of anti-Semitism among all Germans—successfully captured by the Nazis for the project of eliminating all Jews from the face of the Earth—but of the extraordinary amount of energy that was required to turn many German nationals into instruments of the Final Solution.

The huge apparatus of Nazi media and spectacle, the tireless circulation of racialized propaganda and officially circulated rumors, and the self-fulfilling performances (in which degraded Jewish populations were seen as evidence of the subhuman qualities of Jews) were a remarkable feat of active ideological and political engineering. Even in themselves they could be seen as evidence of the effort required to build a successful national consensus in favor of the campaign against Jews as a central platform of the Third Reich. One could also argue that the engagement of civilians in police battalions, death camps, and forced marches, which were part of the machinery of the Final Solution, were themselves among the massive political performatives through which Jews were successfully rendered subhuman and that those Germans who were directly involved were drawn, by violent action, into the consensus about Jews as national filth.

There is a great deal more that could be said about Nazi anti-Semitism and the larger national project of National Socialism. For the purposes of this argument, the main point is that once the project of Germanness became defined in ethnoracial terms and the logic of purity came into play, a variety of minorities became sites of rage about incomplete purity: homosexuals, the aged and infirm, Gypsies, and, above all, Jews. Jews were painted in Nazi propaganda as representing various kinds of social, political, and economic threats, but they were above all seen as a cancer, as a problem for the purity of German-Aryan blood, for the almost perfect project of a nationally pure and untainted ethnos. German identity, as mobilized by the Nazis, required the complete elimination of Jews from the German social body, and, since the German project was a project of world dominion, it required their elimination worldwide.

The Nazi project of eliminating many minorities from the Earth also casts light on another aspect of the way predatory identities are mobilized. In this case, perhaps for the first time in the history of humanity, two contradictory impulses were mobilized in the project of genocide. The first was the mechanical, technological, and bureaucratic side of the project, captured in Hannah Arendt's memorable phrase about "the banality of evil."[5] The second, however, is the degradation, abuse, and horrifyingly intimate violence that was wreaked by German soldiers, conscripts, camp guards, militias, and ordinary citizens at every level and in every site of the Final Solution. This is the contradictory intimacy generated by predatory identities. One way to understand this contradiction is that reducing target populations to subhuman states facilitates the work of large-scale murder by creating distance between killers and killed and by providing a self-fulfilling proof of the ideological argument that the victims are subhuman, vermin, insects, scum, garbage, and yet a cancerous part of the valued national body.

Yet there is more to the degradation that frequently accompanies large-scale genocidal violence. I would suggest that it is precisely the smallness of the gap between national totality and minority presence that produces the anxiety of incompleteness and creates the frustration and rage that drive those forms of degradation that shock us most, from Nazi Germany to Rwanda, from Kosovo to Mumbai. Again we must review some arguments about the narcissism of small differences, which I do later in the chapter.

The Nazi example might appear to be an extreme case that has little in common with such recent liberal majoritarianisms as those of India, Pakistan, Britain, or Germany (among others), all of which are more open to social difference than the Nazis were. The Hindutva ideology in India, for example, the "sons of the soil" ideology in Malaysia, or various ideologies of citizenship in Europe might be seen as liberal majoritarianisms, that is, as majoritarianisms that seek to be inclusive. Are these majoritarianisms fundamentally different from the more "totalitarian" ones that the Nazis installed in Germany in the 1930s and 1940s? My suggestion is that all majoritarianisms have in them the seeds of genocide, since they are invariably connected with ideas about the singularity and completeness of the national ethnos.

The difficult question is to assess how and under what conditions liberal majoritarianisms might turn illiberal and potentially genocidal. When does the fact of incomplete national purity become susceptible to translation and mobilization in the service of building a predatory identity? There are two ways of answering this question without entering into an elaborate empiricist study of causes, conditions, and comparisons. One is to suggest that liberal thought has a fundamental ambivalence about the legitimacy of collectivities as political actors and, as a result, is always open to the manipulation of arguments about quality disguised as arguments about quantity. This approach is explored below in this chapter.

The second is a more generally historical and tentative answer to the question of when the condition of incomplete purity propels an argument for genocide. The historical ingredients for this transformation or tipping point appear to include the following: the capture of the state by parties or other groups that have placed their political bets on some sort of racialized nationalist ideology; the availability of census tools and techniques that encourage enumerated communities to become norms for the idea of community itself; a felt lack of fit between political borders and community migrations and populations, yielding a new alertness to politically abandoned ethnic kin or to ethnic strangers claiming to be one's kinsmen; and a successful campaign of fear, directed at numerical majorities, which convinces them that they are at risk of destruction by minorities, who know how to use the law (and the entire apparatus of liberal-democratic politics) to advance their special ends. To these factors, globalization adds its specific energies, which are discussed at the end of this chapter. This set of factors is not intended to be exhaustive or predictive. It is intended to suggest that the Nazi project may have been extraordinary in its consistency and the reach of its genocidal imagination. But as an ideology of majoritarianism turned predatory, it does not allow us to imagine that liberalism is immune from the conditions that produce majoritarian genocide. India in the past two decades is a prime case of the latter possibility.

The Nazi case certainly invites us to see how predatory identities are formed and to recognize that the reflexive theory of the other, in which scapegoats (often minorities) are viewed as a functional requirement for the building up of feelings of we-ness, is both mechanical and partial. The mobilization of feelings of we-ness, especially in the strong form that I have here called predatory, depends on the tension between ideas of the sacred wholeness of the national demos and the statistical idea of a majority. Majoritarianism thrives where majorities become seized of the fantasy of national purity, in that zone where quantity meets—but does not completely define—quality. This issue opens up another dimension of the problem of small numbers, which is the link between number, quantity, and political voice.

Number in the Liberal Imagination

Numbers have an ambivalent place in liberal social theory, and the relationship between numbers and categories is today at the heart of some central tensions between liberal social theory and democratic norms. The issue of majorities in the modern nation-state allows us to examine these tensions in a productive manner. From a certain point of view, the critical number, for liberal social theory, is the number one, which is the numerical sign of the individual. Insofar as the individual is at the normative heart of liberalism and is shared ground even among competing liberalisms, the number "one" is the smallest important number for liberalism. As the smallest integer, the number "one" has a number of properties of interest to mathematicians, but for liberal social theory, it is in some sense the only important number, other than zero. The number zero is almost as important because it is the key to converting integers into numbers in the hundreds, the thousands, the millions, and so on. In other words, zero is the numerical key to the idea of the masses, which is one of the categories around which liberal and democratic thought part ways. Lenin is quoted as having said: "Politics is where the masses are, not where there are thousands but where there are millions, that is where serious politics begins."[6]

Much liberal thought imagines large groups as aggregations of individuals (that is, of infinite combinations of the number one). A significant part of the utilitarian tradition in liberal thought, from Bentham to Rawls, tries to imagine collective life as organized around forms of aggregate decision making that privilege the individual or a number of persons no larger than one. In this way, liberal thought, in terms of theories of representation, of the collective good, and of social science, imagines aggregations of individuals as constituted by the addition of large sets of the number one. Put another way, the appearance of collectivities, in the central traditions of liberal thought, is a matter of the aggregation of singular interests and agents seeking solutions to the fact that they are forced to interact with one another. This is, of course, only a way of restating the standard characterizations of market models in neoclassical economics and of the images of collective life that lie behind them. In this sense, liberal thought imagines collectivities to be social forms whose logics, motives, and dynamism can always be inferred from some method for understanding the aggregation of interested individuals.

For liberal thought, from its very beginnings, the problem about democracy is the possibility that it could encourage the political legitimacy of large numbers. The sharp contrast between the people and the masses is constituted in liberal thought around what happens to the number "one" when many zeros are added to it. The idea of the masses (as in Ortega y Gasset's classic book, *The Revolt of the Masses*) is associated in liberal thought with large numbers that have lost the rationalities embedded in the individual, in the number one. Thus, the masses are always seen as the product and the basis of fascism and totalitarianism, both because of the sense of their being composed of nonindividuals (or individuals who have lost their mental capabilities to exercise their own rational interests) and of the sense of a collectivity orchestrated by forces outside itself, such as a state, a dictator, or a myth that was not produced by the deliberative interaction between individuals. The quotation from Lenin captures precisely what liberal thought fears about large numbers. It is because of this potential affinity between large numbers and the birth of the masses that much liberal thought has rightly been characterized by a fear of large numbers. This much seems intuitively clear. But where then does the fear of *small* numbers come in?

Except for the number one, which is a special case, small numbers are troubling to liberal social thought for a variety of reasons. First, small numbers are associated with oligopolies, elites, and tyrannies. They suggest the possibility of what today is called "elite capture" of resources, privileges, and the very capacity to mediate. Small numbers are also a worry because they raise the specter of conspiracy, of the cell, the spy, the traitor, the dissident, or the revolutionary. Small numbers introduce the intrusion of the private into the public sphere and with it the associated dangers of nepotism, collusion, subversion, and deception. They harbor the potential for secrecy and privacy, both anathema to the ideas of publicity and transparency that are vital to liberal ideas of rational communication and open deliberation.

More broadly, small numbers always carry the possibility of what in the liberal vernacular of the United States are called "special interests" and thus pose threats to some idea of the "general interest," which is believed to be best served when individuals deliberate or negotiate as individuals with *all other individuals* in the polity, through some legible mechanism of representation.

Minorities are the only powerful instance of small numbers that excite sympathy rather than distrust in the liberal imagination, and that is because they incarnate that numerical smallness of which the prime case is the number one, the individual. So once liberal thought becomes intimately connected to electoral democracy and to deliberative procedures in legislation, the idea of the minority acquires a powerful valence (as with the great regard shown for minority opinions in the US Supreme Court). In fact, the idea of a minority is in its political genealogy not an ethical or cultural idea but a procedural one, having to do with dissenting opinions in deliberative or legislative contexts in a democratic framework.

Thus, in the history of liberal thought, the positive interest in minorities and their opinions has much to do with dissent and little to do with difference. This distinction is an important contributor to the contemporary fear of minorities and requires careful examination.

Dissent and Difference in Contemporary Polities

The initial positive value attached to minorities in Western liberal thought is fundamentally procedural. It has to do with the valuation of rational debate, of the right to dissent, of the value of dissent as a sign of the larger value of free speech and opinion, and of the freedom to express dissenting opinions on matters of public moment without fear of retribution. The US Constitution is perhaps the best place to examine the centrality of dissent to the very idea of freedom. But if we are not careful we are likely to reverse the course of history and place more value on a relatively recent development, what we may call *substantive* dissent (for example, the right to express even morally monstrous opinions, the right to criticize the policies of the state, or the right to question the religious opinions of the majority), than on what we may call *procedural* dissent, which is the original context for the positive value placed on minorities, and especially on minority opinion. The key word here is opinion, for procedural minorities are not cultural or social minorities, they are temporary minorities, minorities solely by and of opinion. Social and cultural minorities, what we may call substantive minorities, are permanent minorities, minorities that have become social and not just procedural.

If we look at the history of Western laws and ideas pertaining to minorities, they take on their full liberal force largely after the birth of the United Nations and in the various conventions pertaining to human rights produced after the birth of the United Nations. Of course, there were various piecemeal ideas about the protection of minorities before the formation of the United Nations, but it was only in the second half of the twentieth century, as the idea of human rights became the major currency for negotiating international agreements about the elementary entitlements of all humanity, that substantive social minorities became critical foci of constitutional and political concern in many democracies throughout the world. The rights of minorities, seen under the larger rubric of human rights, acquired a remarkably wide credibility during this period and, in different national settings, became the basis for major juridical and constitutional struggles over citizenship, justice, political participation, and equality.

This process, in which social and cultural minorities became universally seen as bearers of real or potential rights, conceals a poorly theorized, even unanticipated, transfer of normative value from procedural minorities and temporary minorities to substantive minorities, which often become permanent social and cultural collectivities.

This unintended displacement of the liberal concern with protecting the opinions of procedural minorities (such as minorities on courts, councils, parliaments, and other deliberative bodies) onto the rights of permanent cultural minorities is an important source of the current, deep ambivalence about minorities in democracies of all varieties. The many debates about multiculturalism in the United States and Europe, about subordinate nationalities in various parts of the ex–Soviet Union, about secularism in India, about "sons-of-the-soil" in many countries in Asia, about "autochthony" in many regions of Africa, and about the rights of "indigenous people" throughout Latin America and in places as far apart as New Zealand, Canada, Australia, and Hawaii are different in important ways. But they have in common a concern about the rights of cultural minorities in relation to national states and various cultural majorities, and they always involve struggles over cultural rights as they relate to national citizenship and issues of belonging. In many cases, these struggles have been directly related to the emergence of predatory ethnic identities and of successful efforts to mobilize majorities in projects of ethnic cleansing or ethnocide. These conflicts accelerated during the 1980s and 1990s, during which many nation-states had to simultaneously negotiate two pressures: the pressure to open up their markets to foreign investment, commodities, and images and the pressure to manage the capacity of their own cultural minorities to use the globalized language of human rights to argue for their own claims for cultural dignity and recognition. This dual pressure was a distinctive feature of the 1990s and produced a crisis in many countries for the sense of national boundaries, national sovereignty, and the purity of the national ethnos, and it is directly responsible for the growth of majoritarian racisms in societies as diverse as Sweden and Indonesia as well as Romania, Rwanda, and India.

Muslims in India: Appeasement and Purity

The case of India is instructive in regard to the argument about substantive and procedural minorities that I have been developing. The Indian nation-state was formed in 1947 through a political partition that also produced Pakistan as a new nation-state, formed as a political haven for the Muslims who lived in Britain's Indian Empire. There is a huge and contentious scholarship surrounding the story of Partition, the politics that led to it, and the bizarre geographies it produced (with East and West Pakistan flanking an independent India from 1947 to 1973 when East Pakistan succeeded in seceding from West Pakistan, giving birth to Bangladesh, a new nation on India's eastern borders). I will not take up the politics here, except to note that it produced a permanent state of war between India and Pakistan; spawned the apparently unsolvable crisis of Kashmir; created an alibi for the identification of India's Muslim citizens with its major cross-border enemy, Pakistan; and laid the groundwork for India's current crisis of secularism.

The story of this crisis is also too complex to be told here. What is noteworthy is that as Hinduism and its political mobilizers evolved a cultural politics in the course of the nineteenth and twentieth centuries, the birth of Pakistan created a new link between the Hindu sense of we-ness, the constitutional concern about the rights of minorities, and the rise of a major Hindu political coalition to power in the 1990s. This coalition, of political parties and various affiliated social movements (sometimes called the Sangh Parivar), is virtually coterminous with India's exposure to the pressures of globalization, and it has been bracketed by two of the most horrendous attacks against Muslims in India since the massacres of the Partition: the 1992 destruction of the Babri Masjid, a sixteenth-century mosque in North India, which was preceded and followed by a wave of genocidal riots against Muslim populations throughout India, and the murderous pogrom against Muslims in the state of Gujarat in 2002. The decade that is bracketed by these events also witnessed the national consolidation of a large body of Indian public opinion, including those of its educated and once-liberal middle classes, against the inclusive, pluralist, and secularist ideals of the Indian constitution and of Nehru, India's first, and most charismatic, prime minister. In its place, the coalition of grassroots movements and political parties, led by the Indian People's Party (the Bharatiya Janata Party or BJP), succeeded in creating a deep link between the memory of Hindu humiliations by the pre-British Muslim rulers of India, the dubious patriotism of India's Muslim citizens, the known wish of Pakistan to destroy India militarily, and the growth in militant actions by Muslim terrorists connected with anti-Indian aspirations in the contested state of Kashmir.

Much scholarly and journalistic attention has been paid to this remarkable story in which the world's largest democracy, born with a constitution that pays remarkable attention to religious inclusion, secular tolerance for religious difference, and a general concern with protecting the "weaker sections" of society, could, within forty years of its birth, have turned into an aggressively Hinduized polity, which repeatedly and systematically sought to identify India with Hindus and patriotism with Hindutva (Hinduness). This Indian development casts a particular light on the fear of minorities that is worth examining in some detail.

My argument needs to recognize, at this stage, a major interruption from the world of political events. Since the first draft of this essay was written in October 2003 and revised in August 2004, a momentous and unexpected electoral event occurred in India.[7] The Hindu right-wing coalition, led by the BJP, was resoundingly defeated in the recent general elections, and a new coalition, led by the Congress Party of the Nehrus, returned to power. This extraordinary democratic revolution, not the first in the history of independent India, shocked even the canniest political pundits (not unlike the fall of the Soviet Union in 1989). Though the significance of this major change is still being digested by the experts, there is general agreement among most analysts that the defeat of the BJP coalition expressed two messages. One was that the Indian electorate (both rural and urban) was fed up with the message of Hindutva and did not see it as any substitute for plans and policies concerning the economy and everyday polities at the local level. The second was that the bottom half of the Indian electorate (both rural and urban) was also fed up with seeing the benefits of globalization being consumed by a small group in the ongoing circus of state corruption and elite consumption, with few tangible benefits for themselves. In other words, callous globalization and cynical anti-Muslim mobilization were no longer viable platforms for a national coalition. So we have another novel moment in Indian politics, where the Congress and its allies steer a difficult course between economic justice and global markets and between localized and caste-based politics and a larger, postethnic and pluralist politics.

But it remains crucial to ask why many of India's political parties, a significant part of its population, and a shocking number of cosmopolitan, liberal intellectuals turned to the Hindutva message in the period between 1985 and 2004, a historical period that covers a third of India's history as an independent nation. And the question is not simply historical or academic. The forces of Hindu majoritarianism have not simply disappeared, and its methods, values, and techniques are still very much alive in the Indian polity. We are in a moment of respite [in 2004], and in order to ensure that the Hinduization of Indian politics remains history, we need to think through this period with as much care as we can summon.

The rise of the Hindu Right as India's major and majoritarian political coalition and its capture of mainstream national opinion largely in the 1980s, after decades of being a fragmented and marginal set of political movements, was connected to four major developments that relate to the issue of numbers and minorities. Each of these developments has something instructive to say about other nations and locations elsewhere in the world.

The first development had to do with minorities who are linked to global movements, identities, and networks. Muslims in India have always been subject to the charge of being more loyal to the wider Muslim world than to India, and their alleged sentimental links to Pakistan (often strenuously repudiated by Indian Muslims) have always been read in the context of the resources and political aspirations of global Islam. In India in the 1980s, the Hindu Right took a special interest in the flow of resources from the Muslim Middle East to religious and educational institutions in India, arguing that this sort of subsidy of Indian Muslims needed to be monitored and restricted and that it justified a controversial policy of reconversions undertaken by the Hindu Right, especially among poorer rural and tribal populations, alleged to have been duped into conversion by the forces of global Islam. Such reconversions were also instituted with Indian Christian communities and remained a major platform for the grassroots violence and political strategy of the Hindu Right. In its early manifestations in the 1980s, this battle of conversions was underwritten by the invocation of the size, power, and influence of global Islamic interests and forces, which were seen as the Trojans hidden within the relatively small number of Muslims in Indian communities. Thus, to put the matter crudely, the relatively small numbers of Muslims in India were seen as a mask for the large numbers of Muslims around the world. This picture of militant, transnational Islam beame virtually naturalized in the discourse of Islamic terrorism, especially in the wake of 9/11.

In the Indian case, this picture of Indian Muslims as instruments (and objects) of global Islamic movements (usually portrayed as violent, antinational, and anti-Hindu) was supported by the ongoing commitment of Indian Muslims to going on the Haj (a specially sacred pilgrimage to Mecca, seen as a desirable action at least once in the life of any devout Muslim) and by the growing traffic between Indian workers (of all kinds and classes) and the oil-rich sheikdoms of the Middle East, especially Saudi Arabia, Dubai, Kuwait, and Bahrain, starting in the 1980s. Among these migrants to the Persian Gulf was a significant number of Indian Muslims, though there is little sign that this was anything other than an economic option for them. Nevertheless, the traffic between India and the gulf was the site of a great deal of moral and political anxiety, which expressed itself in such bureaucratic innovations as the creation of the office of "The Protector of Immigrants," a government agency designed to ensure that Indian workers were not being exported to the gulf for immoral or fraudulent reasons. In a related moral drama, there was a great deal of attention paid to the growing practice of marriages arranged between richer (and often older) Arab men from the gulf and Muslim women (often very young) from poor families in impoverished Muslim communities in cities such as Hyderabad, Lucknow, and Agra. This picture of Muslim male depravity and polygamy, targeting the already exploited community of Muslim women, was circulated in the popular press and in such commercial films as *Baazaar*, which were calculated to excite the worst stereotypes of this marriage market.

It is highly likely that these commercial and popular images of the abuse of poor Indian Muslim women by decadent Arab men and money lay behind the celebrated legal controversy surrounding a Muslim woman called Shah Bano, who sued her husband for support after he divorced and abandoned her, in accordance with Muslim personal law (one subset of the specialized body of law applicable to many aspects of family and civil life for different religious communities in India).[8]

The Shah Bano case, which was one of the most publicized legal dramas in India after independence, pitted the state against the judiciary, Hindus against Muslims, feminists against each other, secularists against traditionalists. Since Shah Bano's appeal was against the customary family laws of her own community, it also created a deep and harmful opposition between the interests of women and those of minorities. The case showed every sign of rocking the stability of the regime of Rajiv Gandhi, the then prime minister of India, who represented the Nehruvian tradition of secularism and evenhandedness toward all religious communities. The Hindu Right, led by the then rising BJP, exploited the Shah Bano case mercilessly, painting themselves as the true protectors of the abused Muslim woman and of women's rights generally, while using the public interest in the case to disseminate vicious messages about the authoritarian power of the Muslim community over its women and the generalized sexual immorality and irresponsibility of Muslim men. The case was eventually resolved through a series of legal and political compromises, but it created a major public doubt about the benefits of secularism and laid some of the grounds for the bizarre idea that the Hindu Right was a more responsible protector of Muslim women's rights than anybody else. It also laid the foundations for a debate, unresolved right up to the present, about the desirability of a Uniform Civil Code (UCC), which is now seen as problematic by most political parties and progressive women's groups but is actively supported by the Hindu Right, for which it is a major vehicle for Hinduizing the personal laws of all minority communities.

The Shah Bano case points up the ways in which issues surrounding minorities, in a complex multireligious democracy like India, can become flash points for fundamental debates about gender, equality, legality, the boundaries of state power, and the ability of religious communities to police themselves. The point here is that small numbers can unsettle big issues, especially in countries like India, where the rights of minorities are directly connected to larger arguments about the role of the state, the limits of religion, and the nature of civil rights as matters of legitimate cultural difference.[9] In a very different context, India's long history of actions and litigations concerning affirmative or remedial action, in the context of the scheduled castes, produced the national convulsions over the 1980 report of the Mandal Commission, which sought to give teeth to a policy of job reservations for castes considered to have been historically the victims of discrimination. The Hindu Right recognized the tension in the rise of the lower castes, signaled by the Mandal Report, and was active in its efforts to take advantage of the rage of the Hindu upper castes, who saw themselves as threatened anew by the political aspirations of their poorer fellow Hindus. Many scholars have pointed out that the Hindu Right, throughout the 1980s, mobilized the politics of the Masjid (the Mosque) against those of the Mandal Commission, (which fueled the intra-Hindu battle over reserved jobs for lower castes). It has also been noted that the effort to create a unified Hindu caste front, in the face of the caste battles unleashed by the Mandal Report, made the Muslim minority a perfect "other" in the production of a mobilized Hindu majority. Most important for the issue of numbers, Amrita Basu, a distinguished student of the politics of communal violence in North India, has observed that the idea of a Hindu majority actually hides the numerical minority of upper caste, landed Hindu castes who have much more to fear from the rise of the lower castes than they have to fear from Muslims in their own localities.[10] When we place this concern against the general politicization and mass mobilization of the lower castes in public politics throughout India, arguably the single greatest transformation in the political landscape of India over the past half century,[11] we can see that the fear of small numbers is further inflected by the Hindu minority, which actually has the most to gain from the cultural fiction of a Hindu majority.

The Hindu majority is a double fiction in contemporary India, first because the category of "Hindu" is unthinkable in contemporary politics apart from its birth in colonial ethnographies and census categories and second because the deep divisions between upper and lower castes, always a feature of life in agrarian India, has grown into one of the most important fissures in the politics of North India in the past two decades. Thus, the Hindu majority is demonstrably a project, not a fact, and like all racialized categories and all predatory identities, it requires mobilization through the discourses of crisis and the practices of violence. The existence of minorities, such as Muslims, is an important aspect of these crises and practices, but the relation is not one of simple contrast and stereotyping, as I proposed earlier.

The relationship between Hindu caste politics and the anti-Muslim propaganda of the Hindu Right, especially since the 1980s, is also tied up with a major feature of Indian electoral politics since Indian independence, which is captured in the discourse of the vote bank. Indian elections are frequently seen, especially at the rural, local level, as turning substantially on the power of this or that party or candidate to capture a whole set of votes from a particular caste or religious community, which is bought off through its elites and constitutes a vote bank. Bringing together the associations of an elite-manipulated, collectivized vote and of a vote bought corruptly, the image of the vote bank, which is freely used by all Indian politicians against one another, captures the deep history of links between the census and British colonial ideas of community and electorate, notoriously institutionalized in the separate electorates created early in the twentieth century for Hindus and Muslims in local elections under colonial rule. These enumerated communities[12] remain a major nightmare for liberal thought in India because they catch the liberal abhorrence both of mass politics and its special corruptions and of the negative drag of ascription and kinship in a modernizing democracy. Today, the importance of vote banks has been somewhat undercut by the growing power of independent grassroots movements that resist wholesale manipulation by politicians as well as the cynicism with which politicians often make and break alliances and affiliations. Still, the Hindu Right never lost an opportunity to raise the specter of the Muslim vote bank, often accusing its major competitor, the now victorious Congress Party, of pandering to Muslims in an effort to capture the Muslim vote bank in local elections and, by implication, in state and national elections. The amazing defeat of the BJP in the 2004 general elections showed that this particular bogey was not enough to buy the loyalty of the largely rural Indian electorate.

This point brings us to the final feature of the fear of minorities in India, which has wider implications. The Hindu Right, especially through its dominant political parties, has consistently accused the Congress Party (the party historically associated with Nehruvian secularism, pluralism, and active tolerance of Muslims as a cultural minority) of appeasement in its dealings with Muslims' demands, complaints, and claims on the state. The discourse of appeasement is fascinating, because it is deeply linked to the slippage I earlier discussed between the sense of being a majority and the frustration of incomplete identification with the undivided ethnos of the polity. When the Hindu Right baits secular parties and movements with the charge of "appeasing" Muslims, it implies both a certain opportunism and cowardice on the part of the secularists and simultaneously (as with the Nazis and Munich) creates an image of the slippery slope that leads from the fear of giving in to this or that local demand of Muslim communities to giving in wholesale in the militarized, now nuclearized, battle with Pakistan, which is the large-scale backdrop of all militant Hindu propaganda in India. The discourse of appeasement is the link between minority claims within national boundaries and the struggle with enemy states across the border, in this case Pakistan.

Thus, appeasement is another discursive device that allows the small numbers of Indian Muslims to be swollen and impregnated with the threat of Pakistan and, beyond that, of the militant multitudes of the world of global Islam. In the period immediately following the 9/11 attacks, as I have argued above in this chapter, these connections were revived and re-imagined through the global invocation of Islamic terrorism. I turn now, by way of conclusion, to the figure of the suicide bomber, born in the struggles between Tamils and Sinhalas in Sri Lanka in the 1970s, and the relationship of this solitary figure to issues of number, minority, and terror.

How Small Are Small Numbers?

Minorities, Diasporas, and Terror

The suicide bomber, whether in Israel, Sri Lanka, New York, Iraq, or London, is the darkest possible version of the liberal value placed on the individual, the number "one." The suicide bomber today is the ideal type of the terrorist, since in this figure several nightmares are condensed. He or she, first of all, completely closes the boundary between the body and the weapon of terror. Whether by strapping bombs to his or her body or by otherwise disguising explosives in his or her body, the suicide bomber is an explosive body that promises to distribute its own bloody fragments and mix them in with the bloody parts of the civilian populations it is intended to decimate. Thus, not only does the suicide bomber elude detection, he or she also produces a horrible mixture of blood and body between enemies, thus violating not only the soil of the nation but the very bodies of the victims, infecting them with the blood of the martyr. Second, the suicide bomber is a revolting version of the idea of the martyr, highly valued in Christianity and Islam, for instead of being a passive martyr, he or she is an active, dangerous, exploding martyr, a murderous martyr. Third, the suicide bomber, as with the brainwashed agent in *The Manchurian Candidate*, is invariably portrayed as being in some paranormal state of conviction, ecstasy, and purpose, often built up through quasi-religious techniques such as isolation, indoctrination, and drug-induced hallucination, on the eve of the suicidal attack. This image is the very antithesis of the liberal individual acting in her interest, for the idea of a willingly exploded body does not fit easily into most models of rational choice. Fourth, imagined as an automaton, the suicide bomber, while a terrifying example of the individual, the number "one," is in fact always seen as an instance of the crazed mob or mass, the victim of propaganda and extrarational conviction, a perfect example of the mindless regimentation of the masses and of the dangerous unpredictability of the mob.

In all these regards, the suicide bomber is the pure and most abstract form of the terrorist. In this sense, the suicide bomber also captures some of the central fears surrounding terror. As a figure that has to get close to the place of attack by appearing to be a normal citizen, the suicide bomber takes to the extreme the problem of uncertainty that I discussed earlier. In one suicide bombing in Israel, a suicide bomber disguised himself as a rabbi, thus subverting the very heart of the visible moral order of Israeli Jewish society. Likewise, the suicide bomber thrives in the spaces of civilian life, thus producing a form of permanent emergency that also requires a new approach to the problem of civilians and civil life in the age of globalized terrorism. This brings us to a final feature of the problem of small numbers in an era of globalized networks of terror, such as those that became a full part of public consciousness after 9/11.

Small Numbers and Global Networks

The events of 9/11 are now sufficiently behind us that we can begin to sift through the xenophobia, sentimentality, and shock that the attacks produced to ponder the more persistent images that remain from that event, now to be seen via the dark glass of the war on Iraq.[13] Osama bin Laden is almost certainly alive, the Taliban are regrouping in Afghanistan and Pakistan, various warlords keep Afghanistan in a profound state of dependency on foreign money, arms, and soldiers, and there is a fierce insurgency against American forces in Iraq. The Iraqis, subdued initially by shock and awe, seem to hate Americans as much as they did Saddam Hussein, and the weapons of mass destruction seem to be alibis for the weapons of mass construction, largely in the hands of Bechtel and Halliburton. In both Afghanistan and Iraq, most especially in Iraq, the United States appears to be experimenting with a new political form, which may be called "long-distance democracy," a strange form of imperial federalism, where Iraq is treated as just another American state, operating under the jurisdiction of the National Guard and various other Federal forces from Washington in order to handle a disaster (produced in this instance by the decapitation of Saddam's regime).

The problem of numbers, minorities, and terror is alive and well in Iraq, along with the question of whether an Iraqi "people" can be produced out of the chaotic megapolitics of Shias, Kurds, and other large minorities.

On one hand, the US administration in Iraq faces the bewildering problem of minorities, such as the Shias, who are in absolute numerical terms very large and well connected to the ruling regime of Iran, or the Kurds, who span the borders of Iran, Iraq, and Turkey and constitute a huge minority. As the United States completes its nonexit, having rushed in teams of experts to build an Iraqi constitution overnight (just as they did in Afghanistan), there is a deep conceptual logjam involving large numerical minorities, the insistence among most Iraqis that the new polity has to be "Islamic," and the sense that a real democracy cannot be Islamic, except in the thinnest sense. Struggles over the nature of such basic ideas as constitutionalism, election, democracy, and representation go on in Iraq in the shadow of tank battles and full-scale warfare in places like Najaf and Falluja.

Two points about the ongoing Iraq debacle are relevant to the problem of small numbers and the fear of minorities. One is that even after ending the career of a truly murderous despot, likely feared and hated by many Iraqis, the US military is still dogged by the fear of small numbers, those small groups of militia, civilians, and others who conduct sneak attacks on the US forces and sometimes take suicidal risks to inflict damage and kill US soldiers. Fully embedded as they are within the civilian population, finding these "terrorists" is a nightmarish task of divination for US forces that counted on total Iraqi surrender after one evil individual—Saddam Hussein—had been toppled from power. Thus the United States, as an occupying power in Iraq, faces the fear that the small numbers who are continuing to torment and kill its soldiers are true representatives of the Iraqi people, who were originally scripted to greet the Americans as liberators and unfold the spectacle of a civil society underneath the carcass of the dictator.

Iraq also represents the more abstract challenge of producing a national people from what seem to be only large ethnic or religious minorities. In both Iraq and Afghanistan, the United States found itself between a rock and a hard place as it embarked on the project of building long-distance democracies: either they must allow these countries to constitute themselves as Islamic republics, thus recognizing that the only way to create peoples is by placing the very religion they most fear at the heart of the definition of the nation, or they must find ways to assemble coalitions of numerically large minorities, thus conceding that civil society in Iraq and in many places like Iraq has to be built over a long period of time, and that all there is to work with are minorities. But these are minorities with global connections and large populations associated with them. In facing this difficult set of choices, after starting a war that refuses to end, the United States has to engage with issues of minority, uncertainty, terror, and ethnic violence that plague many societies in the era of globalization. There are indications that some Iraqis may already be engaged in what has been called ethnic dry-cleaning in preparation for more brutal ethnic cleansing. If that scenario comes to pass, we will need, more than ever, to find new ways of negotiating the distance between groups of small numbers that provoke rage in the world's mobilized majorities, whose large numbers Lenin presciently saw as marking the beginnings of what he considered "serious politics."

Globalization, Numbers, Difference

I now return to two important themes: one is the issue of minor differences and the other is the special link between globalization and the growing rage against minorities. In my view, these themes are not unrelated. Michael Ignatieff[14] is perhaps the most articulate analyst to invoke Freud's essay on "the narcissism of minor differences" in order to deepen our sense of the ethnic battles of the 1990s, especially in Eastern Europe. Mostly informed by his deep knowledge of that region, Ignatieff uses Freud's insight about the psychodynamics of narcissism to cast light on why groups like the Serbs and the Croats should come to invest so much in mutual hatred, given the complex interweaving of their histories, languages, and identities over many centuries. This is a fruitful observation that can be extended and deepened by reference to some of the arguments developed here.

In particular, I suggested that it was the small gap between majority status and complete or total national ethnic purity that could be the source of the extreme rage against targeted ethnic others. This suggestion—what I earlier glossed as the anxiety of incompleteness—allows us a further basis for extending Freud's insight into complex, large-scale, public forms of violence, since it allows us to see how narcissistic wounds, at the level of public ideologies about group identity, can be turned outward and become incitements to the formation of what I have called "predatory identities." The underlying dynamic here is the inner reciprocity between the categories of majority and minority. As abstractions produced by census techniques and liberal proceduralism, majorities can always be mobilized to think that they are in danger of becoming *minor* (culturally or numerically) and to fear that minorities, conversely, can easily become *major* (through brute accelerated reproduction or subtler legal or political means). These linked fears are a peculiarly modern product of the inner reciprocity of these categories, which also sets the conditions for the fear that they might morph into one another.

And this is also where globalization comes in. In a variety of ways, globalization intensifies the possibility of this volatile morphing, so that the naturalness that all group identities seek and assume is perennially threatened by the abstract affinity of the very categories of majority and minority. Global migrations across and within national boundaries constantly unsettle the glue that attaches persons to ideologies of soil and territory. The global flow of mass-mediated, sometimes commoditized, images of self and other create a growing archive of hybridities that unsettle the hard lines at the edges of large-scale identities. Modern states frequently manipulate and alter the nature of the categories through which they conduct their censuses and the statistical means through which they enumerate the populations within these groups. The global spread of improvised ideologies of constitutionalism, with elements drawn from the United States, France, and England, provokes new globalized debates about ethnicity, minority, and electoral legitimacy. Finally, the multiple, rapid, and largely invisible ways in which large-scale funds move through official interstate channels, quasi-legal commercial channels, and completely illicit channels tied up with networks like Al Qaeda are intimately tied up with globalized institutions for money laundering, electronic transfers, and new forms of cross-border accounting and law, all of which constitute that form of finance capital that virtually defines the era of globalization. These rapid, often invisible, and frequently illicit movements of money across national boundaries are widely, and rightly, seen as creating the means for today's minority to become tomorrow's majority. Each of these factors can contribute to the exacerbation of social uncertainty—the subject of detailed analysis throughout this chapter—and thus create the conditions for crossing the line from majoritarian anxiety to full-scale predation, even to genocide.

Thus, the fear of small numbers is intimately tied up with the tensions produced for liberal social theory and its institutions by the forces of globalization. Minorities in a globalizing world are a constant reminder of the incompleteness of national purity. And when the conditions—notably those surrounding social uncertainty—within any particular national polity are ripe for this incompleteness to be mobilized as a volatile deficit, the rage of genocide can be produced, especially in those liberal polities where the idea of minority has, in some way, come to be a shared political value affecting all numbers, large and small.

Notes

This essay is the fourth chapter (with minor editorial changes), "Fear of Small Numbers," in *Fear of Small Numbers*, Arjun Appadurai, pp. 49–86. Copyright 2006, Duke University Press. All rights reserved. It is republished by permission of the copyright holder, www.dukeupress.edu.

1. Hinton, ed., *Annihilating Difference.*

2. Appadurai, "Grounds of the Nation-State."

3. Appadurai, *Fear of Small Numbers*, 8.

4. Goldhagen, *Hitler's Willing Executioners.*

5. Arendt, *Eichmann in Jerusalem.*

6. Merton and Sills, eds., *Social Science Quotations.*

7. Of course, events in India have continued, with multiple elections and scholarly analysis since this was originally published in 2006.

8. Das, *Mirrors of Violence.*

9. I owe this important point to Faisal Devji, who made it in the context of a lecture on the partition of British India at Yale University in fall 2003.

10. Basu, "When Local Riots Are Not Merely Local."

11. Jaffrelot, *India's Silent Revolution.*

12. Kaviraj, "Imaginary Institution of India."

13. As in India, the situation in Iraq and Afghanistan and the leadership of Al Qaeda has changed since this was originally published, although the analysis of minorities remains relevant today.

14. Ignatieff, *Warrior's Honor.*

5

Developing a Critical Consciousness

Feminist Studies in Religion

Judith Plaskow

Judith Plaskow visited the University of Alabama as the third Aronov
lecturer. The following essay is a version of the lecture that she
presented to the university and local community on March 3, 2005.

My life's work has focused on exploring and seeking to transform the
ways in which Judaism and Christianity have supported unequal power
relationships between women and men. I have been writing and speaking about feminist studies in religion since the beginning of my career. It
is a field that I have found continually interesting because it has grown
and developed, expanded and changed since I started working on one of
the first feminist dissertations in religion in the early 1970s. I believe that
feminist perspectives on religion are profoundly important because religious attitudes and arguments are crucial ingredients in the continued
subordination of women. Not only are many people in the United States
affiliated with religious institutions that function as significant sources of
identity, values, and community in their lives, but even those who are in-
different or hostile to religion have difficulty escaping its influence. How
many people first see reproductions of Michelangelo's God and Adam on
the Sistine Chapel ceiling when they are children and have forever en-
graved in their consciousnesses the notion that God is an old white man
with a white beard? Or how many famous paintings of the snake talking
to Eve establish a visual link between women and temptation that affects
even those who have never read the creation stories in Genesis? Biblical
images and symbols have shaped American national consciousness from
the beginnings of US history, and biblical values have influenced American law. The legal doctrine of coverture that regulated married women's
lives through the nineteenth century and that held that a woman's legal
rights were subsumed by those of her husband was rooted in the biblical notion that husband and wife are one flesh, that flesh being the man's.

When women fought for the vote in the first part of the twentieth century, some of the most passionate opponents of suffrage were clergy who waved their Bibles and argued that women were to keep silent and be subordinate to their husbands. Religious convictions about the appropriate roles of women and men continue to play an important role today in public debates about sex education, abortion, sexual harassment, workplace equality, and many other issues.

My studies have presented me with many intellectual challenges and have shaped the way that I see the world. Yet in the last two decades—especially since the attacks on the World Trade Center and Pentagon on September 11, 2001—I have asked myself what I have learned over the last many years that is of value to people who do not share my particular interests and passions. What methods and approaches central to my work might have resonance beyond it? There are, after all, many aspects of US society aside from male dominance that cry out for critical examination. Since 9/11, many Americans feel more vulnerable in the world, and yet there is little agreement on how to use the nation's power to manage and respond to perceived threats. Economic inequality has increased dramatically over the past three decades; wages for many Americans have stagnated or declined; unemployment—even long-term unemployment—is high, and many jobs—even white-collar jobs—have gone overseas. A college education is no longer a guarantee of satisfying employment as it was in my day; and it certainly does not mean that one can find a good job in an institution and count on staying there for one's working life. In addition, global communication has raised awareness about dramatic inequalities worldwide: for example, a large percentage of people in the world do not have clean water to drink, and diseases that have been eradicated in the United States still stalk people in other parts of the globe, where there is not money either for expensive drugs or for simple measures of prevention. What does the field of feminist studies in religion have to say to these challenges?

What it offers, I want to argue, is a model of engaged critical consciousness: tools for reflecting critically on unequal power relations in religion and society with the goal of creating more just religious and social institutions. I do not mean to claim that such consciousness is unique to feminist studies in religion. Many people would say that it is the essence of education, and it certainly can be found in many places. Yet because such consciousness is crucial to feminist studies, the field provides numerous concrete examples of what it looks like and how it works. I believe critical consciousness is something that Americans sorely need to cultivate at this historical moment. Barraged by fake news, many people find it difficult to know whether and when to believe what they hear. Close to half of Americans are convinced that climate change is not a threat despite the overwhelming preponderance of scientific evidence suggesting that human action is raising global temperatures. Only 40 percent of Americans believe in the theory of evolution, despite its providing the foundations for modern biology. It is challenging to sift and evaluate conflicting information, whether it comes from Wikipedia or other Internet sites, the government, or the hundreds of ads to which the average American is exposed daily.

For many people, moreover, even those accustomed to looking at other ideas and institutions with a discerning eye, it is particularly difficult to bring critical reflection to bear on religion. Some people find religion to be so fundamentally wrongheaded and obscurantist that it is simply not worth engaging. For them, to bring a critical consciousness to bear on religion is by definition to dismiss it as dangerous and absurd. For others, religion is divinely created and sanctioned and therefore immune to criticism. Many people are taught to see religion—or at least their own religion— as only a positive influence in the world. Since 9/11, many in both the US government and the Muslim community have insisted that terrorists do not represent "true" Islam, just as many Christians would say that Timothy McVeigh was not a "real" Christian. And it is certainly hugely important not to demonize Islam by identifying it with its radical fringe. But one of the basic things that feminists have learned from looking at the role and status of women in various religious traditions is that all of them contain a mix of elements that empower and liberate with those that marginalize and demean. Feminists in religious studies hold many different views of the origins of particular traditions and the extent to which they combine divine and human aspects. But even those who affirm divine revelation would also point out that revelation is experienced by human beings whose particular social locations shape the ways they receive and understand it. It is necessary to examine all traditions critically and to ask where they have supported inequality and violence and where they have helped and encouraged people to live more humane and peaceful lives.

I want to talk about feminist studies in religion from the perspective of this crucial notion of critical consciousness. I do so with a dual purpose. I want to share something of the history of this area of study and my own work. And I want to present an *approach* to religious and social problems that envisions everyone as potentially an active critic and shaper of religious and social institutions. Feminist studies models ways in which people can pause, think, and ask questions about the barrage of information and opinions that constantly assaults them—not in order to become cynics and nay-sayers but rather informed participants in the social structures and decisions that shape their lives.

The Emergence of Feminist Consciousness

The first moment in the emergence of critical consciousness and in the development of feminist studies in religion is the most crucial in that it lays the foundations for everything that follows. It involves beginning to *notice* inequalities of power that may have long been taken for granted and whose invisibility is crucial to the smooth running of the world. I grew up in a very nontraditional synagogue, for example, where many of the practices— such as men not covering their heads during prayer—violated Jewish law or custom. Yet the rabbi was opposed to the ordination of women because it was "against tradition." I was never happy with his style of leadership, but it was not until I became a feminist that I was able to name the profound contradiction between his hostility toward women's ordination and his willingness to jettison other aspects of tradition. Or later, when I was in graduate school, I was never assigned a single book or article written by a woman. But it took me over a year and becoming involved in a feminist group at Yale before I even noticed this. After all, I was studying theology, and all theologians were men. Who else would I be reading?

Feminist studies in religion had its origins in a new kind of *attention* to women's status and roles in religious institutions and to the images of women in religious texts. On a grassroots level in churches and synagogues and on an intellectual level within the academy, women and men began to look at their experiences with a more critical eye and to ask questions that had not occurred to them previously. In some sense, this first moment of feminist awakening was a bit mysterious because it could be triggered by many different experiences and it was discontinuous with what went before. *Ms.* magazine in its first issue called this moment the "click!"— the moment in which a lightbulb or explosion goes off in one's head. It is the instant in which the question that might have been niggling at the back of one's mind suddenly takes shape: wait, why is it your *mother* who gets up from the table when your *father* wants the ketchup? Why is the girls' soccer team playing with hand-me-down equipment while the boys' team gets the new stuff? Why do innumerable advertisements use women's sexuality to sell products that have nothing to do with women or peddle images of female beauty that are virtually unattainable?

In the case of feminist studies in religion, women began asking why so many religious roles were unavailable to them—why girls and women who wanted to be altar girls or priests, rabbis or ministers found the doors shut in their faces. Or in the words of one woman writing in the early 1970s, why did women in the church serve every supper except the Lord's?[1] Women suddenly began to notice their linguistic exclusion from the "brotherhood of man" and also from the divine image. How *did* God come to be thought of as male, and was there a relationship between the traditional picture of the old man with a white beard and the exclusion of women from religious leadership? In the Jewish tradition, since halakha (or Jewish law) plays a central role, Jewish feminists began to look at the legal disabilities that affect women's religious and family roles. Why were women not counted in the quorum of ten Jews needed to conduct a full religious service? Why could only a man write a bill of divorce? Why are things the way they are, and how did they get that way?

Feminists were not raising these questions just to be troublemakers. They were seeking full participation in the religious traditions that had been passed on to them; they wanted access to all the rights and responsibilities of Jewish or Christian life. But for some people at least, these first questions about basic fairness quickly led to deeper ones about the very nature of the Jewish and Christian traditions. It is often the case with critical consciousness that initial questions generate new ones as the process of questioning meets accommodation or resistance. The reality today is that in liberal Protestant and Jewish denominations, the rights women sought in the early 1970s have largely been won. Most mainstream Protestant groups ordain women and have for some time, as do the three non–Orthodox Jewish denominations—Reform, Reconstructionist, and Conservative. Even the Catholic Church has opened some roles to women such as altar girl and lay Eucharistic minister. But in achieving equality or imagining what it might look like, some feminists began to see contradictions between access and the *content* of tradition. Certain Catholic feminists, for example, began asking themselves whether they wanted to be ordained in a hierarchical church. What would it mean for women to be priests in an institution in which only priests can celebrate the sacraments and the laity as a whole is disenfranchised? If women sought the priesthood, would it be a celibate priesthood? What if there was a connection between the suspicion of sexuality and the body that lay at the basis of priestly celibacy and the insistence that women could not be priests? If that were the case, then equality between women and men would have to entail a thoroughgoing transformation of tradition and not simply insert new faces into established roles.

Jewish feminists too began to notice contradictions between women's increasing access to leadership and the substance of the tradition they were hoping to hand on. They began to ask what it meant to argue that a bat mitzvah (a Jewish coming-of-age ceremony for a girl) should be the same as a bar mitzvah (a Jewish coming-of-age ceremony for a boy) when a girl might be called to the Torah the week that the portion contained the laws for selling a daughter as a slave or described how a rapist should pay the girl's *father* a fine and be forced to marry her. They began to ask why, in a tradition with blessings for so many events and aspects of daily life—seeing a rainbow, eating the first watermelon of the season, going to the bathroom—there were no blessings for childbirth, the onset of menstruation, or other important biological events in women's lives. Feminists began to see that their traditions were not created by or for women and that this fact had implications for every aspect of tradition, not just for who filled certain roles.[2]

While these developments were taking place in churches and synagogues, quite analogous and interconnected processes of deepening critique were happening on an academic level. It is important to note that the academic and grassroots questions fed each other, partly because they were sometimes asked by the same people and partly because feminists doing academic work were intent on responding to real-world injustices and women in the pews were eager for analyses that could give depth and context to their own emerging insights. Those of us who were theology students in the late 1960s and early 1970s began to *notice* how many of the religious thinkers we were reading had dreadful things to say about women. Thomas Aquinas opined that women are naturally subject to men because men are wiser and more governed by reason. Echoing this sentiment over six hundred years later, the prominent twentieth-century theologian Karl Barth said that women are properly behind and subordinate to men and should not complain even if men encroach on their rights. Martin Luther said that women were created with big hips in order that they stay home and sit on them, while the church father Tertullian called women the "devil's gateway."[3] The Talmud—the masterwork of rabbinic Judaism—says that ten measures of idle talk were given to world, nine of them to women, and that it is better for a man to walk behind a lion than behind a woman.

When female graduate students pointed out such passages to our fellow students, we were given the equivalent of a verbal pat on the head and urged to ignore them. After all, we were told, they reflect the attitudes of earlier times and have nothing to do with the ways that these thinkers understand important topics such as God, salvation, or creation. We should think of them simply as personal opinions that could be mentally snipped out of the texts and set aside. And perhaps we initially hoped that this was true, if only we could look past the sense of being affronted. But such was the nature of our growing critical consciousness that we gradually began to draw connections between these individual offensive statements and fundamental theological concepts. Some Christian feminists, for example, began to see a connection between Karl Barth's view of the relationship between women and men and the hierarchal dualisms that pervade his theology. Women's "proper" subordination to men is for him analogous to the proper subordination of humans and the world to God.[4] Some Jewish feminists began to ask whether women were full members of the covenant community.[5] In Genesis 17, God's covenant with Abraham is identified with male circumcision, a rite from which women are obviously excluded. "This is my covenant which you shall keep, between me and you and your descendants after you," God says to Abraham, "every male among you shall be circumcised" (Gen. 17:10). In the book of Exodus, when the community of Israel is preparing to enter into the covenant on Mount Sinai, Moses turns to the assembled people and says, "Be ready for the third day; do not go near a woman" (Exod. 19:15).[6] At this central moment of Jewish history, the community is addressed only as men. These Christian and Jewish examples suggest that individual negative statements about women, so far from being distractions from central theological concepts, may in fact provide windows into deeper patterns of thought at work in particular thinkers or traditions.

Moreover, as one critical insight led to the next, feminists noted that women were hardly the only group depicted as "others"—as outside the holy community—by texts considered sacred. The Hebrew Bible repeatedly says that the Hebrews should give no quarter to idolatry, that they should tear down the altars and kill the adherents of foreign gods. The picture of Canaanite religion in the Bible is a caricature of what it means to use images in worship; its purpose is to set off the "true religion" of the Israelites from that of the people of the land. A similar process takes place in the New Testament, which presents the Pharisees in extremely negative terms as rigid and legalistic, even though from a Jewish perspective, they were the creative and innovative religious thinkers of their time. Like the Hebrew Bible's image of the Canaanites, the New Testament's view

of the Pharisees emerges out of competition between the old and new religions; it is designed not for accuracy but to demonstrate the superiority
of the new way of life.[7] In a somewhat different vein, womanist—that is,
black feminist—scholars have pointed to the role of Hagar in the Hebrew
Bible as the other's other. A slave of Sarah, who is herself already a periph-
eral figure in the covenant between God and Abraham, Hagar provides
a paradigm of the situation of black women as, in Zora Neale Hurston's
words, "the mule of the world."[8] In other words, the process of identity
formation, for Jews and Christians as well as many other groups, takes
place partly through defining the self against numerous others who are
perceived as "what the self is not" and who therefore become legitimate
targets of domination and persecution.

Let me point out a couple of crucial aspects of this first moment of developing critical consciousness. First of all, once one enters into the process
of asking critical questions, it can become habit forming! Seeing evidence
of the subordination of women in one place in a tradition may be the start
of seeing it in many places and then moving on to discern the deeper patterns that connect various attitudes and practices. From there, one might
begin to notice other forms of "othering" that are embedded in religious
texts. It becomes difficult to deny the many ways that "real" Judaism and
Christianity have been oppressive to women and other groups. Secondly,
the feminists asking these questions have generally been engaged critics
willing to give voice to difficult and painful parts of their own traditions.
They have not pointed fingers from outside so much as demanded that
their traditions live up to their own best insights and commitments to justice. And that means acknowledging where their own traditions have been
problematic or wrongheaded.

Why, one may ask, would anyone want to raise critical questions about
religion or about any aspect of their lives? Why spoil a relationship to
a tradition that one might have been raised to see as perfect or beyond
questioning? Or, more broadly, why confront the problems with education,
the economic system, or any aspect of society instead of simply accepting
things as they are? Wouldn't seeing such things make a person angry, and
why would anyone want to be angry? I can think of a number of answers
to these questions. Firstly, the initial "click" moment, the moment when
someone suddenly notices something that perhaps bothered them in the
past but that they have never been able to name clearly, sometimes comes
unbidden; it is not always a choice. And once someone's eyes are opened
to an oppressive dynamic, it can be almost impossible to unsee it, just as
Adam and Eve could not have pasted the apple back onto the tree once

they bit into it. But more substantively, the negative aspects of a tradition do not go away just because people do not want to name them. Religious traditions are complicated; they contain an intricate and often contradictory welter of stories, beliefs, customs, and practices. I think there is a tendency on the part of many people to focus on those aspects of their traditions that they find meaningful or agree with and to ignore the rest. If I were to ask you to list important Christian values, for example, I would be surprised if sexism were among those you named. Most people think of values as positive and assign negative values to some outer darkness that, again, is not viewed as part of authentic tradition. But the subordination of women has been a very central value in both Judaism and Christianity. As I began by suggesting, religious views of men's and women's roles influence the way in which people think of themselves today, even when they are unaware of the sources of their attitudes. Becoming conscious allows people to decide which values to affirm and which to modify or discard. And that brings me to my third point: asking critical questions provides a foundation for change. Such questions are not just tools for taking things apart; they are a starting point for putting them back together again. The purpose of critique is to clear the ground in order to allow space for new possibilities to emerge.

Constructive Feminist Thought

In fact, feminists in religious studies found that at the same time we needed to keep asking hard, critical questions, it was also important to explore what our traditions might look like if the lives and experiences of women were taken as seriously as those of men. The first moment of feminist research involved becoming aware of and paying attention to the awful and constricting things that had been said about women in various religious texts and traditions. But uncovering negative attitudes quickly led to new questions: What was the reality of women's participation in various traditions and what would these traditions look like were women's histories included? However women have been *defined* by men—whether as misbegotten men, the devil's gateway, or something else—they are and always have been subjects and actors. Despite all the misogynist things that have been said and written about them, women have always continued to live their lives, care for their children, do sustaining work in the world, and engage in religious practices—either those they shared with men or those of their own creation. Feminist scholars therefore began to ask not what have men said about women but where were the women; what were they doing in particular periods and contexts? What would it mean to look at Jewish or Christian history as the history of women and men? What changes, what new insights and discoveries would emerge?

Thus, from early on, feminist work was characterized by a dual focus: on what was said *about* women by men in important religious texts and on what these same texts as well as other sources might have to say about women's activities and lives. Two early volumes of feminist essays, one edited by Rosemary Radford Ruether and the other by Ruether and Eleanor McLaughlin, nicely illustrate these two very different sets of questions. The first book, *Religion and Sexism*, published in 1974, focused on male *images* of women in the Jewish and Christian traditions. A central concern of the chapter on the New Testament, for example, was Paul's attitudes toward women. Author Connie Parvey asked whether Paul was an emancipator of women or a product of his time and place who wanted to keep women subordinate to men. Parvey argued that he sometimes appealed to established customs—for instance, in saying that women should remain silent in church and cover their heads when they pray—but that he also taught that the old world order was in the process of being overturned by the coming of Christ and that in a new age, differences of race, sex, and economic status would be transcended.[9] Similarly, the chapter on medieval theology examined several types of male-authored texts that shaped perceptions of women: the theology of Thomas Aquinas, writings on marriage and the spiritual life that idealized virginity as the most positive choice for women, and a frankly misogynist sermonic literature that mentioned women only in connection with sensuality and lack of intellectual development. Author Eleanor McLaughlin suggested that it was through the sermonic literature that high theology came to have an impact on ordinary people. Cleric after cleric wrote of the insatiable sexuality of women— even nuns, of the ways in which they used cosmetics to disguise their sins and the ugliness of their bodies and of their danger to the chastity of men and to the tranquility of the contemplative life.[10]

Women of Spirit, published five years later, revisits much of the same historical territory but from a very different perspective. In that volume, the chapter on the New Testament does not ask about Paul's attitudes toward women but about what his letters and other New Testament texts say about the actual roles of women in early Christian communities. Author Elisabeth Schüssler Fiorenza argues that there is significant evidence for women's leadership in the early church. Women were founders and promoters of house churches, which were decisive institutions in the development of early Christianity. They were missionaries who worked with

Paul on an equal basis. They were prophets who, together with men, were important sources of divine revelation. While historians of early Christianity have tended to overlook the significance of women's leadership and to downplay the importance of titles such as deacon when they are applied to women, the New Testament sources probably represent only the tip of an iceberg indicating how much of women's contributions were lost to a patriarchal editing process.[11] The chapter of *Women of Spirit* on medieval Christianity, again by Eleanor McLaughlin, explores a range of ways in which women sought holiness within the monastic life. *The Life of Christina of Markyate*, for example, a twelfth-century text written by an anonymous monk who clearly knew Christina personally, provides evidence of how the ideal of sanctity allowed women to defy family and social expectations and to pursue lives they chose for themselves with the support of the church. Christina, the daughter of a prominent English family, vowed at a young age that she would be the spouse of Christ and none other. When her parents tried to marry her off, she repeatedly and creatively fended off her suitors, finally disguising herself as a boy in order to escape from her home. After a period of hiding in the cell of a hermit who became her friend and protector, she gradually gained fame as a holy woman who was sought out by pilgrims from all over Europe. Christina is only one among many medieval women whose monastic vocation enabled them to resist marriage and motherhood and forge a meaningful spiritual life.[12]

The same juxtaposition of images and history has also been explored by Jewish feminists. The two Talmuds (Jerusalem and Babylonian) say many things about women, from the downright scurrilous to the deeply appreciative. Women are depicted as excessively talkative, sharp-tongued, arrogant, quick to anger, and drawn to witchcraft. Yet they are also seen as filled with compassion, solicitous on their husbands' behalf, and strong in faith.[13] The question facing feminist scholars is whether documents that are basically a record of debates that took place in male rabbinic academies from the second to the fifth centuries tell readers anything about the actual lives of women. While it can be very difficult to get behind the interests of the Talmuds' authors and editors to judge to what extent its laws and narratives reflect historical reality, there are places where they seem to offer glimpses of the actual roles women may have played in historical, social, and religious events of the day.[14] The most fascinating Talmudic figure from a feminist perspective is a woman by the name of Beruriah—the only woman mentioned in rabbinic literature who can be said to be a Torah scholar. The earliest sources associate her with a particular legal decision about ritual purity that is not terribly important in its own right but that is the only decision in Jewish legal literature transmitted in the name of a woman. Later sources elaborate on her significance, saying that she learned three hundred traditions from three hundred rabbis in a single day, and depicting her as instructing a number of men in textual interpretation. In an especially interesting vignette, she chides a (male) student for asking her directions in a wordy way, pointing out that the rabbis say "not to speak much with a woman." The story both underscores Beruriah's knowledge of the law and depicts her as commenting on male attitudes in an ironic way.[15]

In moving from exploring what religious texts say *about* women to asking whether it is possible to get behind male images to the historical reality of women's lives a new layer of critical questions emerges. Most of the sources available to feminist scholars were written by men for men and were not intended to convey the history of women. How does one read between the lines, then; how does one ferret out information from literature meant to serve other purposes? This is a crucial question, and asking it has yielded a great deal of interesting and important information. But feminists have gone still further. The examples I have just cited of individual women or women's roles are drawn from mainstream religious texts and accept standard definitions of historical importance. Not surprisingly, when feminists first began to look for women's history, they looked in canonical texts and at mainstream religious movements. Scholars of the Christian tradition asked: Were there women in the circle around Jesus? What roles did women play in the earliest Christian missions? Were there any women among the group of thinkers who defined church teaching? Was there anything distinctive about the teachings of mystics who were women? Similarly, scholars of Judaism turned to the key texts of that tradition to see what they revealed about women's lives. But it is also possible to ask other and still deeper sets of questions: How do certain texts or movements come to be defined as normative or as most important in the first place? Judaism as it exists in the world today is rabbinic Judaism. The forms of Jewish expression developed by the rabbis in the first centuries still shape contemporary Jewish life. But were the rabbis equally influential in their own time? Did the majority of Jews accept their authority, or were they essentially talking to themselves and a small circle of followers? How did their power come to be established? What competing forms of Jewish belief and practice contemporaneous with the rabbis have since disappeared? Were the roles of women in nonrabbinic Judaism different from those prescribed by the Talmuds and other rabbinic texts? Could it be that the disappearance of competing views of Judaism was linked in any way to their views of women? In other words, feminists came to appreciate the truth that it is always the winners who write history. And in perceiving this truth, they became eager to try to see around and underneath the evidence that the winners left in order to unearth a more complex reality.

Elaine Pagels's work on Gnosticism raises such questions and concerns for the Christian tradition. Gnosticism was a religious movement widespread in the ancient world that taught that knowledge—gnosis—is the way to salvation of the soul. Though Christian Gnosticism was rejected as heretical by what became the orthodox Christian community, surviving Gnostic texts, including noncanonical gospels, offer interesting contrasts to the canonical gospels and their orthodox interpretation. Two distinctive features of Gnosticism were its use of female images for God and the importance of women's leadership. Some Gnostic sources describe God as containing both male and female elements, as primal father and the mother of all things. Women functioned in some Gnostic groups as prophets, healers, teachers, priests, and even bishops. One set of Gnostic texts claims to have received the secret teachings of Jesus through James and Mary Magdalene. The notion that Mary Magdalene was Jesus's beloved disciple and wife, a claim popularized by *The Da Vinci Code*, has its origins in Gnosticism. The *Gospel of Mary Magdalene*—a text that obviously did not make it into the New Testament canon—describes how Mary tried to lift the spirits of the disciples after the crucifixion by sharing with them teachings that Jesus had conveyed to her privately. Peter is depicted as furious, however, at the suggestion that Jesus loved Mary more than the male disciples and had shared with a woman knowledge denied them. Mary replies to him, "What do you think? Do you think I made this up in my heart? Do you think I am lying about the Lord?" This dispute between Mary and Peter about the place of women in Jesus's circle and in early Christianity raises the question of whether the prominent role of women in some Gnostic groups was part of what led to the rejection of Gnosticism as heretical. While Pagels refrains from drawing a direct line between female imagery and leadership and the label "heresy," she does raise the critical questions: What is the process through which a tradition becomes tradition and what is at stake for women in that traditioning process?[16]

A Jewish example of a rather different sort also illustrates the importance of looking for women's history in noncanonical sources. The Mishnah, a very important second-century code of Jewish law that forms the basis of the Talmud, sets out an elaborate procedure for divorce, which, based on Deuteronomy 24, is entirely male initiated. A man may give his wife a bill of divorce (called a *get*), but that right is not reciprocal. The

Mishnah and the Talmudic commentaries on it form the basis of Jewish law today, and the inability of women to divorce their husbands is one of the most serious disabilities of women under Jewish law, as it potentially leaves women whose husbands refuse to write a *get* chained to dead marriages. There is some evidence, however, that in early nonrabbinic communities, divorce may not have been entirely male initiated. The Gospel of Mark (10:12) seems to testify to a different Jewish practice, as Jesus says that a man who divorces his wife commits adultery and so does a wife who divorces her husband. The notion that there were competing Jewish views on this subject is borne out by the discovery of other first-century documents that indicate that, while the right of women to divorce their husbands may have been controversial, there were individual women who initiated divorce or reserved the right to do so in their marriage contracts.[17]

These and other contradictions between the picture of women's lives that emerges from canonical literature and that available through noncanonical texts and evidence such as archeological finds raise many critical questions about whether normative texts reflect historical reality or express primarily the wishes, ideals, and general worldview of their authors. Who were the authors and editors of particular canonical texts, and what interests and perspectives do they represent? Who do they envision as their audiences? Were there women among the circle of writers, readers, or hearers, and what is the significance of their presence or absence? How do people come to believe that there is only one authentic Judaism or Christianity, and what if the popular picture of Jewish or Christian history were expanded to include noncanonical sources? These questions have important implications for women's history, but they also suggest a broader view of religious traditions as complex and contested, shaped by multiple interests and interpretations, and evolving historically as much through positions and practices cast out as nonnormative as those defined as orthodox.

Jewish feminists have another critical tool that expands on the notion of multiple approaches to tradition and makes it possible to imagine how Judaism might look different had women's voices been included in its formation. *Midrash* is a classical mode of Jewish religious reflection employed by Talmudic and later rabbis that begins with noticing gaps or contradictions in biblical texts. Creators of midrash bring their own questions to troubling texts, expand on them to answer those questions, and assume that the expanded texts are part of the original meaning. Many biblical texts are extremely condensed, for example, preserving only those narrative elements that serve a particular purpose and leaving out many details that might be of deep interest to readers. Thus the Bible opens with the universal stories of creation and the flood and then, in Genesis 12, suddenly focuses on God's call to Abraham without any background information or explanation. Why of all the people on earth should Abraham have been chosen to enter into a covenant with God? The rabbis asked this question and answered with a very well-known midrash depicting Abraham as the first monotheist. According to their story, Abraham's father owned an idol shop, and one night, after his father had left, Abraham destroyed all the idols in the shop and left a cudgel in the hands of the largest idol. When his father asked in horror who had ransacked the shop, Abraham pointed to the largest idol and said, "He did." The father replied, "How can that be when he is just a thing of stone that I created?" Abraham asked, "So why do you worship a thing of stone rather than the one God of heaven and earth?" The rabbis not only filled in gaps in biblical texts, they also explored seeming contradictions between them. They noticed, for instance, that there are two different creation accounts in the first chapters of Genesis—that in Genesis 1, men and women are created equally and simultaneously, while in Genesis 2, Eve is created from Adam's rib. They asked whether Adam had a first wife, and they answered, yes, Lilith. Lilith, like Adam, was created from the dust of the ground and because her origin was the same as Adam's, she insisted on complete equality with him. When he tried to subordinate her, she uttered God's holy name and flew away. God then created a second wife for Adam, named Eve.[18] Many years ago, I created a midrash that expanded on this one, but the story I have just described is the rabbis', not mine, and it points to the feminist potential of midrash.

Jewish feminists have used midrash to powerful effect, raising critical questions about the silences in biblical texts and writing them forward in ways that try to imagine the difference that inclusion of women's perspectives and concerns might make to the biblical narrative. A favorite subject of feminist midrash is the story of the binding of Isaac because the text begs for a response to the question of where Sarah was when Abraham took the son that she had borne in her old age and carried him to the top of a mountain to offer him as a sacrifice. The rabbis asked this question too, and noting that the chapter on the binding of Isaac is immediately followed by a report of Sarah's death, said that Sarah died when she heard from Satan what Abraham had done.[19] In feminist midrash, however, Sarah questions or rejects Abraham's choice to follow God's command. Sometimes she responds to events from a position of powerlessness. One midrashic Sarah intuits where Abraham had gone when she sees her angry and defeated son returning home with his father, but she knows in her heart that Abraham misunderstood God's decree. Other feminist Sarahs are more proactive. One follows after Abraham and Isaac, hiding in a bush and sending out the ram as an alternative offering. One is that she herself is asked to sacrifice her son and boldly answers no, saying she will not be chosen and neither will her son.[20]

Another frequent subject of feminist midrash is Miriam, the sister of Moses and Aaron. While Miriam was clearly an important figure in the early Israelite community because she appears in conjunction with the crossing of the Red Sea, a founding event in Jewish history, the biblical portrait of Miriam is frustratingly sketchy. She leads the women in prayer on the far side of the Sea (Exod. 15:21); she challenges Moses's authority along with her brother Aaron, only to be punished much more harshly than he (Num. 12); she dies when the community is encamped in the wilderness (Num. 20:1). Feminist midrash imagines many Miriams: a brave singer standing by the shores of the sea who momentarily hesitates to enter the water but then discovers that the ground beneath her is firm; an old maid elbowing her way to the front of the crowd at Mount Sinai, past the women with children straggling in the rear; a bitter Miriam bewailing the unfairness of her punishment for challenging Moses; a Miriam arguing for her place as prophetess and her equality with Moses and Aaron.[21] These creative reimaginings of biblical narratives represent a very different approach to canonical texts from the effort to use them as historical sources. Yet they also raise critical questions about what is missing from those texts. They encourage reflection on how Jewish tradition—or any tradition—might be reconfigured if women had an equal hand in shaping it. And they ask how a reconfigured tradition might provide different models of what it means to be a person of faith.

Conclusions

I could have used many starting points other than reconfiguring history for talking about the development of feminist critical consciousness. No aspect of either Judaism or Christianity has been left untouched by feminist questions. Feminists have thoroughly explored gender relations in the Bible, not only using it as a source for women's history but also analyzing its stories as culture-shaping narratives. They have written new theologies, raising searching questions about the dominant image of God as male and also reinterpreting Christology, Torah, sin, and salvation from feminist perspectives. They have reconfigured Jewish and Christian liturgy, created inclusive language lectionaries, reworked traditional Jewish blessings, and developed new ceremonies for significant events in women's lives. But my primary purpose has not been to describe the specifics of feminist studies in religion so much as to explore the nature of the engaged critical consciousness that is manifest in this area of knowledge. Central to feminist thought is a deep aversion to letting hoary truths go unexamined or taking things for granted. It repeatedly manifests a willingness to look at how power is consolidated and defined and to wrestle with the hard places in tradition: to confront the ways in which particular traditions support sexism, ethnocentrism, and other forms of inequality that disfigure the world. Feminist thought also moves into the space opened up by criticism in order to participate in the process of change. The relationship between critique and transformation is a dialectical one. Raising difficult critical questions generates an agenda for change. But the process of reimagining a tradition as fully a tradition of women and men leads to new critical questions that push the quest for change still deeper. Thus, as I have tried to show, each set of questions begets both new questions and new ideas for change in a continuing spiral.

Let me conclude by saying a bit more about why I see this process as important. To look at the world through critical lenses is to come to a deeper understanding of one's own history and situation. Whether one is trying to comprehend economic policy, the role of religion in public debates, or the significance of the media in shaping perceptions of national priorities, critical consciousness makes it possible to look past sound bites and simplistic analyses in order to think about complex causes and nuanced solutions and to act purposefully on the basis of one's own priorities. To begin to perceive the intricate mixture of ideas in various religious traditions and the ways in which they have shaped social attitudes is to begin to understand what it is in those traditions that allows them to be invoked for particular political purposes. How is it that the Bible could be used in the nineteenth century to support slavery or oppose women's suffrage, and what permits it to be cited today to turn back the clock on a host of issues pertaining to gender and sexuality? The reality is that there are conflicting strands in all religious traditions, that none developed inevitably in a particular direction, that again and again they came to crossroads at which significant battles were waged and choices made. What are the crossroads at which particular traditions and societies are standing today, and how can their members participate in the decisions that will shape the future? Where do they want their religious communities and societies to be headed? If "real" religion is meant to foster justice, peace, and compassion, how can it actually manifest those values? How is it possible to address the problematic aspects of tradition so that they are not left to do their work in the world? Feminist studies in religion provides models for looking critically at important dimensions of religion and society in the service of encouraging everyone to become thoughtful agents of change.

Notes

1. The idea of the "click" moment appeared in O'Reilly, "The Housewife's Moment of Truth"; Emswiler, "How the New Woman Feels," 5.
2. Plaskow, *Standing Again at Sinai*, introduction and chapter 1.
3. Daly, *Church and Second Sex*, chapter 2, *Beyond God the Father*, introduction.
4. Christ, "Barth on Man-Woman Relation."
5. R. Adler, "I've Had Nothing Yet."
6. Plaskow, *Standing Again at Sinai*, 25.
7. Plaskow, "Jewish Anti-Paganism," 110–13.
8. Williams, *Sisters in the Wilderness*, especially chapter 1.
9. Parvey, "Theology and Leadership of Women," 123–35.
10. McLaughlin, "Equality of Souls, Inequality of Sexes," 250, 252.
11. Fiorenza, "Word, Spirit, and Power," 32–44, 57.
12. McLaughlin, "Women, Power, and Pursuit of Holiness," 108–14.
13. Hauptman, "Images of Women in Talmud," 197–205.
14. Ilan, *Integrating Women*, 5.
15. Ilan, "Beruryah."
16. Pagels, "What Became of God the Mother?" 107–19.
17. Brooten, "Could Women Initiate Divorce."
18. Ginsberg. *Legends of the Jews*, 1:214, 65. This is a seven-volume set that contains hundreds of examples of midrash.
19. Ibid., 286–87.
20. Umansky, "Creating Jewish Feminist Theology," 196; Rogow, "Akedah"; Wilner, *Sarah's Choice*, 21–23.
21. Sohn, "I Shall Sing," 768–69; Weissler, "Standing at Sinai," 91–92; Canady, "Miriam," 41–43; Romm, "Miriam Argues for Her Place," 11.

6

Religious Practices and Communal Identity of Cochin Jews

Models, Metaphors, and Methods of Diasporic Religious Acculturation

Nathan Katz

Nathan Katz was selected as the eighth Aronov lecturer. He presented a version of this essay at the University of Alabama on November 17, 2009.

Models, Metaphors, and Methods

The term *diaspora* is borrowed from the Greek for "dispersion," which, in turn, was used to translate Judaic concepts of being away from home and a feeling of religious estrangement. There are two closely allied Hebrew terms that traditionally were subsumed under the concept of Jewish Diaspora: *tefutzot* and *galut* (or *golah*). In rabbinic literature, *tefutzot* refers to Jewish settlements anywhere, and *golah/galut* refers to Jewish life outside of Israel. In responsa literature, for example, the word *ha'tefutzot* occurs only 10 times, while such compounds as *tefutzot ha-Mizrach* ("settlements in the east"), *tefutzot Israel* ("settlements in Israel"), and *tefutzot ha-Golah* ("settlements in exile") are found 330 times. The tern *galut* or *golah* is found 500 times.[1]

In modern Hebrew, *tefutzot* is used to apply to Jewish settlements outside the land of Israel during periods of Jewish sovereignty over the land. The latter term, *galut*, is more significant for religious studies, as it carries with it a sense of forced exile, estrangement, alienation, and longing for a return.

In modern usage, then, the word *tefutzot* refers only to the Jewish community in Egypt during the First Temple period, communities throughout the Greco-Roman world during the Second Temple period, and to Jewish communities outside of Israel since the establishment of the modern state in 1948.[2]

When, however, foreign powers ruled over Jerusalem, the condition of those Jews forced to live outside the land of Israel was subsumed under the concept of exile (*galut* or *golah*). This term is used for the period of the Babylonian Exile (597–538 BCE) when much of the population of Israel was taken captive and sent to Babylon, but this brief exile was understood as but a precursor to the exile that commenced with the Roman sack of Jerusalem and destruction of the Second Temple in 70 CE and lasted until the establishment of the modern state of Israel in 1948. "Only the loss of a political-ethnic center and the feeling of uprootedness turns Diaspora (Dispersion) into *galut* (Exile)."[3]

In our attempts at understanding the religious life of communities outside of the Jewish homeland, this modern Hebrew distinction between *tefutzot* and *galut* is useful. Perhaps we need to understand differently the religious lives of those whose exile is forced upon them—Jews between 70 CE and 1948, Tibetan Buddhists in India, Vietnamese and Cambodian Buddhists in North America today, people of African descent in the Americas, Zoroastrians in India, Baha'is worldwide, most native peoples in the world (who, although often remaining on ancestral lands, nevertheless experience the loss of political control over these lands as a variety of exile)—and those whose dispersion is voluntary and therefore of a more gentle variety—Hindus in Europe and the Americas, Jews since 1948, Muslims outside of traditional Islamic societies, and so on.

In both cases, however, religious life in exile is experienced as the opposite of being at home, a sense amplified when a return home becomes impossible due to political circumstances. Life in exile severs the primal connection of land, religion, people, and language, four factors taken by nativists to be inseparable but which unravel once the condition of exile is brought into play. A person outside of his or her homeland, who speaks a language other than an ancestral tongue or who confronts an ethnic or religious other far vaster than one's own community, can no longer imagine that his or her Weltanschauung is unchallenged or that his or her traditional ways are normative universally. The condition of exile implies a plurality of meanings, customs, rites, and worldviews. And it is in this sense that exile is the precursor of postmodernity's relativism.

An example of this is when the Dalai Lama of Tibet, leader of a people whose exile began in 1959, invited a delegation of rabbis and Jewish scholars to his palace in 1990. He wanted to learn what he termed the "Jewish secret" for preserving a religion and a culture despite the loss of a homeland. He reasoned that if the Jewish people were able to persevere for nearly two thousand years, then his Tibetan people ought to be able to benefit from their experience. In the ensuing dialogue, the Dalai Lama was especially fascinated by Judaism's confrontation with modernity. Paul Mendes-Flohr of Hebrew University in Jerusalem aptly articulated the dilemma: "personal fulfillment" is the watchword of modernity, whereas "communal responsibility" is the hallmark of tradition. While the Jews' entry into exile in the year 70 CE anticipated the confrontation with modernity in the Jewish Enlightenment (*Haskalah*) by more than 1,600 years, peoples such as the Tibetans, who began their exile during the twentieth century, must confront exile and modernity virtually simultaneously. Nevertheless, the connections between the experiences of exile and of the modern world were vivid.[4] In dialogue between Jews and Asian communities in North America, Jews are often idealized as the first people to strike a balance between accomplishment in the modern world on its own terms and traditional values of the community.[5] Thus, when a religion goes into exile it becomes modernized, at least in some senses.

Models of Religious Acculturation

To ask about religion in exile or a diaspora is to ask how a religion travels; that is, we want to understand what happens when a religion and the community in which it is embedded moves from a place where it is "at home," where it is in the majority, where it enjoys political and cultural authority, to a place where it is a stranger, where it becomes a minority, where it flourishes or suffers at hands other than its own. In short, we want to develop models, metaphors, and methods for the process of religious acculturation of an exiled community. And as noted above, the process may look different for a religious community in *tefutzot* from one in *galut*.

There have been two dominant, interrelated models for understanding how a diasporized religion accommodates itself to its new cultural context: the concept of religious syncretism and the anthropological distinction between "high" and "little" traditions. The concept of religious syncretism was introduced by anthropologist Melville Herskovits in his descriptions of Afro-Caribbean religions, as a way of explaining the dual identity of many of the folk deities of Cuba, who were simultaneously Yoruban gods and Catholic saints.[6] More recent studies of religions of the African diaspora have been critical of Herskovits's implicit assumption that the process by which these dual identities came to be was a "mere mixture" or a simple "translation" from one theological system to another.[7] Rather, a more deliberate, conscious, and judicious model for the interactions between the diasporized and the host religious cultures was suggested, a need that I hope to address in this chapter.

Another pivotal model for this type of religious interaction was suggested by the concept of "high" and "little" traditions. According to this perspective, the "high" traditions are those with a literature, male literati, and rituals performed in public space. "Little" traditions are those of non-literate peoples, often with female leadership, whose central ritual performances are done in the home.

The high/little traditions model has been used to analyze the adaptation of a "high" religion to its "little tradition" environment, such as the coming of Christianity to pagan Europe or of Buddhism to Sri Lanka and Southeast Asia. This model has been very useful in understanding how "'universal' concepts that from a doctrinal point of view are ethical norms for all mankind are 'contained' within a map of Ceylon, i.e., the universalistic concepts are embodied in a pluralistic (national) framework."[8] No doubt, this model is effective in certain cases, but it cannot account for the complex interactions between two "high" traditions such as diasporized Judaism and host Hinduism in the case of the ancient Jewish community at Cochin, in southwest India. As will be shown, the accretion of Hindu temple practices into synagogal worship in Cochin was no "mere mixture" but a judicious borrowing within the framework of Judaic law (halakha). And the well-intended but demeaning characterization of "little tradition" could not possibly be applied to either side of the Hindu-Judaic interaction in Cochin.

An Alternate Metaphor

Rather, we look outside of the field of religious studies to Gestalt psychology to find a metaphor more finely attuned to the data we wish to consider, such as Fritz Perls's metaphor of figure and (back)ground, or of foregrounding and backgrounding.

According to Perls et al., visual perception involves the construction of a *figure*, "the focus of interest—an object, pattern, etc." over and against its *background*, "the setting or context." As Perls elaborates, "The interplay between figure and ground is dynamic, for the same ground may, with differing interests and shifts in attention, give rise to different figures; or a given figure, if it contains detail, may itself become ground in the event that some detail of its own emerges as figure."[9] Perls's psychological theory can be applied to the type of religious interaction we are considering when the diasporized religion itself, in this case Judaism, is understood as the ground, and the particular expression of Judaism in a context, in Cochin, is understood as the figure. The "shifts in attention" are the cultural demands of the host culture, in this case the Hinduism of the dominant Nayar and the priestly Nambudiri castes of Kerala.

To extend this approach, if it can be shown that diasporized Judaism in Cochin is configured according to the cultural values and norms of Kerala's Hinduism, albeit within the normative framework of Judaic law, then it is to be expected that we can account for the unique expression of Judaism in China, or in America, in terms of this same figure/background process. We assume Judaism, like any religion, to be enormously complex, and the Judaic ritual behaviors and symbol complexes that rise to the foreground do so in response to the host religious culture.

For example, let us imagine how an American Jew might respond to an inquiry about what the essence of his or her religion is. Especially among the Conservative or Reform sects, the response might likely include the belief in one god and a divine imperative to work toward social justice. Without doubt, these are Judaic values. But these are values among other values, and they would be foregrounded only in the context of a dominant religious culture that upholds just those values, namely in Protestant America. By way of comparison, let us consider briefly the self-understanding of the Jews of Kaifeng in China. Before they built their synagogue, the Kaifeng Jews erected a stele in 1488 that, in effect, proclaims the similarity if not virtual identity between their religion and indigenous Chinese traditions. The stele reads, "Although our religion agrees in many respects with the religion of the literati (Confucianism), from which it differs in a slight degree, yet the main design of it is nothing more than reverence for Heaven, and veneration for ancestors, fidelity to the prince, and obedience to parents, just that which is included in the five human relationships."[10]

Anyone familiar with Confucianism will recognize immediately the Chinese nature of this self-characterization. After proclaiming the close similarity between Judaism and Chinese traditions, the Jews gloss their religion first as "reverence for Heaven." This reflects a coincidence of metaphors in Hebrew and Chinese. In Hebrew, *yirat Shamayim*, literally "fear of or reverence for Heaven," is one of many metaphors expressing submission to God. In Chinese, "Heaven" (*Tien*) is the most widely used metaphor for the transcendent. It is significant that the Jews selected the one metaphor for God that most closely approximates the Chinese. The Jews then highlight "veneration for ancestors," a tradition of memorializing the departed during certain festivals and on death anniversaries. While this is certainly part of normative (halakhic) Judaism, I do not think Jews anywhere else in the world would make this the second most important feature of their religion. But the Chinese Jews did, clearly reflecting Confucian values. "Obedience to parents" (*kibod ab v'em*) is a value shared by Judaism and Confucianism, but what makes the Kaifeng metaphor so Confucian is the subsequent reference to the "five relationships," a mainstay in Confucian tradition.[11]

As we shall see, the Jews of Cochin similarly reflected Hindu values in their self-understanding. What is important to note at this juncture is how the self-understanding of a diasporized religion, which we are calling the figure or the foreground, emerges out of a complex background in response to the demands of the host culture. As American Judaism is so very Protestant, so Chinese Judaism is very Confucian, and as we shall see, so Indian Judaism is very Hindu. But all three Judaisms remain Judaism; that is, this figure/background process is mediated by the framework of normative Judaism as defined by halakha.

Three Methods of Religious Acculturation

The Jewish community of Cochin has had at least one thousand years, and perhaps twice as long, to evolve unique ways of adapting to its host culture. According to their traditions, they arrived on the tropical, verdant coast of what is now India's southwestern state of Kerala and enjoyed prestige, power, and piety in a multireligious culture under the suzerainty of Hindu kings. They flourished in agriculture, in the military, and in the lucrative spice trade. Such a hospitable environment facilitated their acculturation, but the local caste system prevented their assimilation. Thus, identity was preserved at the same time as social harmony was maintained until a variety of factors—including Indian independence in 1947 and the establishment of the state of Israel a year later; the elimination of the role of the maharajahs, who had been their patrons; the redistribution of land; and the nationalization of private enterprises undertaken by the elected Communist government of Kerala during the 1950s—led to their emigration to Israel over the past three or four decades. At the dawn of the twenty-first century, fewer than fifty Jews remained in Kerala. Nevertheless, their long experience in India makes them an ideal case for analyzing the process of religious acculturation.

After intensive study of the Jewish community of Cochin in South India,[12] three strategies for religious acculturation were identified and analyzed. These three methods are (1) the narration of an appropriate historical legend; (2) the creation of a place within the caste hierarchy of Kerala that simultaneously reflected this hierarchy within the Jewish community; and (3) the ritual enactment of Hindu symbols of purity and nobility within the halakhic, or parameters established in Judaic law, framework. It is suggested that some version of these strategies of narration, social structure, and ritual enactment might be found among other diasporized religions, especially those that find themselves in a hospitable host culture as the Cochin Jews did.

Narration As Acculturation

The first step in the process of the religious acculturation of the Cochin Jews is the narration of an appropriate historical legend. In narrating such a legend, the Cochin Jews did what everyone does when asked to tell who they are: they tell a story that, in part at least, meets the inquirer's expectations.

Reflecting certain recent theoretical developments in hermeneutics, a person's identity is understood to be "a narrative construct" and points to "the continuous need for narrating experience in order to exist as a meaningful human subject, and the function of narrative interpretation in generating a continuity of identity, of self."[13] As an individual's narrative construction of self orders the data of past experiences, so the Cochin Jews constructed a self acculturated into its Hindu context; and their legend interweaves Jerusalem, the holy city for Jews, with Cranganore, the ancestral home for the elites of Kerala. Their legend highlights their lavish, royal welcome into Keralite society and emphasizes the relationship between avuncular Cheraman emperors of Kerala and their Jewish vassals, a theme ritually reenacted in Cochin Jewish weddings. It is a story of long-standing honor and privilege, interweaving Judaic and Hindu status-generating motifs.[14] And it is a story that arises in response to the expectations of the day; as recently as 1686, when a delegation of their coreligionists from Amsterdam visited them, they told an entirely different legend that reflected the Dutch Jews' quest for lost tribes. At that time, the Cochin Jews reported that they were the lost tribe of Menassah. When we recall Perls et al.'s comment as to the "dynamic" nature of the figure/background process, the shifting frames of reference for the legends become less surprising.

Acculturation and Social Structure

The Jews also reflected Kerala's hierarchical social structure within their own community, and this was the one feature of their life in India that deviated from, even defied, halakhic standards.[15]

It is fairly typical of caste behavior for a caste to proliferate into sub-castes. The Cochin Jews, who were viewed by their neighbors as a caste, did just that. They developed a social system that European visitors apprehended along racial lines as the infamous "white Jew/black Jew/brown Jew" system of religious discrimination, labeled "Jewish Apartheid" by a rabbi from South Africa.[16]

As early as 1520, the Cochin Jews sent a letter to Rabbi David ibn Zimra of Cairo, the Sephardic world's leading legal authority of his century. Like other middle to upper castes in India, the Jews were slaveholders. According to Judaic law, a Jewish slave must be freed every seventh (sabbatical) year, after which he or she is known as a *meshuhrar*, that is, one with a bill of manumission (*shihrur*). In Cochin, many non-Jewish or half-Jewish manumitted slaves converted to Judaism. The letter writer, hoping for a negative answer, contrasted these *meshuhrarim* with his own group of *meyuhasim*, or those with attestable descent from Israel. He asked whether it is permissible for a *meshuhrar* to marry a *meyuhas*. But Rabbi ibn Zimra cited the legal principal that a convert (*Ger*) is indistinguishable from one who is born Jewish and that it would be a breach of halakha to impose any religious disabilities on the *meshuhrarim*. The Cochin Jews ignored the rabbi's admonition, and some years later they wrote to his successor with the same question, hoping for a response more to their liking. They were disappointed, and this dispute continued until the mid-twentieth century.

What the Cochin Jews were doing was very Indian; for them, membership in a caste (*jati*, which literally means "birth") was a matter of blood, not a matter of ritual conversions. While they accepted the *meshuhrarim* as Jews, they could not bring themselves to consider them their equals. And by so doing, they reflected Indian sensibilities.

This halakhic deviation was entirely Indian in origin, and its resolution was also thoroughly Indian. In the 1930s, the *meshuhrarim* and their descendants, led by a fiery attorney known as "the Jewish Gandhi," A. B. Salem, began a series of *satyagraha* demonstrations against the synagogue, just as the Mahatma led similar campaigns on behalf of the untouchables' quest to gain admission into caste-Hindu-only temples. Like his mentor, Salem eventually succeeded.

Ritual Enactment of Acculturation

The final method for religious acculturation is the ritual enactment of Hindu symbol complexes within a halakhic framework.

Among the most distinctive features of Indian civilization are two separate sources of power, of social prestige, and of position. Ever since Manu's

fourth-century codification of social law, the Brahmin priests and the nobility (usually Kshatriyas, but in Kerala they were Nayars, traditionally
a lower-caste community) derived status from separate sources, the ascetic and the noble respectively. The Brahmins, who occupy one of the
two apexes of the Indian hierarchy, are distinguished by symbols of purity: their pure food, their white clothes, their ascetic lifestyle, and their
self-distancing from such sources of pollution as animal carcasses and
meat, low-born people, and agriculture. This distance has been maintained
through an intricate, hierarchical system of social interdependencies, customs, and taboos. Such purity is deemed an essential prerequisite for the
efficacious reenactments of ancient rituals that constitute the Brahmins'
means of livelihood. In Kerala, the chaste rituals of the Nambudiri Brahmins, the religious elite, are counterbalanced by the colorful, riotous deity
processions of the Nayars, who are the dominant caste politically and eco-
nomically. The Nayars' object of worship is not some abstract metaphysical
concept but rather the life-embracing, erotic warrior-prince god, Lord
Krishna, who embodies the Kshatriya ideal.

The nobility, residing at the second apex of the Indian hierarchy, have
traditionally employed the symbols of royalty, conquest, and wealth. Not
the homespun white cotton of the Brahman but fine silks and jewels be-
deck the Kshatriyas and the maharajas.

In their *minhagim*, or local religious practices, the Cochin Jews have
foregrounded the symbols of purity and nobility inherent in Judaism at
the same time as they have adapted some of the priestly and royal symbols of Hinduism, making for one of the most intriguing systems of Jewish observance found anywhere in the Diaspora. They appropriated certain royal symbols in their unique Simchat Torah (the culminating day of
the month-long autumn cycle of holy days) observances as well as in their
marriage customs, and they borrowed Brahmanical-ascetic symbols into
their Passover traditions. Moreover, they managed this syncretism judiciously so as not to contravene halakha.

During Passover many Jews add "additional observances" (*hiddur mitzvot*) to those required by halakha, "which express the Jew's love of the
mitzvot, divine commands, by embellishing them."[17] Passover preparations
in Cochin are striking in this regard. In several ways they are more fastidi-
ous than those found in other traditional Jewish communities.

For example, according to the standard codebook of Judaic law, the
Shulhan 'Arukh, preparations for Pesah (Passover) should begin right after
Purim, or thirty days before the festival.[18] But in Cochin, preparations
began soon after Hanukkah and increasingly consumed the Jews' time

and attention for about one hundred days. During this time, wells were emptied and scrubbed, interior walls were whitewashed, and exterior walls were freshly painted. Individual kernels of wheat to be used for the ceremonial flat bread, known as matsah were inspected for defects thrice. Wine was pressed laboriously, wooden furniture was polished, special pots, pans, crockery, and cutlery were removed from special rooms and cleaned in preparation. All of this "Pesah work" culminated in "matsah day," when the women (and a few of the men) of the community baked the flat bread over charcoal fires during the peak of Kerala's sweltering hot season.[19]

Such *halakhically-excessive* preparations reflect an ascetical sensibility akin to the Brahmins, and the methods of preparation of "emblematic" foods in *particular*—matsah, wine, and other consumables—exceed halakhic norms at crucial points that resemble high-caste Hindu taboos about possible pollution by contact with *kaccha* (cooked) food.

Seclusion and isolation are common ascetic practices, and there was an intriguing variant of this form among the Cochin Jews. Usually very gregarious, they became increasingly isolated from their non-Jewish friends during the month or two prior to Pesah, culminating in an almost total isolation during the eight days of the festival itself. This gradual and increasing isolation became apparent by the festival of Purim, one month before Passover, by which time "Pesah work" had become so dominating and consuming that there was little time for interactions outside of the community. Cochin Jews generally enjoy sharing food and conversation with their Hindu, Christian, Jain, Muslim, and Parsi friends on any occasion. In fact, the intercommunal exchange of special foods, such as special cakes for the Jewish New Year, Rosh Hashanah, is particularly enjoyed—but not during Passover.

The Cochin Jews believed that the only way to ensure the avoidance of "*chamets*" (leavened food) was to avoid their non-Jewish friends. "For eight days I cut off everything. If I see my friends," Isaac Ashkenazy said, "they may offer a cup of tea or some food. Actually, Pesah is a very hard time for us." Sarah Cohen warned, "Don't go outside [of Jew Town]. You might make a mistake and eat or drink something you can't have." While they would have enjoyed a visit with friends or to the local Brahmin vegetarian restaurant, such visits were avoided. "The main thing," according to Reema Salem, "is that we take nothing from outside."[20] During the Passover festival, the universe of the Cochin Jews did not extend beyond Synagogue Lane. Thus, their avoidance of *chamets* translated into the temporary avoidance of non-Jews.

A celebratory reaggregation into Kerala society culminated this period, which resembles the liminal phase observed in African coming-of-age rites by Victor Turner.[21] The liminality that had temporarily suspended normal societal interactions, which are of necessity hierarchical in Kerala, led to a reaffirmation of that hierarchy after a ritualized reaggregation in a party hosted by a Gentile neighbor during which Jews again ate foods that are prohibited during Pesah.[22] The meal ritually reintegrates the Jews into the larger Kerala society and hierarchy. The Jews' high status thus ritually reestablished, they returned to and reaffirmed the society in which they had lived so happily for so long.

Every spring in the ritual observances of the Passover festival, the Cochin Jews reassert their high place in the caste hierarchy by demonstrating their purity in accordance with the Brahmanical-ascetic pole of power. Every autumn, on the other hand, in the ritual enactments of the High Holy Days and in particular Simhat Torah, they give precedence to a different set of symbols, symbols of royalty and wealth, in accordance with the Kshatriya—a noble pole of power represented in Kerala by the Nayars. This emphasis on symbols of royalty represents a natural extension of the liturgical theme of the autumn High Holy Days, which celebrates God's kingship *(malchut* in Hebrew).

Concluding the fall cycle of holy days is the two-day festival known in Cochin as Shmini. Most synagogues in the West observe two separate festivals, Shmini Chag Atzeret and Simchat Torah. In Cochin, Shmini is of enormous significance, arguably the community's most distinctive autumn observance.

The synagogue, brilliant and colorful at any time, was utterly dazzling on Shmini. The whitewashed walls and dark wooden benches were covered with golden satin. The effect of the shimmering walls reflecting the blazing oil lamps encircling the *tebah* (pulpit) suffused the dainty prayer hall with a light that bordered upon the supernal. All around the upper half of the walls were *parohets*, "curtains" made of deceased Cochin women's festive sarongs, in green, gold, blue, red, and white embroidered silks. The impact was enhanced by an olfactory stimulus as well. Hanging among the many chandeliers and oil lamps were string upon string of freshly plucked jasmine flowers.

The most striking decorations transformed the *Aron Hakodesh* (Holy Ark), the focal point of synagogues where the Torah scrolls are kept. A special temporary ark, known as a *kule*, was constructed between two tall silver pillars. The platform was covered with red- and gold-embroidered Banarsi silk. All seven Torah scrolls, replete with gold, jewel-encrusted crowns, and silver *rimomim* (finials), were proudly displayed. The effect was completed by a canopy of red and gold silks, topped off with the lid of the synagogue's solid gold kiddush cup.

Elsewhere in the Jewish world, Simhat Torah celebrations include seven *haqafot* (circumambulations around the *tebah* with the Torah scrolls) during evening (*Arbith*) and morning (*Shaharit*) services. But the Cochin Jews add three *haqafot* in the courtyard outside of the synagogue building during the afternoon (*Mincha*) service, a *minhag* unique among Jews throughout the world.[23] The entire liturgy for the afternoon *haqafot* was composed in the Jews' ancestral home in Cranganore, according to local tradition. So significant was the unique service that when a Hebrew-Malayalam printing press was first established in Cochin in 1877, the very first book they published was the distinctive liturgy for the Simhat Torah *Mincha* service (*Seder Mincha Simhat Torah*), which includes the longest Kaddish prayer in world Jewry.

Following *Mincha* was another unique Cochin observance. The Torah scrolls were placed on chairs and benches, and as everyone—men, women, and children—sang *shir'ot* (liturgical songs) in the synagogue hall, the congregation dismantled the temporary Ark. It was demolished ritually and methodically: the Banarsi silks were carefully removed, followed by the silver pillars, and, finally, the wooden planks were disassembled.

Three aspects of the Cochin *minhag* for Simchat Torah are creative responses to their Hindu environment in Kerala: the displaying of their Torah scrolls on a temporary ark, the addition of afternoon *haqafot* outside of the synagogue building, and the ritual dismantling of the ark. Specifically, Hinduized symbols of royalty and nobility have been appropriated.

Each and every Hindu temple has its own deity and an annual festival for that deity. During the festival, the deity image is generally displayed on a wooden cart (*ratha,* a royal chariot). Often these carts are enormous, such as the one in the festival at the Shri Jaganath Temple in Puri, Orissa. More than a million Hindus participate in Shri Jaganath's annual festival, pulling the three-hundred-foot cart down Puri's main road. At the conclusion of such annual temple festivals, the deity's image is ceremoniously disposed of, often by tossing it into a river or ocean.

The three elements characteristic of Hindu temple festivals—display, procession, and disposal—are also characteristic of Simhat Torah in Cochin. Like a Hindu deity, the Torah scrolls are removed from their usual holy abode, the Jewish *Aron Hakodesh*, paralleling the Hindu *garbha griha*, and displayed on a temporary structure, the Jewish *kule*, paralleling the Hindu *ratha*. Like the deity, they are carried through a public area, in this case the synagogue courtyard. As the deity's image is disposed of at the end of the festival, so the temporary Ark—not of course the Torah scrolls—is demolished ritually. It is precisely these three aspects of the Cochin *minhag* that are unique and that serve as the means by which Hindu royalty symbols and rituals are adapted and Judaized.

The ingenuity of these adaptations is an elegant instance of the Jewish acculturation. How to participate in the Gentile world while maintaining fidelity to Jewish observance has been the challenge to Jews in all four corners of the Diaspora. In India, a culture not merely tolerant of religious diversity but affectionately supportive of it, Jews adapted to Hinduism while adhering to normative Judaism's standards. Theirs has been a well-balanced, ritually established identity. Traditional Jewish metaphors and symbols of nobility and royalty have been judiciously merged with borrowings from Hindu practice in order to connect Jews with one of India's poles of power and thereby to integrate the Jews into Kerala's predominately Hindu social order.

There are essentially two analytical methods by which Western scholars have understood caste or *jati*: Louis Dumont proposed an attributional approach in his classical study, *Homo Hierarchicus*,[24] and McKim Marriott offered an interactive model.[25] The former regards inherent traits in a community, especially its perceived purity or impurity, whereas the latter observed how communities interact, with special regard to food behaviors. The Cochin Jews' high-caste status can be understood in both ways, which tend to reinforce one another. Their hereditary priesthood, dietary code, purity concerns regarding women in particular, and, paradoxically, foreign origin all indicate inherent high-caste characteristics. On the other hand, their narrative of social proximity to the maharajas, as well as their social and culinary isolation during Passover, demonstrate the drama of hierarchical intercaste interactions.

Concluding Remarks

The Cochin Jews provide a particularly fine example of how a small religio-ethnic community can acculturate itself within a tolerant, larger society.[26] By narrating an appropriate historical legend that interweaves motifs from both diasporized and host religious cultures, by reflecting the host culture's social structure within its own community, and by a periodic ritual enactment of the symbols representing the poles of power in the caste hierarchy of Kerala, a secure place in that hierarchy is achieved. In some instances, strands from within the guest community's traditions that are congruent with, or parallel to, the symbols of the host culture are foregrounded, while in other cases the host's symbols are borrowed directly. By so doing the guest community retains its unique identity at precisely the same time as it locates itself within the larger host society.

Notes

A prior version of the essay was published as "Understanding Religion in Diaspora: The Case of the Jews in Cochin" in *Religious Studies and Theology* 15, 1 (1996): 5–17. This revised version of the essay is published with permission of the copyright holder, Equinox Publishing.

    1. Personal electronic communication from Joseph Rivilin of Bar Ilan University (November 21, 1995).

    2. *Encyclopedia Judaica*, s.v. "Diaspora," 8.

    3. *Encyclopedia Judaica*, s.v. "Galut," 275.

    4. See Katz, "Jewish Secret and Dalai Lama."

    5. Katz, "How the Hindu-Jewish Encounter Reconfigures."

    6. Herskovits, "African Gods and Catholic Saints."

    7. Here I follow the work of my former student, Raul Canizares, in his *Walking the Night*, 39–40. Canizares quotes Murphy, *Santería*, 121, and Bastide, *African Religions of Brazil*, 270.

    8. Obeyesekere, "Religious Symbolism and Political Change," 60.

    9. Perls, Hefferline, and Goodman, *Gestalt Therapy*, 25.

    10. Perlmann, "History of Jews in China," 183–83. See also Katz, "Judaisms of Kaifeng and Cochin," 118–40.

    11. Smart, *Religious Experience*, 167–69.

    12. Katz and Goldberg, *Last Jews of Cochin*.

    13. Kerby, "Adequacy of Self-Narration," 232–34.

    14. See Katz and Goldberg, *Last Jews of Cochin*, 1–7.

    15. See Katz and Goldberg, "Jewish 'Apartheid' and Jewish Gandhi," 147–76.

    16. Rabinowitz, *Far East Mission*.

    17. Chill, *Minhagim*, xx.

    18. Zalman, *Shulchan 'Arukh Orech Chayyim*, 3:1.

    19. Pesah preparations of Cochin Jews were first described by Johnson in "'Our Community' in Two Worlds." Johnson's insightful observations were corroborated and amplified in Katz and Goldberg, "Asceticism and Caste in Passover," 52–83.

    20. Quotes come from the author's fieldwork among Cochin Jews.

    21. Turner, *Ritual Process*.

    22. By ending the Pesah partial fast as guests of Gentile neighbors, the Cochin Jews resemble the Jews of Morocco. See Deshen, *Mellah Society*, 22–23.

    23. Hallegua, "Simchat Torah in Cochin," 6.

    24. Dumont, *Homo Hierarchicus*.

    25. Marriott, "Interactional and Attributional Theories."

    26. Acculturation in an intolerant host culture may involve quite different models, metaphors, and methods than those employed by the Cochin Jews, who enjoyed an especially hospitable milieu.

III
Righting the Discipline

7
Regarding Origin
Beginnings, Foundations, and the Bicameral
Formation of the Study of Religion

Tomoko Masuzawa

Tomoko Masuzawa presented "Return of the What?—or Why We
Should Care about the (Mere) Concept of Religion" as the fifth
Aronov Lecture at the University of Alabama on March 7, 2007. The
following chapter reflects some of the ideas of her broader work on
the field of religious studies.

In the beginning stands an onerous thought: nowadays, whatever else may
be said about it, the term "origin" is loaded. One has the impression, indeed, that it is somehow *overloaded*. Certainly, origin can mean very many
things in diverse contexts, and perhaps too many things have been already
said and written about it. These meanings and opinions are abundant beyond control and, on the whole, wildly polymorphous and richly incon-
sistent.

On the one hand, it would seem that this is just as it should be because
origin in the strong sense—in the sense of *absolute* beginning, say, out of
nothing—must mean that *everything* is already contained in it somehow.
If origin is truly absolute, it eradicates any possibility of a precedent, pre-
existing condition, or prototype—in fact, anything other than itself—that
might in any way account for later developments. Absolute origin purports to account for posterity in toto, and as such, origin is the plenum. It
stands to reason, then, that some philosophers have claimed that origin is
an essentially theological idea. For, in the last analysis, the only true origin
in this strong sense would be the originator of absolutely everything, and
Western metaphysics has always assigned this "unique and universal" position to God. (Or at least that's what the whole world has been told lately.)
Following this line of reasoning, it is often said that, to the extent that any
finite thing or person purports to be the origin or originator—whether it
be creative genius of the author, originality of the artist, spiritual founding of a religion or a nation—it/she/he is emulating and approximating

this famous prototype, though of necessity only imperfectly. Here, insofar as the theological tenor of the idea is recognized, an important point of ramification may be mentioned: He who is the absolute origin in this prototypical, theological sense is of course also He who will be there at the end of time and He who will preside over the last judgment or, in the event that things turn out somehow differently from what most theologians have been telling us, He will be the one Who has the last laugh. Be that as it may, this first train of thought about origin can be summarized in two brief statements. In origin is everything. Before origin, there is but nothing.

On the other hand, there is another, equally powerful train of thought, namely, that origin refers to that very nothingness—the blank, the clean slate, the virgin state, the pristine moment before anything particular and delimiting happens, hence, the absolute beginning. In this sense of the term, in order to return to or to recover origin, it is felt that one needs, precisely, to get rid of everything. This is how, for example, the origin of modern philosophy is told. Descartes is generally credited with having ushered scientific modernity into the domain of Western thought. Philosophy, it is said, after meandering in the rough seas of metaphysical nonsense for centuries, finally came into its own with Cartesian soliloquies, *Discourse on Method* (1637) and *Meditations on the First Philosophy* (1641). As Hegel said, "Here we finally reach home, and like a mariner after a long voyage in a tempestuous sea, we may now hail the sight of land; with Descartes the culture of modern times, the thought of modern Philosophy, really begin to appear, after a long and tedious journey."[1] In a somewhat less salutary mode, Descartes himself once likened the quest for the first principle of philosophy, or *prima philosophia*, to the method of groping in a mixed bag—or, to be precise, a basket—of good and bad apples. Instead of drawing out and inspecting the contents of the basket one at a time, he opines, what is necessary at the outset is to empty the basket entirely, thus expelling both the potentially good and the bad at once, only to restore later, one at a time, those truly proven wholesome and unspoiled. Only this way, he claimed, will we be assured that the basket contains no rotten apples, as our philosophical outlook will consist only of sound principles and no erroneous beliefs.[2] As is well known, in order to achieve this unsullied first page of philosophy, Descartes began by doubting everything he possibly could, and he arrived at the famous clean slate of pure, objectless self-consciousness: *cogito*. And everything else, according to his reckoning, eventually followed from it.

It is understandable—one might say that it is structurally inevitable—

that origin, qua that which is at once everything and nothing, should be an object of intense desire. At the same time, it follows with equal certainty and necessity that such a hypercathected object should be subject to strenuous prohibition. For, that which is most acutely and singularly desired is also that which must be most stringently and energetically denied. In short, the fundamental contradiction endemic to the concept (qua everything and nothing), as well as the logical double bind of desire and prohibition that defines and determines its function, together make an impossible object-idea out of "origin." This constitutional difficulty, it appears, haunts every deliberation on the problem of origin, openly or surreptitiously. With this in mind, we may now look at how various attempts at getting at origins have played out, not in philosophy or theology per se, but in the domain more proper to the science of religion (*Religionswissenschaft*).

*   *   *

There is a commonly held opinion today that the quest for the origin of religion was a peculiarly and characteristically nineteenth-century preoccupation. Indeed, we find a number of intellectuals of the period who are said to have identified, correctly or not, the ultimate origin of religion or religions in general. These writers attained certain celebrity and notoriety partly because, by and large, what they thus identified turned out to be something other than the divine source, or, in any case, something other than what traditional religious authorities presumably had been claiming to be the source of religion. This is an indication that by the nineteenth century it had become permissible to look for the origin of religion not in some unknowable supernatural mystery but in human nature or in nature itself, which was assumed to be plainly in view if only we would train ourselves to see it with the rigorously empirical eye of science. Although the naturalistic accounting for the phenomenon of religion can be traced back to earlier centuries—most notably to seventeenth- and eighteenth-century Deism—it is generally felt that the naturalistic explanation of religion came into full force as it became intertwined with various theories of evolution in the middle of the nineteenth century.

It should be remembered that the so-called theory of evolution in the usual, inexact sense—the sense most pertinent to the question of the origin and development of religion—is significantly different from the strictly Darwinian theory. As we may recall, in addition to the controversy over the possible human descent from the apes, the scandal of Darwinism had to do with the notion of natural selection and the survival of the fittest. According to the latter theory, mutations of the species into new forms, and the eventual prevailing of the forms better suited for the given environment and the concomitant elimination of the forms less "fit"—that is, the processes that are tantamount to "evolution" in the properly biological sense—are essentially random and incidental occurrences. The concept of evolution in this biological sense, therefore, is not teleological or goal oriented, and as such it is fundamentally incompatible with the notion of purposeful development, progress, or providence. Indeed, this theory deprived the nineteenth-century Europeans not only of the myth of the paradisiac origin but also of the assurance or even the probability of the divinely guided course of world history or any such narratives that posited *Homo sapiens*, and Europeans in particular, at the helm. With the Darwinian theory of evolution, then, history attained for the first time a real possibility of being nothing but meandering tracks of fortuitous events, patterns of change as pointless as the results of a game of chance, or a case of the proverbial tale told by an idiot . . . signifying nothing.

This, to be sure, is not what is normally meant by the theory of "evolution of religion," or "origin and development of religion," as such a theory is usually attributed to various writers from the nineteenth century. As a rule, in a theory of religious evolution there is a presumption of meaningful and purposeful *development*, a presumption of the human condition generally changing and evolving for the higher and better—though the possibility of "regression" is also admitted—with something like a fulfillment, perfection, or even apotheosis projected at a certain indefinite point in the future. This is as much as to say that these so-called evolutionary theories of religion have less affinity with Darwinism or any such new varieties of natural scientific theory than with the seventeenth- and eighteenth-century Deistic idea of natural history of religion as exemplified, most notably, by the posthumously published treatise by David Hume.

Hume's *Natural History of Religion* (1757) may be considered epoch making in more than one sense, but the sense most relevant to our immediate concern is that this was arguably the first account that placed the origin and development of religion strictly within the domain of *human* history, that is to say, an account not directly linked to the providential, divinely guided history.[3] Earlier Deists—such as Herbert of Cherbury and John Toland—typically presupposed that there was the original, universal, rational, and ethical religion common to all humankind and that with a passage of time this original pure theism became variously "corrupted" with the result that different peoples in different regions of the world came to practice divergent and idiosyncratic religions. Sidestepping these Deistic presuppositions, Hume instead begins by categorically divorcing the question of the (to him) true, rational, and permanent foundation of religion—the very thing that other Deists identified as the original religion—from the temporal domain of nature and history. This separation gets accomplished even before the treatise proper begins. In the author's introduction, he proclaims:

> As every enquiry, which regards religion, is of the utmost importance, there are two questions in particular, which challenge our attention, to wit, that concerning its foundation in reason, and that concerning its origin in human nature. Happily, the first question, which is the most important, admits of the most obvious, at least, the clearest, solution. The whole frame of nature bespeaks an intelligent author; and no rational enquirer can, after serious reflection, suspend his belief a moment with regard to the primary principles of genuine Theism and Religion. But the other question, concerning the origin of religion in human nature, is exposed to some more difficulty.[4]

Thus first erecting the impermeable barrier between the two domains—on one side, what is ahistorical, rational, and assured, and on the other side, what is historical, contingent, and fraught with human frailty—Hume proceeds to explain that only the latter domain will be the subject of the book in question. No sooner than the first chapter opens he asserts, with no sign of uncertainty or scruples, that "polytheism or idolatry was, and necessarily must have been, the first and most ancient religion of mankind." Quoting the learned opinions of his day, he claims that this assertion is readily attested by the experience concerning various "barbarous nations" of the known world: "The savage tribes of America, Africa, and Asia are all idolaters. Not a single exception to this rule."[5]

In retrospect, the lasting impact of Hume's work on the future course of the study of religion has less to do with the particular scenario of historical development he had in mind and far more to do with the fact that he effected the separation of the two domains of inquiry with such authority and finality. By declaring the rational, philosophical, and theological domain to be absolutely foundational and true, he effectively liberated the domain of natural-human history from the biblical constraints and, rather ironically, rendered it invulnerable to dogmatic-theological interventions. This, of course, did not necessarily prevent those who did not share Hume's views from simply disregarding this decree of separation and meddling and interfering freely, as it were, with the affairs of the natural historians of religion. Indeed, Hume must be regarded as the first one to face this reality as the opposition forces made it necessary to suppress the publication of this very work during his lifetime. All the same, with this slim volume, he in effect issued to all posterity a license to forage the field henceforth known as (natural) history of religion(s). It is above all for the impetus Hume generated, that is, to do what one will within the contingent realm of human history, that the book is credited as something of an origin of comparative religion itself.

*   *   *

Following Hume's lead directly or indirectly, many nineteenth- and early twentieth-century writers proffered various accounts as to how religion began, developed, and would likely become in the future. The positivist Auguste Comte sketched world history in terms of a three-stage development: theological (fictive), metaphysical (abstract), positive (scientific). He further subdivided the theological stage into three, and the designations of those substages are identical with the ones delineated by Charles de Brosses in the eighteenth century: fetishism (superstition), polytheism (idolatry), monotheism (ethical religion).[6] The implication here is that, in Comte's own time, very many specimens of the human species known around the world were still inhabiting the earliest stages of this evolution, whereas a few Europeans at the vanguard of history, such as himself, were witnessing the dawn of the positive epoch. Similarly, J. G. Frazer's *The Golden Bough* posited the developmental stages as first magical, then religious, and finally implicitly projecting the age of the scientific.[7] The three-stage schema is also reflected in Freud's speculation on the philogenetic and ontogenetic development of humankind.[8]

There are several recurrent themes in the ways in which these and other writers of their time narrated the "evolution" of religion. To begin with, and most generally, the progression is always from the lowest to the highest, from the mean, primitive, and degraded to the noble, cultured, and refined. This value-laden narrative trajectory also implies a transformation from the particularistic, limited conception of the divinity to the universalistic, genuine conception of the Infinite. The rising level of mental-intellectual sophistication is typically expressed in terms of the movement from materiality to spirituality, from literal, concrete language to symbolic, abstract language, and from helpless and reactive passivity to imaginative and creative activity. This complex of ideas is exemplified well in the familiar "evolutionary" scenario already mentioned: first fetishism (misguided attribution of supernatural power to merely material objects; ignorance of the spiritual), then polytheism (idolatrous worship of finite and often capricious deities in material forms; confusion of the material and the spiritual), and finally monotheism (worship of the universal, ethical deity through symbols; proper apprehension of the spiritual unencumbered by materiality).

There were, to be sure, some writers in this period whose views were more in line with the earlier Deists in the sense that they believed that there was an original, universal religion common to all humankind at the beginning of time and that it was a monotheism. The German theologian Wilhelm Schmidt was perhaps the most renowned of the advocates of the so-called primitive monotheism theory, while Andrew Lang, a prolific Scottish writer on diverse subjects, also came to advocate this idea late in his life and did much to popularize it. It should be noted, however, that, because these writers also believed that the primitive revelation—or at least some form of preknowledge of the one and the only true God— initially fell in the hands of the crudest of primitive humankind, they assumed that this pristine knowledge or revelation could have been only very imperfectly apprehended or, more probably, promptly forgotten by those primitive recipients. For, in the estimation of these writers, the childlike mental abilities of the savage ancestors were such that they were easily swayed by all too human emotions and the material exigencies of everyday life, that is, those factors generally inimical to the rational contemplation of the purely spiritual deity. Therefore, even if there was a time in the mythic past when the world basked in the light of true religion, much of the history of humankind that is known or knowable is tantamount to the same laborious movement from the bottom up. On the whole—as would be obvious to anyone who actually read these texts—the accounts of the history of religion presented by the primitive monotheism theory advocates are not appreciably different from the ones proposed by those who did not believe that any such primordial knowledge existed.

A much more fruitful way of exploring the full range of views held by the historians of religions of this period may be to ask how various writers situated themselves in relation to the aforementioned fundamental division first established by Hume. As we have seen, Hume made his own position clear at the outset. For him, the essential foundation of religion, or rational *grounds* of religion, was not at all the same thing as the merely contingent, temporal *beginning* of religion in human history, even though both of these notions may be taken to mean "origin" in a certain sense. Moreover, he was just as convinced of the loftiness of the rational basis of true religion as he was certain about the humbleness of the beginning of the human religious history. He was in fact interested in both these domains and wrote *The Natural History of Religion* to deal with the latter and a better-known treatise titled *Dialogues Concerning Natural Religion* to address the former.[9]

In the nineteenth century, this division of the realms of inquiry was often expressed in terms of the distinction between "history of religion(s)" (or "comparative religion") and "philosophy of religion." Together, they were thought to constitute the general science of religion (*Religionswissenschaft*). Hence when the Dutch scholar and reputed cofounder (together with F. Max Müller) of this science, Cornelis Petrus Tiele, delivered his Gifford Lectures at the University of Edinburgh in 1896–97, the resulting two-volume compendium was titled *Elements of the Science of Religion*, of which *Morphological*, the first volume, corresponded to the historical-comparative study, whereas *Ontological*, the second volume, explored philosophical issues.[10] This arrangement proved exemplary and was followed by a number of lesser known writers thereafter. In this connection we may note that, by looking at this two-ply legacy of the discipline, we can appreciate better why many scholars today continue to debate, and can never seem to agree, whether theology and philosophy of religion should have a proper place within the science of religion or, alternatively, outside the science and parallel with it.

F. Max Müller was faithful to Hume's legacy to the extent that, while he studiously pursued his immense philological research in the area of history of religions, he continued to proclaim throughout his career his conviction that all humankind without exception harbored in their hearts the intimation of the Infinite, however dimly or poorly this primordial awareness may be conceptually understood in any given society or by any given individual. In comparison to the Deists of the seventeenth and eighteenth centuries, Müller did not stress as much the rational foundation of this knowledge; yet, by his own admission, his spiritual sensibility found the greatest affinity with the rationalist philosophy of Kant. In effect, one might reasonably describe Müller's own theology as an exemplary postulate of German Idealism swaddled in the highly cultivated poetics of Romanticism.[11]

Although no other writer may have been as articulate or insistent as Müller regarding this matter, there were indeed many others whose stance, and whose understanding of the rationale for their scholarly practice, were generally consistent with his. In fact, so long as this paragon of *Religion-*

swissenschaft continued to assert the inviolability and incorruptibility of the knowledge of the Infinite, others could infer that the domain of faith appropriately understood would be secure irrespective of what the science might do. This in turn could be construed to mean that even the most thoroughly naturalistic and secularist enterprises of the history of religion would remain legitimate and safe, as it were, under the protection of the Humean edict, which divided and set apart, in good Enlightenment fashion, the immutable truth of reason from the incidental facts of history. By thus disengaging the operation of the two domains, this edict appears to have served as something of a cover for the self-appointed historians of religion, since it nominally enabled them to get on with their business as soon as they finished paying due respect, à la Hume, to the consummate religion of universal reason. Over time, however, this sacrosanct sphere of theological conviction became less and less a matter of universality and more and more one of *privacy*. As the discursive domain of history of religions gained its academic and public status, the domain of theological conviction lost hold on the universal and in turn became exclusively a personal affair. Henceforth this tightly circumscribed territory of the personal came to shelter and protect, at least in principle, religious predilections of any kind whatsoever—from the most imperiously universalist to the most fanatically exclusivist—so long as they remained strictly within the sphere of scholars' private lives and personal experiences.

* * *

As ingenious and effective as this strategy might have been for the purpose of securing a legitimate position for the naturalistic history of religions, it is not altogether surprising that some theologians grew deeply suspicious of this convenient arrangement devised by several generations of so-called historians of religion. Thus it was that in 1881 Bishop John Wordsworth of Salisbury went on record warning against the half-truths of the natural historical approach:

> It is at present far too common a habit of mind to be satisfied with tracing out the conditions and circumstances under which a belief or a religious custom arises in the world. Some men exhaust themselves in classifying the phenomena of religion under this or that heading of myth or symbol. . . . But, when they have done all this useful work . . . they are in danger, and leave their readers in danger, of tacitly assuming that the subject is closed, and that religion is a natural

development, out of which the positive action of God, as a real existing Being, is excluded. Their mouths are full of the various ways in which other men have thought of God, but He Himself is far from their own thoughts.[12]

In a similar vein, in a publication dated the same year, American Sanskritist William D. Whitney—who was once remembered as a contemporary and ruthless critic of Max Müller—argued that what he termed "the so-called science of religion," unlike the science of language, could never be expected to attain the status of a true science, insofar as it was ultimately nothing more than "a history of men's opinions, as inferred from modes of expression far less clear, objective, and trustworthy than are the records of speech."[13]

If some theologians were wary of the separate and not so equal configuration of the two discursive fields (i.e., natural history vs. religious confession, science of religion vs. theology, the public/academic vs. the private/personal, etc.), perhaps there was a good reason for their circumspection. Nineteenth- and early twentieth-century Europe certainly saw a number of prominent writers who had no compunction about hauling a thoroughgoing naturalist theory directly into the heart of the theologico-confessional domain. For, whatever their individual intent may have been in their respective theory building, each of these theories, if taken seriously, would have the effect of destroying the pith of "religion" as we know it. For example, Ludwig Feuerbach proposed, with not much ambiguity or irony, to "translate theology into anthropology."[14] By that he meant, and wished to demonstrate, that all theological propositions (such as the main precepts of Christianity) can be fully and exhaustively understood in completely naturalistic—or, in his own words, "materialistic"—terms. Such a transcription of theology into "anthropology" makes God and any other allegedly supernatural entities altogether superfluous, nonessential, and ultimately self-alienating from the human standpoint. Sigmund Freud, on the other hand, declared no such mutinous intentions, but there is little doubt that he, too, rendered the traditional, freestanding, self-validating theological discourse either redundant or half-estranged from modern sensibility, in his case, by virtue of the fact that he devised a peculiar newspeak called psychoanalysis, a brave new discourse nearly equal to Christian theology in its hyperintelligence and its voracious explanatory power.

While neither Feuerbach's nor Freud's impact is likely to be slighted by any historian of religions endowed with sufficient hindsight, as regards the actual practices of the hitherto established mainstream *Religionswis-*

senschaft, each of these figures stands as something of a maverick, an intellectual nomad at once inspiring and irritating but never truly constitutive of "the discipline." The legacy of Emile Durkheim, on the other hand, is altogether differently situated. Variously crowned as a founding father of sociology, French anthropology, or the sociology of religion, his accomplishments have been too consequential to be brushed aside as merely of historical interest, despite the fact that much of his data and many of his theoretical propositions have been subsequently disputed. In common accord, the significance of his role in the formation of the nomothetic-scientific study of religion is matched only by that of Max Weber. Not only did Durkheim put forward a prototype (albeit a largely speculative one) for the sociological understanding of religion, by so doing he virtually made Hume stand on his head.

In Durkheim's most famous work on religion, *The Elementary Forms of Religious Life*, he offers no opinion with regard to, say, the existence and the attributes of God, the possible apperception of the Infinite, or any other like subjects of theological import.[15] Unlike Hume, if he had a religious conviction of any kind, he did not reveal it, did not even hint that it should be of any significance whatsoever. Instead, he directly proceeds to state what he terms the "subject of our study: religious sociology and the theory of knowledge." It is here, in the introduction to the five-hundred-page treatise, that his radical transposition of the Humean arrangement is most visible. To begin with, like Hume, Durkheim draws a distinction between the question of the temporary *beginning* of religion and the question of the permanent *basis* of religion, and he also identifies the latter as the realm of rationality. What makes his endeavor radically different from that of Hume is that he purports to direct his naturalist-secularist attention not to the former but to the latter domain. Durkheim was certainly not unaware of the momentousness of this transvaluation of inquiry. There is a remarkable decisiveness and authority in his voice announcing his intentions:

> The study which I undertake is a way of taking up again the old problem of the origin of religions *but under new conditions*. Granted, if by origin one means an absolute first beginning, there is nothing scientific about the question, and it must be resolutely set aside. There is no radical instant when religion began to exist, and the point is not to find a roundabout way of conveying ourselves there in thought. Like every other human institution, religion begins nowhere. So all speculations in this genre are rightly discredited; they

can consist of only subjective and arbitrary constructions without checks of any sort. The problem I propose is altogether different. I would like to find a means of discerning the ever-present causes on which the most basic forms of religious thought and practice depend.[16]

As he makes amply clear in this introduction and elsewhere in the book, he chose to focus on Australian totemism as the most "primitive" form of religion, not because he believed that totemism was historically and chronologically the *earliest* but rather because, in his estimation, it represented the most basic and structurally rudimentary form, consisting only of the minimum, that is to say, the most essential and indispensable elements.

Hence not only does Durkheim transpose the temporal and the timeless in the way he characterizes the object of his naturalistic-scientific inquiry, but by so doing he also brings into the domain of this inquiry the question of reason and rationality, such that it is now possible to speak of the origin of the faculty of reason, or, more specifically, the origin of the categories of thought. As it turns out, according to Durkheim, religion and reason have the same origin, the same basis or grounds. Durkheim claimed that basis to be the sui generis reality of the collective life, that is, the ways in which members of a given societal group act, interact with one another, and represent to themselves their sense of unity and solidarity. In effect, the origin of religion—that is to say, the "ever-present cause" of religion, as well as the ever-present cause of rationality—is *society*, that is, something natural (as opposed to supernatural), contingent and "historical" in a carefully qualified (i.e., not merely chronological) sense of the term.

* * *

As with Hume, the ground-shifting effect of Durkheim's work depended less on the validity of the specific observations he made with regard to what he construed as the most elementary (therefore essential) form of religion than on the overall transformation of the field and of the logic of inquiry. What Hume opened up almost surreptitiously in the eighteenth century as a modest, well-circumscribed area of a novel inquiry under the name of natural history of religion—that is, as an area for activities supposedly harmless to the eternal truths of religion and reason—became a foraging ground for much speculation during the nineteenth century. By the time of Freud and Durkheim, it was as though open season

on big game hunting had been declared; for, as many religionists and traditionalists decried, nothing could be presumed safe and sacred any longer.
According to the opinions and the complaints of these religious protesters,
what the speculative "evolutionists" such as Durkheim and Freud had done
was, by claiming to have identified an origin of religion in a place entirely
different from divine inspiration, effectively to *reduce* the phenomenon of
religion and *violate* its essential integrity—the moralizing terms often employed by many religionists—and improperly convert it into something
else, something other than "religion itself."

Fearing the imminent evaporation of "religion itself" and inferring—
rather injudiciously to be sure—that the denial of the irreducible essential substance of religion would render the science of religion itself baseless
and defenseless, and some even worrying that any such admission might
in turn drive them out of business, many students of religion of subsequent generations protested against the methods as well as the results of
the "evolutionist" search for the origin of religion. These epigonic scholars sought to shift the grounds of inquiry, above all, by shelving the issue
of origin and concertedly declaring the question of the essence or foundation of religion off limits to any scientific probe.

To put this in the words of the best known proponent of this position,
Mircea Eliade, "The historian of religions knows by now that he is unable
to reach the 'origin' of religion. What happened in the beginning, *aborigine*,
is no longer a problem for the historian of religions, though conceivably it
might be one for the theologian or the philosopher."[17] His argument here
is not entirely unlike that of logical positivists; for, he in effect suggests
that what cannot be answered cannot be a problem, as far as the sound-
minded, empirically responsible historians of religions are concerned. This
statement may leave us wondering what Eliade imagined a theologian or
philosopher might be doing, as they continued tackling the seemingly impossible or, worse yet, nonexistent problem. In any event, it is clear that
this declaration of intent not to pursue origins was very much a matter
of *renunciation*, a matter of "ascetic modesty"[18] on the part of those who
were resigned to a life mired in historical documents, which would never
provide answers to questions such as: "What is the sacred? What does
a religious experience actually mean?"[19] Without apparent irony, he lik-
ens this life of a dedicated historian, half-buried under massive data, to "a
kind of *descensus ad inferos*; a descent into the deep, dark subterranean regions where he is confronted with the germinal modes of the living matter"; and in so doing, Eliade adds, the historian risks "a spiritual death; for,
sadly enough, the creativity of the scholar may be sterilized."[20] Cast in this

language, it appears that the life of a historian is but a somewhat novel mode of carrying out a time-honored spiritual discipline, a sort of *imitatio Christi*, recommending pious labor of self-denial. For, according to Eliade, the historian of religion "knows that he is condemned to work exclusively with historical documents, but at the same time he feels that these documents tell him something more than the simple fact that they reflect historical situations. He feels somehow that they reveal to him important truths about man and man's relation to the sacred. But how to grasp these truths? This is the question that obsesses many contemporary historians of religions. A few answers have been proposed already. But more important than any single answer is the fact that historians of religions asked *this* question."[21]

A few things may be said in view of this revised mission statement for history of religions. First, it is clear that the question of origin—or what Eliade terms "obsession with origins"—is hereby suspended rather than resolved, disabled, or eliminated. (Since Eliade himself resorts to pathological terminology here, one might add that, according to psychoanalysis, it is in the very nature of an obsession that it cannot be "renounced" because it is itself a result—a reaction formation, to be precise—of an attempt at renunciation.) It therefore stands to reason that the general work environment of these neohistorians of religions is fraught, even more so than before, with deep ambivalence, owing to the structural tension or contradiction endemic to the very idea of origin—and the double bind of desire and prohibition associated with the idea—to which I referred earlier in this chapter. In the case of Eliade specifically, the ambivalence becomes exceptionally pronounced when his "scientific" dictum to suspend the search for origins is juxtaposed with his pet theory, which holds that, baldly put, the point of religious life or quest is tantamount to a longing for origins and that the aim of ritual acts is the reenactment of events *ab-origine*.[22] This juxtaposition results in a peculiar pair of mirroring images representing the object and the subject of *Religionswissenschaft*: on the one hand, an assembly of "religious men" indulging in the deepest human desire, jubilating among their own kind well beyond the pale of science, and on the other, an ascetic tribe of "scientists of religion" resolutely resisting this desire, feeding among the dry dust of historical documents, waiting for any intimation of "important truths" that their views from afar might yield.[23]

Secondly, this demarcation of subject and object of the science reinscribes and reinforces the Humean edict of separation, except that, with Eliade (as well as with Rudolf Otto), rationality seems to have switched sides altogether and consequently the domain of foundational "truths" (as opposed to the domain of historical facts) can no longer be reached by rational thought but only through some self-authenticating experience unmediated by the usual cognitive faculties. In effect, Eliade would roll back all the liberties taken by the "evolutionists" and "reductionists" since the time of Hume, undo the effects of these violations, and urge the scholars to quit speculating about the dreamtime and to repair to their proper station in documentary history. Yet this newly designated seat of the neohistorian of religions is considerably more constrained and impoverished than the position taken by Hume, who, secure in his belief in the immunity of the Deistic rationalist faith, felt free to construct the "origin and development" of religion in entirely naturalistic terms, from start to finish. In contrast, Eliade's neohistorians are "condemned" to elaborate endlessly on a particularized historical narrative, which may or may not be finally meaningful but from which both the origin and the telos are preemptively bracketed. The proper historian in Eliade's sense is thus reduced to slaving over the deluge of facts, "immersed in his documents, sometimes almost buried under their mass and weight,"[24] all the while straining to eavesdrop on the rumors of angels possibly echoing between the lines of hard, unyielding documentary history.

*　*　*

After Eliade died in 1986, there developed a small industry critiquing his legacy. Today, there may not be as many scholars who profess the Eliadean orientation to be their own, compared to the number of those who do not. In fact, I suspect that the majority of historians of religions now consider themselves to have gotten *beyond*, not only the evolutionist follies and the reductionist fallacies, but also Eliade's own scruples, not to mention his unsatisfactory—still too theological, some say—pseudosolutions. In all their modesty, the contemporary historians seem to feel that they have overcome at least *those* stumbling blocks. Yet, having traced the seemingly intractable origin complex constitutionally ingrained in the enterprise of (natural) history of religions from the beginning, we cannot escape the impression that the very terms in which the contemporary historians often express their sense of difference from their predecessors—"we don't speculate on the origin, the essence or the goal of religion; we just do history"—consign them exactly to the same epistemic regime that has dictated the religious-scientific inquiry, that is to say, to the infernal machine first set in motion by Hume's clever device. To be sure, given the particular configuration of institutional and ideological forces at work in Hume's time and place, there is no question, it seems to me, that his cunning legislation, which marked out a space for "natural history of religion," was enormously enabling. And since that time it has enabled the inquiry not in a monolithic way but allowed it to proceed in many unexpected directions. At the same time, it seems equally obvious that this operating system has compelled generations of scholars to read the same origin-dominated ideological cycle over and over, the cycle that seems to be in perpetual motion, thanks in part to the enduring vitality of the unresolvable contradiction within.

The question we are left with, then, is whether it is possible to write a history elsewhere, that is, in some other register than the bicameral system designed, presumably, both to "protect" and to "keep at bay" the allegedly irreducible being or basis of religion, the system which prescribes not only how history can be narrated but also, and more importantly and fundamentally, determines and dictates the supposed object (i.e., religion) in a particular, essentializing, and ultimately unhistorical way. Can we "do history" otherwise? Is it possible, so to say, to channel history of religions in the direction of what Michel Foucault calls, after Nietzsche, *genealogy*?

Foucault describes genealogy as an alternative strategy for rendering and managing the past. (The past that requires rendering and managing, of course, is that which constitutes the present materially and ideologically.) Genealogy is above all an alternative to the historicist mode of indolent narration, which is always on the side of the dominant ideology and power, as Walter Benjamin would say. Critically marshaling "relentless erudition," genealogy "rejects the metahistorical deployment of ideal significations and indefinite teleologies" and, as such, "opposes itself to the search for 'origins'."[25] What does this mean? "Why does Nietzsche challenge the pursuit of the origin (*Ursprung*), at least on those occasions when he is truly a genealogist? First, because it is an attempt to capture the exact essence of things, their purest possibilities, and their carefully protected identities, because this search assumes the existence of immobile forms that precede the external world of accident and succession. This search is directed to 'that which was already there,' the image of a primordial truth fully adequate to its nature, and it necessitates the removal of every mask to ultimately disclose an original identity."[26]

At this point the neohistorians of religions might interrupt and protest: such an origin quest is precisely what the historians do *not* engage in; there is no allowance for timeless essence, primordial truth, or any predetermined teleology in the historians' modus operandi. Yet, as we have seen, much of this disavowal comes in the form of bracketing, self-restraint, renunciation. The historians may thus resolve to *suspend* the origin quest indefinitely, but the suspension or the renunciation of the hope of satisfaction does not automatically shift and upgrade their scholarly enterprise to a new operating system but rather it makes the same old system all the more opaque, as the latter becomes partially occluded by denial.

Meanwhile, the neo-neo-historians of the post-Eliadean epoch may intervene here, announcing their total disaffection with the metaphysics of origin and possibly even claiming to concur with the genealogist on this point. What, then, follows from this? As Foucault puts it, "If the genealogist refuses to extend his faith in metaphysics, if he listens to history, he finds that there is 'something altogether different' behind things: not a timeless and essential secret, but the secret that they have no essence or that their essence was fabricated in a piecemeal fashion from alien forms. . . . What is found at the historical beginning of things is not the inviolable identity of their origin; it is the dissension of other things. It is disparity."[27]

Perhaps some historians are prepared to abide by this principle wholeheartedly. Of course, since all this is not only a matter of principle but of practice as well, one might duly ask: What does this genealogical outlook do to something like "the history of Christianity"? Or, how does it change the nature of our business when we learn to resist the overwhelming facticity of a theoretical (yet thoroughly naturalized) object, such as "Buddhism"? How do we come to terms with the ideological construction of this facticity, which a genealogy of "Buddhism"—not "the history of Buddhism"—makes visible? Some answers to questions of this kind have been attempted, some already in print. In this regard, Philip Almond's *The British Discovery of Buddhism* (1988), William Pietz's brilliant analysis of colonial genealogies of the discourse on fetishism (1985, 1987, 1988), not to mention Jonathan Z. Smith's fossorial archeology of "religion"/"religions" (1998), among others, may be considered harbingers of this growing body of scholarship.[28]

It may be still too early to tell, however, if and how this new genre of strategic studies have proven effective in engaging, inflecting, and transforming the ways in which the study of religion (and teaching about religion) are regularly conducted. An even more challenging question may be whether such studies can impact, intervene, and destabilize the ideology embedded in the prevailing assumptions about "religion(s)" any time soon, assumptions that have been thoroughly naturalized in our general (nonacademic) discourse. Can the study of religion make evident, with accuracy and precision, the fact that many of the questions that are routinely asked about "religions" today tend to arise from the depth of ideological opacity and from our systemic blindness with regard to the material history that helped constitute these objects, be they "Buddhism," "Hinduism," "Judaism," or "religion" itself? It is only then that the dust-covered scholars of religion will have much to offer, in terms of critical, much needed expertise in the subject of religion today.

Notes

This chapter is substantially revised from its previous publication as "Origins" in *The Guide to the Study of Religion*, edited by Willi Braun and Russell McCutcheon (Bloomsbury Academic, 2000).

1. Hegel, *Lectures on the History of Philosophy*, 3:217.

2. Descartes, *Philosophical Works of Descartes*, 2:282.

3. Hume, *Natural History of Religion*.

4. Ibid, 107.

5. Ibid, 109–10.

6. Comte, *Cours de philosophie positive*; de Brosses, *Du culte des dieux fétiches*.

7. Frazer, *Golden Bough*. The original and subsequent—ever expanding—editions appeared in 1890, 1900, and 1915.

8. Freud, *Totem and Taboo*, originally published 1912–13.

9. Hume, *Dialogues Concerning Natural Religion*.

10. Tiele, *Elements of the Science of Religion*.

11. See Masuzawa, "Our Master's Voice."

12. Wordsworth, *One Religion*, 78–79.

13. Whitney, "On the So-Called Science of Religion," 451–52.

14. Feuerbach, *Essence of Christianity*.

15. Durkehim, *Elementary Forms of Religious Life*.

16. Ibid, 7: italics in the original.

17. Eliade, *The Quest*, 50.

18. Ibid, 48.

19. Ibid, 53.

20. Ibid, 48–49.

21. Ibid, 53.

22. Eliade, *Myth of Eternal Return*.

23. Masuzawa, *In Search of Dreamtime*, 1–6, 25–33.

24. Eliade, *The Quest*, 48–49.

25. Foucault, "Nietzsche, Genealogy, History," 140.

26. Ibid, 142.

27. Ibid.

28. Almond, *British Discovery of Buddhism*; Pietz, "Problem of Fetish, I," "Problem of Fetish, II," and "Problem of Fetish, IIIa"; Smith, "Religion, Religions, Religious."

8
De-Judaizing Jesus
Theological Need and Exegetical Execution

Amy-Jill Levine

Amy-Jill Levine visited the University of Alabama as the fourth
Aronov lecturer, presenting "Jesus and Judaism: Why the Connection
Still Matters" on September 15, 2005. The following essay addresses a
similar issue in the discourse concerning Jesus.

The attempt to understand Jesus of Nazareth in his cultural context is an
admirable one: it can recover the provocation of his proclamations and so
explain why numerous Jews chose not only to follow him; it reveals how
proclamations of Jesus not only as messiah but also as the manifestation
of the divine made sense in an early Jewish context; it shows church and
synagogue our common roots. However, despite advances in our knowledge of early Judaism and despite awareness of how earlier Christian exegesis
falsely and negatively stereotyped Jews and Judaism, many re-creations of
that context still continue to substitute apologetic or political expedience
or misguided liberation theology for rigorous history.

When Jesus is understood as a genius detached from his cultural context,[1] as a universal humanist correcting Judaism's tribal particularism, or even
as a pedagogue of the oppressed seeking to demystify the elitist Temple-
domination system and to dismantle a purity- and honor-obsessed system—
the result is not good history but bad theology. When such anachronistic
projections then infuse church preaching and teaching, bad theology creates ethical damage. And the damage continues to be done today through
combinations of overstated macrosociological approaches, uninformed liberation theology, and the need to present Jesus as a viable figure to nominal
Christians disaffected by church polity or disenchanted by high Christo-
logical claims.

The problematic configuration of early Judaism—and Jesus's detach-
ment from it—rests on four planks. First, Galilee is distinguished from
Judea, with the former romanticized and the latter defamed. Galilee be-

comes the land of charismatic prophets, the wisdom tradition, villages joined in solidarity against the oppression of the Temple and state, while Judea is characterized by cultic centralization and urban elites who promote the "Great Tradition" with its oppressive and expensive purity laws. The utilitarian aspect of these constructs allows liberals today, dissatisfied with urbanization, global capital, and hierarchical structures of church and state to claim Jesus as their own. These constructs then serve to undergird the translation of the New Testament's use of the term *Ioudaioi* as "Judeans" rather than "Jews"—a translation that distinguishes the Galilean Jesus from anything "Judean," that is, Jewish, and at the same time stresses the import of geographical location over religious identity.

Second, for Jesus's fellow Galilean peasants, depicted as impoverished by Antipas's lavish building programs and the triple taxation of the Temple, tetrarchy, and empire, Jesus articulates "a reading of the Torah congruent with the little tradition of the villages and hamlets of Galilee, whose inhabitants supported his vision and work."[2] The libertarian ideal of small government is not far behind.

Third, the Temple is a "domination system" (the phrase has become a technical term,[3] along with Jesus's mission to the "outcast and marginalized"—a phrase that almost inevitably fails to indicate "cast out by whom?" or "marginal to what?") that impoverishes peasants even as its priests and Pharisaic retainers pronounce them unclean for failing to tithe. Complementing this reading is the modern insistence that animal sacrifice—associated with the Temple and thus with Judaism—signifies a violent God who insists on blood offerings. This view is particularly useful to those today unhappy with church leadership structures, whether of bishops or presbyteries or conferences.

Fourth, the Pharisees and the Temple support a purity and honor-based system designed to separate male from female, rich from poor, Jew from Gentile, and Judean from Galilean, always to the advantage of the rich, male, Judean Jew. And this construct then becomes neatly mapped, by liberals, onto any church that would oppose gay or women clergy or the celebration of a same-sex marriage.

In many of these "historical" reconstructions today, Jesus the peasant and his dispossessed, exploited, but politically aware followers represent the true heirs of the "Old Testament": They are the successors of Israel's charismatic prophets and folk wisdom; they stand against Deuteronomy's cultic centralization and Ezra's and Nehemiah's xenophobia. They dismiss the purity laws and challenge the honor codes; they reject the Temple and its sacrifices and the "Great Tradition" however defined. Otherwise

put: the old configuration of "late Judaism" (*Spätjudentum*) has been res-
urrected, while Jesus incarnates the twenty-first-century liberal values of
anti-institutionalism, anticlericalism, antiritualism, populism, universalism, and even anti-Zionism. This construction is the outcome—perhaps
inevitable—of low Christology: if Jesus cannot be seen as divine or as the
Second Person of the Trinity, then distinguishing him from his Jewish
context becomes theologically necessary; the distinction provides the rationale for maintaining Christian identity.

Galileans and Judeans

Recapitulating the arguments that, as William Arnal dryly notes, "animated Chamberlain, Grundmann, and their ilk"[4] are those scholars who
seek to describe a Galilean culture substantially different from that of Judea. Arnal rightfully cautions that the scholars he cites as exemplary of this
move (e.g., John Dominic Crossan, Burton Mack, Richard Horsley) firmly
locate Jesus with Judaism—and do so with the intent to counter Christian
anti-Semitic readings. Yet the results remain troubling.

Arnal's observation has deeper roots. With graduate students in New
Testament studies today reading the latest theorist from the Modern Language Association (not a bad thing, as long as the work is accompanied by
study of the primary sources) and not having the time to read in the history of the discipline, old models are recycled. The Galilee/Judea divide
was already a part of David Friedrich Strauss's 1835 *Life of Jesus* and Ernst
Renan's 1863 *Life of Jesus*. Halvor Moxnes describes how for Renan, "Galilee as a space that inspired visions of the Kingdom of God is an ideal representation of, but also a criticism of, the West; Jerusalem and Judea represent the fanatical Orient, the home of Muslims and Jews."[5]

Thus we hear today that the "Jesus movement is a Galilean movement.
Further, it is a movement of Galilean peasant society. . . . The dynamics
of Jewish society in Galilee and Judaea were quite different, according to
their very different histories, and their different relationship with Jerusalem."[6] Whether seen as cosmopolitan to Judea's more insular "Jewish"
focus or rural compared to Judea's Jerusalem-driven urban focus, Galilee
in the hands of the scholars is *different*. Theologically, it has to be, for Jesus
to be seen as *different* from "the Jews." That Jesus was likely in and out of
Judea during much of his public career, as John's Gospel suggests and as
many scholars are now finding to be likely, usually is ignored in such constructions. That the early church took root in Jerusalem, not Galilee, is another ignored inconvenience.

Today's recuperation of this distinctive Galilean consciousness frequently offers an independent, charismatic north in contrast to the hierarchical, institutional south. For example, the claim that "Galilee was heir in some form to the traditions of the Northern Kingdom. Especially the figures of Elijah/Elisha and Moses seem to have played a key role in popular consciousness. . . . Torah was important, as was circumcision in Galilean society, but not the written and oral Torah as interpreted by the Judaean and Jerusalem retainer class and enforced where they could by the Temple aristocracy. Rather Galilee was home to popular legal and wisdom traditions." All this is to say: "Galilee was also ambivalent about Jerusalem, the Temple, the priestly aristocracy, temple dues and tithes." "On the one hand [Jerusalem] was recognized as the centre of Jewish identity and the holy city. On the other, it was perceived to be the very embodiment of the exploitative system which was destroying peasant society."[7]

Evidence for these claims lies not in texts or archaeological data but in imagination. As Mark Chancey,[8] Morten Hørning Jensen,[9] and others have shown, Galilee was not overly Hellenized: it lacks pig bones and graven images; its coins do not have human figures; numerous *miqvaot* and stone vessels attest to the practice of purity laws. Nor is there strong evidence of a prevailing Roman presence: unlike Judea, Galilee was not under direct Roman rule at the time of Jesus. In terms of the Temple, both Josephus (e.g., *Ant.* 20.118 on the "custom of the Galileans, when they came to the holy city at the festivals") and the New Testament (Luke 13:1: "At that very time there were some present who told him about the Galileans whose blood Pilate had mingled with their sacrifices") attest to Galilean participation in Temple worship. Politically, Galilee appears to have been just as divided as any other location in the Roman Empire: some supported Rome and its client rulers; others did not.

Regarding the Elisha/Elijah and Moses traditions, we have no access to a distinct Galilean consciousness.[10] Nor can Jesus be seen as representing Galilean rather than Judean attitudes: his Galilean movement substantially failed as the curses against Capernaum and Bethsaida suggest (Matt. 11:20–24; Luke 10:13–15), and his followers established themselves in Jerusalem. Stories of Moses and Elijah are by no means limited to Galilee: Philo of Alexandria has extensive discussions of Moses, and Elijah appears in a Coptic pseudepigraphon; both figures are staples in rabbinic midrash; Gospel parallels between Jesus and Elijah made sense to Jesus's followers, wherever located. The extent to which the social dynamics differed between the regions is also unclear: while Judea and Galilee had different histories, they were united under Hasmonean rule; in the first centuries BCE and CE there was migration back and forth; regional differences (whatever they were) were surmounted by a sense of unity—the people were Jews, connected by land, ethnicity, Temple, practice, texts, and self-definition over and against Gentiles and Samaritans.[11]

Once a hypothetical Galilean culture, distinct from a Judean (or "Jewish") one, is in place, the move to translate *Ioudaioi* as "Judeans" rather than "Jews" follows neatly. Some scholars find the ethnic/geographical connotations of "Judean" more historically accurate than the religious connotation of "Jew" because the translation "Jew" privileges a religious identity that is not granted to other groups in antiquity. However, this privileging of the category of religion—connoting both belief and practice—is precisely what the writers in antiquity saw. As Shaye J. D. Cohen states, "The main theme, explicit or not, of all of Graeco-Jewish literature is *Ioudaismos*, the distinctiveness of the Jews within their social and cultural environment." Cohen summarizes, "In the course of the last centuries BCE and the first century CE the ethnogeographical meaning of *Ioudaioi* receded, and a new religious meaning came to take its place. As a religious term, best translated 'Jews,' it designates people of whatever ethnic or geographical origins who worship the God whose temple is (or, after 70 CE, had been) in Jerusalem."[12]

In other cases, the translation "Judean" is based on good intentions. The major New Testament lexicon, Bauer-Arndt-Gingrich-Danker, states: "Incalculable harm has been caused by simply glossing [the Greek word] IOUDIAOS with 'Jew,' for many readers . . . do not practice the historical judgment necessary to distinguish between circumstances and events of ancient time and contemporary ethnic-religious-social realities, with the result that anti-Judaism in the modern sense of the term is needlessly fostered through biblical texts."[13] Omit references to Jews in the New Testament and replace them with Judeans, so this argument goes, and anti-Judaism is omitted as well.

Nonsense. The argument for translating Judean rather than Jew does not resolve anti-Judaism; it feeds it. If there are no Jews in the New Testament, we have a *Judenrein* text, a text "clean" of Jews. To promote the translation "Judeans" immediately distinguishes Jesus from the category, since he and his immediate followers, with the possible exception of Judas Iscariot, are Galilean. Jesus the Galilean vs. the Judean/Jewish population is an argument featured on neo-Nazi, Christian separatist, and other anti-Semitic websites: "Stormfront White Pride," the "New Covenant Church of God," www.Christianseparatist.org, www.Jewwatch.com, and www.Zundelsite.org, among others.

Still other scholars, working within so-called cultural-anthropological rubrics, insist that the term "Jew" cannot be used prior to the codification of the Talmud. The claim is premised on the view that today's "Jews" "largely trace their origin to Turkic and Iranian ancestors who comprised the Khazar Empire and converted to Judaism in the eighth century C.E." Thus, "given the sixth-century C.E. [Talmudic] origin of all forms of contemporary Jewish religion, and given the US experience of Jews based largely on Central European Jews, themselves originating from eighth-century C.E. converts, it would be quite anachronistic to identify any modern Jews with the 'Judeans' mentioned in . . . the New Testament."[14]

The Khazar argument should have died years ago. It eliminates Sephardic Jews in Tunisia and Spain, Yemen and Syria, and Iraq, where the Babylonian Talmud was compiled, let alone Jews who remained in Israel. The argument that all Jews are descended from the Khazars presumes that those Jews responsible for the conversion then disappeared. Even the Khazar website (http://www.khazaria.com) offers a variety of perspectives on the origin of Eastern European Jews; it also includes references to South Asian and sub–Saharan African Jews and mentions how "evidence on genetics . . . shows that Ashkenazi Jews have substantial roots in the Middle East." But why let data get in the way of ideology?

Finally, making the argument that Jesus is not a Jew but a Galilean and then severing Jews today from any connection to the people of Israel in the late Second Temple Period leads to the inevitable conclusion that Jews have no connection—historically, ethnically, spiritually—to the land of Israel. Jesus the Jew becomes Jesus the Galilean, and Jesus the Galilean becomes either Jesus the Aryan or Jesus the Palestinian, crucified by the Israeli army, whose followers hide behind locked doors "for fear of the Jews" (John 20:19).[15]

The Peasant

In this construct of Jesus's context, Galilean peasants are exploited agricultural workers told by the Temple system and its Pharisaic retainers that the prevailing political and economic systems have divine warrant; it is this mystification of the system that Jesus, the Paolo Friere of antiquity, seeks to expose. Further, when threats of landlessness become severe, such as when Antipas's commercialization displaces peasants and creates social disintegration, so does an increase in "social banditry."[16] Thus, the bandits in the parable of the Good Samaritan should be seen as Jewish Robin Hoods (I imagine *Men in Tights and Tzitzit*), who, displaced from family lands by overtaxation and urbanization, are "roving terrorists staging their own form of protest against various types of official and unofficial exploitation of the poor."[17]

Oy, where to start?

First, the peasant model, based in macrosociological study that combines data from fifth-century BCE China and twelfth-century CE feudal France, requires nuance, since not all peasants lived the same lives. A few good harvests and a general peace create a very different life than years of famine, war, or disease. Jesus's exhortations to abandon home and family were received by those who had something to give up: Peter and Andrew with their boats and home; James and John with their father's hired men; Matthew/Levi and his tollbooth. Their poverty was voluntary, not imposed, just as was their choice of fictive kin over biological or marital relations.

Perhaps several years of respite from pressure was precisely what was needed for Jesus's movement to work: a surplus economy, such that itinerants could expect to be fed.[18] Archaeological studies of Sepphoris and Tiberias, Cana and Capernaum, Gamala and Yodefat, as well as cities in the Decapolis and Caesarea Maritima, show flourishing if relatively modest communities.

In terms of protest movements (defined very broadly), they appear to have developed primarily either prior to the reign of Antipas or after he was deposed in 39 CE. Judas the son of Hezekiah (*War* 2.56; *Ant.* 17.271–72) attempted to raid Sepphoris around 4 BCE, at the death of Herod the Great. Athronges (the Shepherd), according to *Antiquities of the Jews* 17.278–84, was stopped by Herod Archelaus that same year as was Simon of Perea (*War* 2.57–59; *Ant.* 17.273–77; Tacitus, *Histories* 5.9.2). Judas the Galilean (*Ant.* 18.4–6 cf; 18.23 on Zealot origins) from Gamala was connected with the census; his sons Jacob (James) and Simon were executed about 47 CE by Tiberius Julius Alexander (see *Ant.* 20.100–103). Josephus (*Ant.* 20.97–98) dates Theudas to the governorship of Fadus (ca. 44–46 CE), the "Egyptian" prophet to the time of Felix (*Ant.* 20.169–71; *War* 2.261–62; ca. 52–58 CE), and the otherwise unknown "imposter" to the time of Festus (*Ant.* 20.188; ca. 59 CE). The "Samaritan prophet" (*Ant.* 18.85–87) fell under Pilate's jurisdiction (ca. 39 CE). Aside from Jesus, the only popular leader under Antipas appears to be John the Baptist, and both the Gospels and Josephus suggest that his program was one of religious renewal, not political protest. Were he anti-Temple—an unnecessary construct in that John's baptism can be seen as complementing rather than challenging Temple worship—it is surprising that Josephus, a priest, does not mention this fact; it is even more surprising to hear that Sadducees were coming to him for baptism (Matt. 3:7; whether historical or not, at least Matthew thought it possible).

Regarding taxation, Horsley and Hanson estimate that as much as 40 percent or more of produce went for taxation and religious dues, although they do not detail their sources.[19] E. P. Sanders and Douglas Oakman arrive at much lower rates; Sanders, for example, estimates the total tax burden on the average peasant was no more than 28 percent in most years.[20]

It is the theorists, not the New Testament, who tell us that Jesus and his followers faced crushing poverty. Parables about day laborers, debts, absentee landlords, the rich abandoning the poor, and so on need not reflect only a Galilean context or a system marked by destitution: even the best of economies have pockets of poverty. Claims that the building of Sepphoris and Tiberias exacerbated pressure on the rural poor also overstate. That peasants may view cities negatively—and here we have no access to what "peasants" in Galilee thought— is not the same thing as explaining how cities impacted their lives. Nor does urban construction necessarily pressure the rural poor: cities are financed variously, and for the cities of Galilee, we do not have the data to determine their funding: cash crops such as dates and balsam? Increased taxes? Tolls or levies? Euergetism?[21] Cities may strain the economics of the countryside; conversely, they may provide work, trade, and opportunities for growth. Claims that Jesus "never goes into Sepphoris or Tiberias, probably because he opposed the political and economic domination they represented," overstate (at best).[22]

Mark 6:22 states that Jesus was a *tekton*, an artisan or a builder (Matt. 13:55 makes him the son of a *tekton*). Definitions of the term range from "handyman," with connotations of unskilled and underpaid laborer to "woodworker," a more upscale title connoting "a fair level of technical skill."[23] The term appears thirty times in the LXX, with the general connotation of "artisan" or "skilled worker." James Carlton Paget notes: "The term carpenter (*tekton* in the original Greek), applied to Jesus at Mark 6.3, could be applied to someone just below a civil engineer. But it is not unambiguously such a term as any glance at a Greek lexicon will show (and we do not know what word in Aramaic, Jesus' mother tongue, was used)."[24]

Artisans are not necessarily peasants; nor are they necessarily impoverished. Rather, compared to peasants, artisans have greater opportunity to interact with the elite. David Fiensy's study of peasant-based movements shows that leaders of such movements tend to be not peasants but "discontented intellectuals, dissident landed aristocracy, priests and other religious leaders, artisans, teachers and village leaders."[25]

Within Jesus's immediate group, along with boat owners, is also Levi (or Matthew), a toll collector (Mark 2:14), whom Mark presents as hosting a banquet (2:15–17; see also Matt. 9:9–11). Luke sets Jesus at three meals hosted by Pharisees (7:36–50; 11:37–52; 14:1–6); Zaccheus the chief tax collector hosts another meal (Luke 19:1–10). Among Jesus's supplicants are a "synagogue ruler" and a centurion; his supporters include Joanna, the wife of Herod's steward, and other women of independent income (Luke 8:1–3), the householder Martha (Luke 10:38–42), the council members Joseph of Arimathea (Mark 15:43; Matt. 27:57 notes that he was "wealthy"), and Nicodemus (John 3:1–2; 7:50; 19:39). My point is not that all of these figures, or any of them, are historical. It is rather that the tradition—across all strata—depicts Jesus in the company of those of a relatively high social status.

Jesus's message does not appear to have taken root among the peasantry—who knew better than to be told not to worry about what they might eat or what they might wear. The tradition from Q to Mark to Matthew and Luke to John is replete with statements presuming an audience of some means. One does not exhort "take no bronze" (Mark 6:8; Matt. 10:9 inflates to "gold, or silver, or copper"), unless individuals had a surplus to take. Further, the message took root in Jerusalem, not in Galilee.

Concerning the idea that artisans only become so when economic pressures force them off the land,[26] cottage industry has existed since the time that individuals required houses in which to live, pots with which to cook, garments with which to clothe their bodies. Artisans who have full-time employment—and the good economic conditions of the Galilee under Antipas as the evidence from Kefer Hananiah suggests—do not appear to be lacking food or turning to material because they were forced off their land.

Some social scientific readers find Jesus's work as an artisan and Paul's as a tent maker to indicate a rejection of prevailing views that denigrated manual labor and so a challenge to Mediterranean honor codes. Herzog, for example, claims that in Roman antiquity "aristocrats viewed all manual labor as degrading, and they considered those who engaged in it as inferior creatures, little better than slaves. As a result, artisans lived on the edge of destitution."[27] He does not explain how he gets from the attitude of the elite to the economic status of the artisan.

Although we cannot facilely distinguish Jewish and Hellenistic culture, the sources suggest different cultural views. Herodotus, Aristotle, and Xenophon, as well as Dio Chrysostom, Cicero, and Lucian of Samosata, regard artisans negatively.[28] Yet, as Fiensy notes, "the same attitude seems not to have prevailed among Palestinian Jews." He cites rabbinic sources that "extol both manual labor (*ARN B* XXI, 23a) and teaching one's son a craft" (*m. Kidd.* 4.14; *t. Kidd.* 1.1 1; *b. Kidd.* 29a); he remarks that "artisans often receive special recognition" (*m. Bikk.* 3.3; *b. Kidd.* 33a), notes that many of the sages were artisans, and finds indications that Josephus highly regarded artisans, especially those connected with the construction of the Temple.[29] To this we can add that the traditions of Israel celebrate the labor of the heroes: Jacob, Moses, and David are shepherds, Amos is an agricultural worker, and so on.

Herzog proposes that Jesus's challenge "was to articulate the meaning of the Sinai covenant in this context of colonial rule and to do so in a way that represented the interests of the peasant villagers in Galilee."[30] Hence the parables focus "on the gory details of how oppression served the interests of the ruling class."[31] Yet Jesus's images are more broadly targeted: not just to peasants but also to artisans and elites. His focus may be less this-worldly and more eschatological (the sociological models discussed here tend to discount an eschatological Jesus); his concerns less with systemic injustices or Roman imperialism (especially since Galilee was not occupied) and more with preparing followers to inhabit the Kingdom of Heaven. Perhaps the construct of Jesus the pedagogue of the oppressed may reveal more about the (usually) American academic, who needs a genius Christ to speak against the Pax Romana the same way that the liberal professor declaims the Pax Americana. That the biblical studies emphasis on empire is more an American than European phenomenon and that it seems to be subsiding with the replacement of President Bush by President Obama may, of course, be coincidental.

The Temple

Popular today are depictions of the Jerusalem Temple as a domination system that overtaxed the poor, promoted exploitative purity regulations that sanction inequity, and equated the poor who cannot pay for the sacrifices with the sinful. Horsley, for example, finds "an inherent structural conflict between the interests of the Temple-based rulers and those of peasant producers."[32] Draper proposes that Jesus, by stating, "The children are free" (Matt. 17:24–27), absolved the people from the obligation of paying the Temple tax even as he "attacked the exploitation exercised by the ruling class and their retainers."[33] Nicholas Perrin describes the Temple priests as invested in "a systematic embezzlement of temple funds."[34] Herzog posits "a peasant population excluded from the Temple because they could not afford to pay their tithes and offerings. . . . They still paid their taxes but, given Jesus' instructions, they could pay their poll tax or tributum capitis not as an act of acquiescence but as an act of resistance, even defiance . . . an act of removing the blasphemous coins from the land."[35] Were I cynical, I would read this as saying that if the Pharisees advocate payment of the Temple tax, it is exploitative; if Jesus advocates payment, it is liberationist.

Often overlooked in such depictions are the positive roles religious institutions play. The Jerusalem Temple welcomed all nations (hence the Court of the Gentiles), resisted assimilation (by proclaiming Jewish worship of the Jewish God), provided a link between heaven and earth and so addressed the spiritual needs of worshipers (had it not done so, Jews would not have attended, defended, and mourned it), celebrated the history of the covenant community, united Israel and the Diaspora by its pilgrimage festivals and the voluntary paying of the Temple tax, provided for the poor, and erased locative barriers between rich and poor, tax collector and Pharisee, high priest and tenant farmer.

We can see the problem of assessment in readings of Mark 12:41–44, the account of the "poor widow" who offered "two small copper coins." Jesus tells his disciples, "Truly I tell you, this poor widow has put in more than all those who are contributing to the treasury. For all of them have contributed out of their abundance; but she out of her poverty has put in everything she had, all her life." Scholars who begin with an anti-Temple basis find here an exploitative Temple system that requires the least and the lost to contribute the last of their funds. But this reading is by no means demanded, and Mark's text sets up a persuasive alternative. Had Jesus found the situation exploitative, he could easily have exhorted, "Madam, save your money." Rather than exploiting the poor, the Temple enfranchises them, since they are welcome in the same corridors as the wealthy, and their generosity is more recognized. The same point holds for any church today that passes the collection plate. Readers who wish to regard the poor solely as needy recipients, who have nothing to contribute, are the ones doing the exploiting and disempowering.

Whether Temple authorities could exclude anyone from worship remains unclear. Albert I. Baumgarten argues that in *Ant.* 18.18–22, *eirgo-*

menoi (18.19) is passive as in "the Essenes were excluded."[36] However, the term can be reflexive: the Essenes exclude themselves. In either case, there is no indication that peasants who did not pay tax or tithe were excluded. How would the priests know?

Looking for evidence of Temple-based domination, Herzog cites [Tosefta] *Menahot* 13:21 and [Babylonian Talmud] *Pesah[im]* 57a.[37] The Baraita reads: "Woe is me because of the house of Boethus. Woe is me because of their staves. Woe is me because of the house of Kathros. Woe is me because of their pen. Woe is me because of the house of Hanin [perhaps Annas]. Woe is me because of their whispering. Woe is me because of the house of Ishmael b. Phabi. For they are high priests, and their sons treasurers, and their sons-in-law supervisors, and their servants come and beat us with staves." This is, by the way, one of the most commonly cited rabbinic texts in studies of the historical Jesus. The situation is despicable. But it has nothing to do with oppression of peasants, taxation, or purity, despite Herzog's conclusion that this "indictment would seem to indicate that the peasants of the land, and no doubt many others, viewed the high priestly houses as part of the problem, not part of the solution."[38]

The sentence preceding the statement in *b. Pesahim* is: "There were sycamore-trees in Jericho which the priests forcibly appropriated for their own use, in consequence of which the owners consecrated them for the use of the Temple." The focus is on landowners, not peasants. That the text comes from sources two centuries removed from the Temple and that it was written by individuals with an ambivalent relationship to it should also be noted. That Temple-based priests did at times exploit their position during the Roman period is not in doubt: the issue is one of systemic exploitation of peasants, and that the sources do not detail. The problems appear to be more in terms of internal intrigue, with a few high priests, of short reigns, overstepping authority.

Under the heading "The Jerusalem Temple as System of Political Economy and Social Archetype," Oakman notes, "The priestly dues can be shown to have increased significantly in the post-exilic period. Not only is this clear from the growth of the temple tax from one-third shekel annually in Nehemiah's time (Neh 10:32) to one-half shekel annually in Josephus's time (*Ant.* 18.312; Matt 17:24); it is also clear from the various dues inferred from priestly traditions."[39] Inferred? From what? Further, no one could enforce payment; even Oakman notes that, at least according to 4Q159 (one of the Qumran scrolls), the "Qumran group" refused annual payment.[40] Finally, whether the people found the Temple taxes "onerous" might, although risking anachronism, be comparable to whether citizens today find their tax burdens "onerous."

Herzog insists that those who refused to pay "faced social ostracism, shunning, and vilification by Temple authorities. It was this situation that seems to have created a growing class of peasants, artisans, and other rural workers known as the am-ha-aretz."[41] The *Temple* creates poverty? These "degraded dirt farmers," as he later calls them,[42] or more generally "the peasantry of Galilee . . . were unable to avoid the Herodian and Roman tribute" and so were "forced to withhold their tithes from the temple in order to survive. The temple responded by condemning the peasants . . . declaring them to be perpetually indebted and unclean."[43] To support these views, he states, "Josephus recounts rulers travelling to the threshing floors to claim their share of the peasants' harvest" (citing *Ant.* 20. 181, 206).[44]

Here is what Josephus recounts:

> About this time king [ca. 59 CE] Agrippa gave the high priesthood to Ismael, who was the son of Fabi. And now arose a sedition between the high priests and the principal men of the multitude of Jerusalem; . . . and when they struggled together, they did it by casting reproachful words against one another, and by throwing stones also. . . . And such was the impudence and boldness that had seized on the high priests, that they had the hardiness to send their servants into the threshing-floors, to take away those tithes that were due to the priests, insomuch that it so fell out that the poorest sort of the priests died for want. To this degree did the violence of the seditious prevail over all right and justice.[45]

This may be the second most-cited rabbinic text. The point is again internal infighting. The grain had already been tithed; the peasants were not suffering because of the tithe, although the poorer priests were.

The "degraded dirt farmer" construct is also extreme. The term *am ha'aretz* first appears in Genesis 23:3–7, where Abraham "bowed to the people of the land." It appears in Exodus 5:4, where Pharaoh states, "The people of the land [i.e., the Israelites] are numerous." For Leviticus 4:2–27 it refers to the common people as opposed to the priests, with no negative connotations. Following Persia's defeat of Babylon, it refers to members of the Judean population who rejected the claims of the returnees. In the rabbinic sources, it refers to those who do not follow rabbinic dictates. The most extensive discussion appears in *B. Berakhot* 47b, an in-house rabbinic discussion—and one usually not cited in these works, perhaps since the text calls the "degraded dirt farmer" construct into question.

> We have been taught: Who is an *am ha'aretz*? He does not eat pro-fane food in ritual cleanness. So said R. Meir. But the sages say: Anyone who does not tithe his produce in the proper way. Our masters taught: Who is an *am ha'aretz*? He who does not read the Shema morning and evening—such is the opinion of R. Eliezer. R. Joshua said: Anyone who does not put on tefillin. Ben Azzai said: Anyone who has not tzitzit attached to his garments. R. Nathan said: Anyone who has no mezuzah at his doorway. R. Nathan ben Joseph said: Anyone who has sons but does not bring them up to the study of the Torah. Others say: Even if he has not read Scripture and studied Mishnah but has not attended upon disciples of the wise, he is an *am ha'aretz*.

The rabbis cited, all of whom were living in the second century or later, write prescriptively not descriptively. Nor does any of this description concern degraded dirt farmers (the description could well fit the elite) or "vilification by Temple authorities."[46]

The Temple tax itself did increase. Exodus 30:11–16 requires all Israelite men between the ages of twenty and fifty to pay a half shekel, once, toward the construction of the *miqdash* (sanctuary). Nehemiah states that the tax was to be one-third of a shekel. *M. Shekalim* (2.4) speaks of the "shekel" or "the shekel dues," and the different currencies used to pay it; the currencies equal half a shekel. An increase from one-third to one-half over four hundred years hardly indicates an onerous increase. The big increase came not with Nehemiah, but with Vespasian. In need of revenue, the emperor removed the upper cap on the age of Jews responsible for the payment and expanded the base to include women up to age sixty-two and children over the age of three.

Other pieces in the anti-Temple literature are the presumptions that sacrifice is violent, atavistic, superstitious, and elitist.[47] That is, "we" don't like it. Missing from this configuration is any understanding of how people in antiquity viewed sacrifice. If the idea of sacrifice were so distasteful, then it is difficult to explain why some of Jesus's followers saw his death in sacrificial terms, and his blood as cleansing (see especially the Epistle to the Hebrews). Apparently, when Jews perform sacrifices, it is bad; when Jesus does it, it is salvific.

Certainly some Jews questioned the legitimacy of the high priesthood. The Hasmoneans usurped the office, Herod appointed his lackeys, and some priests abused their power. But the people continued overwhelmingly to support the Temple, to pay the tax, to participate in its activities. 11QTemple (the Temple Scroll of the Qumran scrolls) anticipates an eschatological temple; Bar Kochba put pictures of the Temple on his coinage; the revolutionaries in the first revolt appointed their own high priest; and the New Testament as well as Josephus connect Jesus's followers with it. All these Jews apparently missed the message of the Temple-domination system.

Purity and Honor

The social science model locates the Pharisees as Temple retainers who "converted the debt codes of the Torah into purity or pollution codes."[48] Herzog's study of Luke 18:9–14, the parable of the Pharisee and the toll collector, provides a good example of this approach. In his analysis, the Pharisee is a "retainer in the Temple system," and, "through the network of synagogues," he and his faction "participated in efforts to enforce the collection of tithes."[49] Pharisees did not run synagogues: "Synagogue leaders" did. Evidence that Pharisees around 30 CE collected tithes is lacking.[50]

Next, Herzog states that in the context of the purity codes, the Pharisee and the tax collector "represent one more incompatible pair, the clean and the unclean."[51] Thus, the toll collector, who "stood far off" (*makrothen*) was "most likely ostracized by other worshipers because of his suspected ritual impurity."[52] The parable says nothing about either ostracism or purity; rather, to enter the Temple one needed to be ritually pure; the tax collector may be a sinner, but he is a ritually pure one. Herzog continues: the Pharisee "participates in the systematic, institutionalized violence originating from the Temple" whereas the toll collector's "behavior in the service of Roman rule threatens the economic interests of the Temple-centered elites and their retainers."[53] What the "institutionalized violence" is remains unclear. Conversely, it is in this Temple where the toll collector finds reconciliation; it is this institution that brings together publican and Pharisee, sinner and saint. If the toll collector is ostracized, it is not because he is impure but because he works for the occupation government. In like manner, the women at the cross (Luke 23:49) are also standing "far off" (*makrothen*), but the issue is neither ostracism nor ritual purity: it is self-distancing from Roman capital punishment.

Despite the facts that Galileans worshiped in the Temple and that the Temple as a place of pilgrimage served to undermine socioeconomic and regional boundaries, scholars continue to impose the hypothesized Galilean/Judean cultural divide onto the parable. For example, Herzog notes, "Following a suggestion made by R. B. Y. Scott, Pheme Perkins believed that the parable was based on a Galilean proverb, 'Better a tax collector than a Pharisee self-righteous before God.'"[54] Perkins states, "The parable may have been based on a Galilean proverb."[55] But Scott himself simply observes, "How easily a parable like that of the Pharisee and the tax collector can be turned into a gnomic couplet."[56] Thus a parable becomes a "Galilean proverb," and so demonstrates Galilean wisdom vs. Judean-Pharisaic Oral Law.

To explain the toll collector's location, Herzog once again seeks a purity-obsessed Temple. He adduces that "the delegation of Israel (Maamad) was responsible for making the unclean stand at the Eastern gate."[57] His citation is to Kenneth Bailey, who in turn cites "Danby 1933, p. 587." "Danby" refers to the Mishnah; the citation by date and page number would be equivalent to citing "Bible, King James Version, p. 42." The citation should be *m. Tamid* 5.6: "When a priest heard the noise of it [the 'shovel'] he knew that his brethren the priests had entered to prostrate themselves, and he ran and came also; and when a Levite heard the noise of it he knew that his brethren the Levites were going into sing, and he ran and came also; and [when he heard the noise of it], the chief of the Maamad [the 'standing' priests from the 24 courses] made the unclean to stand at the Eastern Gate." The citation to *m. Tamid* has now become commonplace in biblical studies, although the literary context tends to drop out. For example, in discussion of this parable, Klyne Snodgrass offers: "The 'unclean' were made to stand in the Eastern Gate (*m. Tam* id 5.6). Whom the Mishnah intends by 'The unclean' is uncertain, but even if it refers only to those who were temporarily ritually unclean, it betrays an attitude that explains why the tax collector stood at a distance."[58]

The identity of the "unclean" is, to repeat, unclear. They might have been people who had been pronounced clean by the priests (see Matt. 8:1–3) and who were waiting to bring their sacrifices (so Maimonides) or priests who had contracted uncleanness [e.g., through genital discharge] and who stood at the gate to show that they were impure rather than idle.[59] In either case, the passage has no relationship to our parable, which, again, never mentions impurity.

The next step in the negative depiction of purity is to insist that it promoted a system that "regarded sickness and misfortune as punishments for sin. It laid the burden of guilt on the victims of society, while absolving the beneficiaries of exploitation. Forgiveness of sins was controlled to the economic advantage of the ruling class by their monopoly of the temple."[60] Here a negative view of "purity" meshes nicely with the emphasis on the peasant, seen as connoting marginalization or being "outcast." Jesus the peasant and his compatriots in Galilee are the impure, the despised, the marginal, and the outcast. The questions "cast out from what?," "by whom?," and "marginal to what?" are rarely asked. It is presumed, rather, that the sick are the outcast.

It is this configuration that gives us such unwarranted claims as the view that, in the Samaritan parable, the priest and the Levite avoid the fellow in the ditch because they are following prohibitions regarding corpse contamination. However, ignored are the facts that the priest is going down (*katabaino*) from Jerusalem, that the Levite is under no law concerning avoidance of corpses, that burying a corpse is a mitzvah (see, e.g., Tobit, *m. Nedarim* 7, Joseph of Arimathea and Nicodemus), that the parable says nothing about purity, that the priest and Levite set up the expected "Israelite" rather than the unexpected "Samaritan," and that the hemorrhaging woman was a social pariah (were she so seen, that crowd would have parted like the Red Sea when she appeared; missing in most exegeses of this pericope is also the fact that hands do not convey impurity).

Herzog, speaking of Mark 2:1–9, describes the social consequences of paralysis: "His social bonds were disrupted and broken, and he was in danger of becoming an outcast."[61] By the next page the danger has been fulfilled with the reference to "outcasts like the paralytic." Against this purity system stands, of course, Jesus. Draper makes the case explicitly: "Jesus absolved people from the obligation of maintaining ritual purity in its rigid form, especially as taught in the oral tradition of the retainer class." Further, "Jesus undercut this [control of forgiveness by the Temple] by declaring sins directly forgiven and demonstrating this by his healing miracles."[62]

The test case of the paralyzed man calls into question the association of purity with illness, and so the connection of illness and outcast. The man is not an outcast: his support system opens a roof for him; he is, rather, an "incast." The majority of sick people in the Gospels are embedded in networks of family and friends. The only people who see the paralyzed man and the "bent over woman" and Peter's mother-in-law as "unclean" and "outcast" are Christian exegetes, not the Gospels, and not—as far as their stories tell us—the individual's Jewish family or friends.

Purity is a means of leveling class distinctions, since all Jews can practice purity. They can all sanctify their bodies, and they can all engage in practices that resist assimilation. Galileans would have been just as much, or as little, invested in purity as were their compatriots in Judea. Jewish sources typically do not equate sickness and impurity (save for specific illnesses such as leprosy or genital hemorrhages), and they do not view the sick as outcast.

The most commonly attested source that does equate the two is, ironically, John 9:2, wherein Jesus's disciples ask, "Rabbi, who sinned, this man or his parents, that he was born blind?" Now the disciples represent the view in which "disease was widely considered to be a judgment of God."[63] On the other hand, *bikhur cholim*, visiting the sick, is a prominent mitzvah. From the Babylonian Talmud, *Nedarim* 39b states:

> "Rabbi Helbo once fell ill. Thereupon Rabbi Kahana went and proclaimed: "Rabbi Helbo is ill!" But none visited him. He rebuked them [the scholars], saying, "Did it not once happen that one of Rabbi Akiva's disciples fell sick, and the Sages did not visit him? So Rabbi Akiva himself entered [the disciple's house] to visit him, and because they swept and sprinkled the ground before him, he recovered. 'My master,' said the disciple, 'you have revived me!' Whereupon Rabbi Akiva went forth and lectured: "He who does not visit the sick is like a shedder of blood."

My point in listing this passage is not to suggest that the attitudes in the passage represent late Second Temple Judaism. It is to show that even those heavily invested in matters of ritual purity, such as the rabbis, did not equate impurity and sickness. The same point can be seen throughout the scriptures of Israel: Job suffered, but he did not sin; Isaac's blindness and Tobit's blindness were not indicative of impurity, and none were "outcasts."[64]

Closing Thoughts

Biblical scholars should use—and will use—whatever resources we find from whatever disciplines we encounter in order better to understand the texts. But at the same time, we cannot neglect the work of history: we must look to the ancient sources and the archaeological remains in order to test the method. Biblical scholars will often use—and should not be forbidden from using—their own values and beliefs in interpreting texts. Nor should scholars be so naive as to think that we begin without presuppositions, in-

cluding presupposed sociological models. Further, we scholars should attend to our own apologetic concerns.

When the "Oral Law" (identified with rabbinic Judaism) becomes associated with an exploitative "Great Tradition," we might ask ourselves
whose interests are being served. When desiderata of the religion of Israel
(wisdom traditions, charismatic leadership, spiritual visions) are associated with Galilee but negatively presented purity codes describe Judea, we
might wonder whose history is being inscribed. When Galilee in the 20s
and 30s CE is seen as a place of rampant exploitation, oppression, and poverty, and Jesus and his immediate followers are seen as fighting the good
fight against those elite Pharisees and that blighted Temple, we might inquire: is the argument fact, hypothesis, apologetic, a bit of all?

I too am driven by my own ideological concerns—it is those concerns
that prompted me to address the social science conclusions in the first
place. But it is my hope that hypotheses can also be supported by hard evidence, respect for the cultures we seek to understand, recognition of our
own investment, and careful research into the primary sources.

Notes

An earlier version of this chapter appeared as "Theory, Apologetic, History: Reviewing Jesus' Jewish Context" in *Australian Biblical Review* 55 (2007): 57–78;
some of this material was presented to the Cambridge New Testament seminar
in March 2012.

1. The genius model recapitulates both the late nineteenth-century neo-
Romantic approach to history and the categorization of *Spätjudentum* from which
the genius Jesus was distinguished. See Theissen and Winter, *Quest for Plausible
Jesus*, 44–63. Winter summarizes, "Jesus was seen as the genius beyond compare,
the great independent heroic individual who arises at crisis time, repudiates Jewish legalism and ushers in a new historical era, before being crucified because he
is dangerously new" (Winter, "Saving Quest for Authenticity," 144).

2. Herzog, *Prophet and Teacher*, 60. Herzog distinguishes this "little tradition"
from "the 'great tradition' that emanated from Jerusalem" and which "was focused
on the Torah as interpreted by the oral Torah of the Pharisees or the readings of
other groups like the Sadducees and Essenes. . . . In the villages, peasants kept
alive the prophetic traditions associated with Elijah and Elisha" (59). The terms
"little tradition" and "great tradition" come substantially from James C. Scott's
work (for example, "Protest and Profanation"). Overstated but nevertheless apt are
the comments by Dunn on the import of this terminology into New Testament
studies: "It is used by Scott in reference to a colonialist situation in Southeast Asia,
which has little bearing on a Jewish Galilee ruled by a client Jewish king" (*New

Perspective on Jesus, 100–101n65). The question is not whether there were distinct versions of the tradition but whether those versions can be so neatly correlated to region.

3. On Friday, May 18, 2012, I put the words *temple, domination*, and *system* into Google and received "about 11,100,000 results." The first hit was a website called "A Portrait of Jesus from Galilean Jew to the Face of God"; the epigraph, from Marcus Borg, reads "Context: Social/Cultural World of Jesus. The political situation of first century Jewish Palestine was a domination system marked by peasant society, purity society, and patriarchal society." Much of the site displays the types of ahistorical, overstated readings this essay discusses.

4. Arnal, *Symbolic Jesus*, 23.

5. Moxnes, *Jesus and Rise of Nationalism*, 15, cf. discussion 59–60, 71–72.

6. Draper, "Jesus and Renewal."

7. Ibid.

8. See, e.g., Chancey, *Myth of Gentile Galilee*, and *Greco-Roman Culture*.

9. Jensen, *Herod Antipas in Galilee*.

10. Nickelsburg, "Enoch, Levi, and Peter," reads portions of 1 Enoch as "closely resembl[ing] explicit polemics against the priesthood" (584) and as finding "sacred space" in the Galilee, but he also notes that "at several points, 1 Enoch asserts the geographical centrality and ultimate sanctity of Jerusalem" (585).

11. Even Sean Freyne—who sees a distinctive Galilean ethos—notes, "As a result of the archaeological evidence, I am now dubious about my earlier views that an old Israelite presence was maintained in Galilee over the centuries. . . . [The archaeological data] point to the essentially conservative nature of the Jewish settlements in Galilee (Upper and Lower) in religious terms" ("Galilean Questions," 72).

12. S. Cohen, "Judaism and Jewishness," 513. See also, in the same volume, Garroway, "*Ioudaios.*"

13. Bauer, et al., *A Greek-English Lexicon, Ioudaios*, ad loc.

14. Malina and Rohrbach, *Social-Science Commentary on Gospel of John*, 44. Malina concludes: "Thus most US Jews are essentially Khazar Americans rather than 'Jewish' Americans. The same is true of the majority of people living in the Jewish State" (Malina, "Was Jesus a Jew?").

15. Ateek, "Pentecost and Intifada," 70. The volume has no Jewish Israeli contributor. As a consultant for both Americans for Peace Now and for Churches for Middle East Peace, I find myself often critical of Israeli policy. However, the divisive rhetoric that strips Jesus of his Jewish identity and uses anti-Jewish (not anti-Israeli but anti-Jewish) tropes to make a political argument prevents those interested in a two-state resolution from working together.

16. See especially Horsley, *Jesus and Spiral of Violence*, and "Bandits, Messiahs and Longshoremen"; Horsley and Hanson, *Bandits, Prophets and Messiahs*. See also Freyne, "Bandits in Galilee."

17. Ringe, *Luke*, 158.

18. Jensen, *Herod Antipas in Galilee*, 247, states: "It seems indisputable that the rural area was able to sustain its livelihood and even expand it in this period." See also Chancey, "Review of *Herod Antipas*," which concludes that the volume "convincingly demonstrates that recent scholarly claims that the reign of Antipas resulted in the impoverishment of the Galilean countryside have little basis in the currently available evidence."

19. Horsley and Hanson, *Bandits, Prophets, and Messiahs*, 52–63. See discussion in Harland, "Economy of First-Century Palestine."

20. Following Harland, "Economy of First-Century Palestine," 521. The Sanders citation is to *Judaism*, 146–69. Harland adds: "The fragmentary nature of the evidence when it comes to quantifiable estimations of taxation, rents and other expenses helps to explain the difficulty in assessing the economic situation of the peasantry and the varying results of scholars on the extent of the tax burden." Finding the primary source data, however, is as difficult as finding tax money in the mouth of a fish. Josephus (*War* 6.335 [noting annual payment]; *Ant.* 14.110; 16.163–73; 18.312) and Philo (*Spec. Leg.* 1.77–78) indicate that the half-shekel tax to the Temple was paid from communities in Asia and Europe as well as Galilee and Judea.

21. Suggestions in Reed's "Reappraising the Galilean Economy".

22. Houlden, *Jesus in Thought and History*, 474.

23. Meier, *Marginal Jew*, 1:280, 281.

24. Paget, "Education: Was Jesus a Chartered Surveyor?"

25. Fiensy, "Leaders of Mass Movements," 7.

26. Herzog, *Prophet and Teacher*, 63, proposes that "peasants usually turn to trades and handicrafts to augment their resources only when they are finding it difficult to survive on . . . their agricultural production alone." He disagrees with Douglas Edwards that the village of Kefer Hananiah, which produced pottery sold throughout Galilee, demonstrates the existence of a "capitalistic market economy." See Edwards, "First Century Urban/Rural Relations," 174.

27. Herzog, *Parables as Subversive Speech*, 63.

28. See primary source citations in Fiensy, "Leaders of Mass Movements," 22.

29. Fiensy, "Leaders of Mass Movements," 22.

30. Herzog, *Prophet and Teacher*, 14.

31. Herzog, *Parables as Subversive Speech*, 3.

32. Horsley, "Innovation in Search of Reorientation," 1150.

33. Draper, "Jesus and the Renewal".

34. Perrin, *Jesus the Temple*, 110.

35. Herzog, *Prophet and Teacher*, 190.

36. Baumgarten, "Josephus on Essene Sacrifice." See *m. Eduyot* 5.6 on the possible exclusion of Akabya b. Mahalaleel (the attributed citation is from Rabbi Judah ha-Nasi, ca. 200 CE). *Ant.* 18.19 reads, "And when they send what they have dedicated to God into the temple, they do not offer sacrifices, because they have more pure lustrations of their own; on which account they are excluded/exclude

themselves from the common court of the temple, but offer their sacrifices themselves; yet is their course of life better than that of other men; and they entirely
addict themselves to husbandry."

37. Herzog, *Prophet and Teacher*, 48, gets the citation from Horsley and Hanson, *Bandits, Prophets and Messiahs*, 42. He repeats the citation in his "Why Peasants Responded to Jesus," 49–50. Readers, unless they had familiarity with rabbinic literature, would presume the first reference was to the Mishnah.

38. Herzog, *Prophet and Teacher*, 48.

39. Oakman, "Culture, Society, and Embedded Religion," 6.

40. Ibid., 7.

41. Herzog, *Parables as Subversive Speech*, 181, following Borg, *Conflict, Holiness and Politics*, 33.

42. Herzog, *Parables as Subversive Speech*, 191.

43. Ibid., 54, cf. 62.

44. Ibid., 52.

45. Josephus, *Antiquities of the Jews*, 20:8:8.

46. Along with Oppenheimer, see also Zeitlin, "The Am Haarez" for rabbinic
references.

47. Jonathan Klawans details the resurgence of anticultic views among Jewish
as well as Christian scholars: the move begins with the denigration of the Priestly
code. For example, Israel Knohl describes "elitist Priestly circles" who "generated
the ideology of a faith that is completely detached from social, national or material needs" (*Sanctuary of Silence*, 11) cited in and discussed by Klawans, "Methodology and Ideology," 91.

48. Herzog, *Parables as Subversive Speech*, 182, following Belo, *Materialist
Reading of the Gospel of Mark*, 37–59. This formulation permits a separation of the
(good) Torah from the (bad) Pharisaic/rabbinic interpretation of it.

49. Herzog, *Parables as Subversive Speech*, 182.

50. See Neusner and Chilton, *Quest of Historical Pharisees*.

51. Herzog, *Parables as Subversive Speech*, 183, cf. 184. Oddly, Herzog notes on
187 that toll collectors "do not seem to have been considered ritually defiled by
virtue of their work."

52. Ibid., 185, following Donahue, *Gospel as Parable*, 189.

53. Herzog, *Parables as Subversive Speech*, 191.

54. Ibid., 176.

55. Perkins, *Hearing Parables of Jesus*, 171.

56. R. B. Y. Scott, *Way of Wisdom*, 77.

57. Herzog, *Parables as Subversive Speech*, 185, citing Bailey, *Through Peasant
Eyes*, 149.

58. Snodgrass, *Stories with Intent*, 468.

59. Danby, *Mishnah*, 587.

60. Draper, "Jesus and Renewal."

61. Herzog, *Prophet and Teacher*, 84.

62. Draper, "Jesus and Renewal."

63. Herzog, *Prophet and Teacher*, 84.

64. For discussion of purity within the social science framework in connection to gender and sexuality and for the social science argument for translating *Ioudaios* as "Judean" rather than "Jew," see Levine, *Misunderstood Jew*.

9

How to Theorize with a Hammer, or, On the Destruction and Reconstruction of Islamic Studies

Aaron W. Hughes

> Aaron W. Hughes came to the University of Alabama to present the ninth Aronov Lecture on March 29, 2011. The following essay is a revised version of the lecture that he presented.

As many will no doubt recognize, the title of my chapter—and, I trust, the spirit that guides its analysis—draws its inspiration from Friedrich Nietzsche's *Twilight of the Idols*, subtitled "or, How to Philosophize with a Hammer." One of the goals that Nietzsche sets for himself in that work is to expose what he considered to be the lack of sophistication—what he called the decadence—associated with German intellectual culture of his day. In particular, he accuses its intellectuals of employing shoddy think-ing as a tool for self-preservation.[1] The fictions of such pseudophiloso-phers, for him, present a make-believe world, a consolation, based on a confusion of cause and effect, in which they project their own subjectivi-ties onto the world they claim to elucidate.

Turning from Nietzsche, but informed by the tenor of his critique, I wish to make the provocative statement that the study of Islam, espe-cially as carried out in departments of religious studies, is not qualita-tively different from the types of pseudointellectualizing of which Nietz-sche was so critical. Taking my cues from him, I submit, and without mincing words, that the academic study of Islam as carried out in depart-ments of religious studies is apologetical, decadent, and based primarily on the self-preservation and self-promotion of those who engage in it. The unfortunate result is that we know very little about Islam, both syn-chronically and diachronically, because what we are largely presented with is liberal Muslim theology, ideological apologetics, and a soft version of postcolonial theorizing in which—as one scholar writes—the "other" is afforded "the integrity that they are due."[2] What we are rarely presented with is hard, sober, and critical scholarship.

Nietzsche raised his metaphorical hammer to smash what he considered to be the decadent infrastructure that propped up European thought and culture. Mine is aimed at the equally decadent, although I would add apologetic, regnant discourses associated with the academic study of Islam. Many of these discourses are so over the top and borderline offensive to academic ears that the destructive force of a hammer must be used to clear the way for new conceptual and nonapologetical models.

Before I proceed, however, two caveats are necessary. First, lest it be misunderstood that "I want to hit Muslims with hammers," this chapter, like my work more generally,[3] is not interested in Muslims or Islam. Rather, my goal is to provide a meta-analysis of the study of Islam; in particular, the contorted hermeneutics associated with its academic study. Why do we write about and present Islam so apologetically when we do not necessarily do the same things for other religions?[4] Why do we talk, for example, about the literary strata of the Old Testament and the New Testament—the Js, Es, Ps, Ds, Qs, and so on—but present the Quran as if it fell from heaven? Why do we employ such strange rhetoric—this is real or authentic Islam, whereas that is a hijacked or bastardized version? To reiterate: I am not analyzing or making value judgments about Muslims or Islam here. There are far too many people that do this but not nearly enough that seek to study those who study Islam.

The second caveat is that my hammer is directed primarily at those who study Islam in Departments of Religious Studies. I refer to these discourses collectively as "Islamic religious studies."[5] This term has two advantages. First, it articulates and accurately defines the largely apologetic claims put forth by scholars of Islam who work under the larger canopy of religious studies. Secondly, it conveniently differentiates it from some of the more philological and historical work carried out by Islamicists in other disciplines, such as history or Near Eastern studies. Although I should add here that I do not mean by this that all is well with the study of Islam outside of Departments of Religious Studies, or even with the academic study of religion more generally. We would do well to remember that the larger discipline of religious studies—as scholars such as Russell McCutcheon have well noted—is saturated with theological, inherently phenomenological assumptions that are largely based on liberal Protestant categories.[6] "Islamic religious studies" is, thus, a convenient rubric that nicely designates its Islamic equivalent.[7] Two things follow from this. One is that I do not have the time or the energy to go after all those who study Islam in cognate departments. And, two, I should note that not every scholar of Islam working within Departments of Religious Studies engages in the apologetical arguments that I will showcase shortly. There are certainly a few that are self-reflexive, although they certainly form a minority. Unfortunately many self-reflexive Islamicists are not at places where the majority of graduate students are trained.[8] This means that the system perpetuates itself in ways that the introduction of changes associated with new theories and methods becomes very difficult.[9]

I divide what follows into three overlapping sections. In the first part, I provide a series of exempla of the apologetic discourses of Islamic religious studies. These exempla take us directly into the apologetical discourses that I have just described. These examples are not anecdotal but, as I suggest in the second part, iterations of a much larger and systemic problem that plagues the field. Following this analysis I move, tentatively, in part three toward reconstruction, the articulation of what I hope will one day be a "new Islamic studies" carried out using the terms and categories of critical discourses produced within certain subfields of the academic study of religion. This "new Islamic studies" must possess a foundation that is radically different from the set of unchecked assumptions that govern so-called "Islamic religious studies."

I

Let me begin my analysis with my conclusion, which I will spend the remaining parts of this chapter seeking to prove. The study of Islam as carried out in Departments of Religious Studies has become so apologetic that it has largely ceased to function as an academic discipline, preferring instead to propagate a theological and apologetical representation of itself. My interest in what follows is in examining both why and how this came about.

Before an analysis of the problems besetting the field of Islamic religious studies can begin, it is first necessary to articulate the problem. In order to do this I begin with a series of examples taken from my colleagues who work within the larger field of Islamic religious studies. I will confine myself to six examples and it should not be difficult to see, fairly quickly, that they all highlight, in various ways, the types of discourses that I have just labeled as "theological" or "apologetical."[10]

The first comes from Omid Safi, professor of Islamic religious studies at the University of North Carolina, Chapel Hill, and his book *Memories of Muhammad*.[11] In the preface to the volume, Safi—a scholar—informs us that his methodological framework is based on the fact that "my primary audience has been and remains my children. . . . I have spent my adult life figuring out how to make the wisdom and spirituality of these texts intelligible to my own children, and their children. I hope that they will have meaning to your children as well."[12] Although this is certainly a nice statement from a doting father, it is, I think safe to say that such a hermeneutic will not lead him to an interest in hard or critical questions. A quick perusal of the work backs this up. Despite the appearance of the word "memory" in the title, for example, Safi is decidedly not interested in how memory vectors or creates Muhammad, let alone rival Muhammads. Rather than argue, for example, that the only Muhammad that now exists does so solely in the memory of later generations, Safi straightforwardly and unabashedly writes that "the reader has every right . . . to be assured that the Muhammad presented and confronted here [i.e., in his book] is authentic, real, and recognizable."[13] Talk of *the* Muhammad, much less *the authentic, real, and recognizable* Muhammad, is extremely problematic. Safi's tone instead is primarily confessional: "For me, Muhammad represents the completion of the possibilities available to us as human beings, not because he is superhuman, but precisely because he embodies the meaning of what it means to be fully human. The fullness of his humanity is particularly important to me in his life as the ideal father, husband, friend, leader, and prophet. He ascended to God and out of compassion returned to lead others so that they too might ascend to God. These are facets of my memory of Muhammad, and aspects that I seek to transmit to my children."[14] Such words, I submit, are problematic in the extreme coming from a scholar of Islam, who, in theory, is charged with presenting objective accounts of the religion to students (both Muslim and non-Muslim) and others. After all, Safi had earlier argued that "scholars trained in the field of Islamic Studies" represent the true experts of Islam and that their lives are made more difficult by the "dilution of the standards of scholarship" presented by the media and other imposters.[15]

Words like those quoted above clearly reveal that Safi is not interested in a, let alone the, historical Muhammad. "The facets of [his own] memory" cloud his understanding of Islam's prophet and what he ultimately presents is a theological apology for his own belief. This is fine except that, to reiterate, Safi writes from a position that is legitimated by the institutional authority of his university position, which presumably also includes the backing of Islamic religious studies.

As an aside for the non-Islamicist: We know nothing about the historical Muhammad. All the sources we possess about his life come from at least 150 to 200 years after his death. The creation of an "authentic, real, and recognizable" Muhammad is historically impossible. To bypass the difficulties associated with reconstructing the early community of Muhammad, Safi employs a hermeneutic that replaces historical impossibility with reading as many sources as possible. For example, Safi "consult[s] the widest range of sources about Muhammad."[16] Two scholars whom I shall discuss shortly also employ this trope of "hard work" to reassure their readers. Asma Afsaruddin, for example, informs us that she reads the later sources with "careful, judicious scrutiny."[17] Tariq Ramadan presents an account that, according to him, "is strictly faithful to classical biographies (as far as facts and chronology are concerned),"[18] but nowhere mentions that these classical biographies date to much later generations. Wide-ranging, judicious, and/or faithful readings, however, cannot make later sources miraculously appear as early ones.

Before I leave Safi's analysis of Muhammad, allow me one further reflection of his work that reveals the state of Islamic religious studies. *Religious Studies News* (*RSN*), one of the official publications of the American Academy of Religion (AAR), encourages the program unit chairs of the annual meeting to "recommend two to five books which they consider influential, pivotal, seminal, or otherwise important publications in their field—publications that someone within the broad field of religion and theology might be interested in, even if the topic is outside of their area of specialization or concentration."[19] One of the works on the list of the Islamic Mysticism Group's top five "influential, pivotal, seminal, or otherwise important publications" is Safi's *Memories of Muhammad*.[20]

My second example comes from the aforementioned Asma Afsaruddin, professor of Islamic religious studies and Near Eastern languages and cultures (NELC) at Indiana University, Bloomington. In her *The First Muslims: History and Memory*, she writes that

> there is no reason to prevent us from regarding this corpus of material [she refers to the material about Muhammad that comes from a much later date] as less than a largely reliable reflection and reconstruction of actual events in their own time as well as their later perception . . . despite the assertion of the minority rejectionist camp, which has based its contrarian position on its own rather tendentious reading of the sources and unsubstantiated speculations. *The majority of careful and responsible scholars* have not found this camp's position unassailably convincing and the scholarly consensus remains that the traditional historical, biographical, and prosopographical works together constitute an invaluable and indispensable source for the study of the formative period of Islam.[21]

Despite such a bold claim, however, Afsaruddin herself presents no compelling evidence to back up her claims. She is certainly correct to posit that scholarly consensus regards these sources dealing with Muhammad as historically accurate. This consensus, however, is based more on lethargy, on maintaining the status quo, and on apologetics than it is on solid evidence. Because they attempt to break out of the status quo she labels those who disagree with her as cynical "rejectionists," whose "contrarian" nature is based on a series of "tendentious" readings. Cynicism, rejectionism, and contrarianism, however, are for me the hallmarks of sober scholarship and they neither emerge from nor reduce to tendentiousness.

Having convinced herself that she can truly understand the earliest sources as accurate reflections of earlier times, Afsaruddin proceeds to inform us that at the time of Muhammad, there existed a "message of social justice and gender egalitarianism."[22] In the "late medieval" period, however, this egalitarianism was replaced with "construals of 'proper' Muslim women who are demure, retiring, and, above all, who prefer seclusion in their homes to activity in the public sphere."[23] Afsaruddin here invokes a trope that we will see time and again in this apologetical literature: that the pure, pristine message that Muhammad introduced into sixth- and seventh-century Arabia was liberal, inclusive, feminist, peaceful. Only in subsequent generations was this message co-opted by illiberal, exclusive, misogynist, bellicose male elites. My interest is not who is right and who is wrong in such rival constructions, only to show the various ways that modern scholars create early Islams that correspond to their own visions of what the tradition should be.

My third example comes from Tariq Ramadan, the cause célèbre of the AAR.[24] In the introduction to his *In the Footsteps of the Prophet: Lessons from the Life of Muhammad*, Ramadan writes, "Our aim is more to get to know the Prophet himself than to learn about his personality or the events in his life. What is sought is immersion, sympathy, and essentially love. . . . This is indeed the primary ambition of this work: making of the Messenger's life a mirror through which readers facing the challenges of our time can explore their hearts and minds and achieve an understanding of questions of being and meaning as well as broader ethical and social concerns."[25] From this quotation, we see that the main hermeneutic for Ramadan with which to understand Muhammad and his life is love. Let me put this in perspective. I know of no other discipline where one would see a "scholar" from the University of Oxford (more precisely St. Antony's College) writing an "academic" monograph with Oxford University Press and making such claims. Could a scholar of Christian origins get away with writing in an academic monograph published by, say, Cambridge University Press that the main way to understand Jesus and the early Jesus movement was through love? And would such an individual subsequently be doted upon by the American Academy of Religion and invited to give plenary lectures at its annual meeting as an authority on the scholarly approach to religion?

Example number four comes from Omid Safi's colleague at UNC–Chapel Hill, Carl Ernst, the William R. Kenan Jr., Distinguished Professor of Islamic Religious Studies. I am not going into a full-scale critique of his work here, something that I have done elsewhere.[26] Within the present context, I mention only his resistance to critical scholarship—and suggest that it is symbolic of much of the discipline. In his celebrated *Following Muhammad*,[27] he writes critically of those who question the largely unquestioned narratives of Islam's origins and contest Islam's subsequent uncontested development. Such individuals are referred to as Orientalists or as Islamophobes, and their arguments, to quote Ernst, can and should remain "safely buried in obscure academic journals."[28] The arguments to which Ernst here refers are not those books that present Muhammad as a "terrorist" or Islam as an inherently evil religion (books that are, incidentally, easy to dismiss) but scholarly articles and monographs that seek to question the chronology of sources and help us rethink the nature and function of the "historical" Muhammad, whomsoever he may have been. Ernst makes it clear that such critical scholarship has little or no room in his vision of Islamic religious studies.

Example number five comes from John Esposito—the 2012 president of the American Academy of Religion, a position elected by the general membership. In *Who Speaks for Islam?* Esposito addresses the issue of women. Notably, he does so under a chapter titled "Culture" as opposed to the one on "Religious Doctrine," and there he writes that there are no crimes committed against women in Islam. He cites a survey and claims that "research indicates that 69.4% of the men who committed honor killings in Jordan did not perform their daily prayers, and 55% did not fast. That these men fail to observe the most obligatory rituals of Islam suggests that their act of murder is not motivated by religious zeal or devotion."[29] Such statements are truly unbelievable, not to mention highly insulting. Esposito, based on his false dichotomy between "religion" and "culture," acts as the arbiter of what gets to count as an authentically "religious" act and what does not. Because those "Muslim" men who kill their daughters or sisters do not pray on a daily basis or fast during Ramadan, they are, according to him, not really Muslims! Esposito manipulates his data to skew his conclusions. The bad or the uncomfortable is never mentioned and instead we are presented with a sugarcoated and apologetic treatment of the tradition.

So that I am not misunderstood here, let me be crystal clear: I am certainly not trying to make the case that Islam is inherently more patriarchal than any other religion. My point is not to side with the many hostile critics of Islam that appear in various neoconservative venues. On the contrary, my goal is simply to expose the theoretical and methodological inconsistencies of Esposito's approach to his data.

Example number six is perhaps the most insidious, and for this reason I will spend a little more time analyzing it. In their *Rethinking Islamic Studies: From Orientalism to Cosmopolitanism*, Carl Ernst and Richard C. Martin seek to "rethink" the field of Islamic studies. They largely fail, however, because they work with vague notions of what exactly needs to be rethought. This categorical failure stems, in part, from the fact that nowhere do they clearly define any of the key terms that sit together in the title of the book: "Orientalism" and "Cosmopolitanism." The editors tell us, for example, that "Orientalism remains for most scholars the bête noir in the expanding family of Islamic Studies today."[30] Why? Says who? Recent years have seen many important monographs—ones that greatly extend our understanding of the formative and other periods of Islam—that we or their authors might comfortably label as "Orientalist."[31]

Using the term "Orientalist" in a pejorative sense, in the manner that the editors do here, is a matter of ideology, a way of drawing disciplinary boundaries that define who is in and who is out. Linking these comments with those of Safi, Afsaruddin, and Ernst, we see the dismissal of all those who take a critical perspective when it comes to dealing with the historicity of early and other Muslim sources. Even though the editors ostensibly call for a "rethinking" of the discipline, they are instead attempting to establish parameters for what gets to count, at least for them, as authoritative Islamic studies in the future. To categorize neatly their critics under the omnibus rubric "Orientalist" is both misleading and unfair. Am I, for example, an "Orientalist" because I have criticized a number of the authors in *Rethinking Religious Studies I* on methodological grounds? Is anyone who takes a scholar of Islam to task for presenting an overly apologetical or theological portrait of Islam guilty of the charge of being an "Orientalist" (or, worse, an "Islamophobe")? I would certainly hope not. And while I am aware of the current political situation and the often hostile presentation of Islam and Muslims in the media and popular culture, we must not use this as an excuse to curtail historical analysis.

The second ambiguous term of the subtitle of *Rethinking Islamic Studies* is "cosmopolitanism," which, given its invocation and placement, seems to function as a hermeneutic to replace the recently and, as I have just argued, all too easily dismissed "Orientalism." By this new term, the editors seem to refer to an overlapping set of noncritical, nonskeptical, and nonoutsider approaches to deal with Islam. It appears, even though it is not completely obvious from their introduction, that the editors have in mind Kwame Anthony Appiah's notion of cosmopolitanism articulated in his 2006 book, *Cosmopolitanism: Ethics in a World of Strangers*. Therein, Appiah writes ethat "two strands intertwine in the notion of cosmopolitanism": "One is the idea that we have obligations to others, obligations that stretch beyond those to whom we are related by the ties of kith and kin, or even the more formal ties of a shared citizenship. The other is that we take seriously the value not just of human life but of particular human lives, which means taking an interest in the practices and beliefs that lend them significance."[32] Okay, but what does this mean? How does this term function as a critical hermeneutic to interpret Islamic data—or for that matter any other datasets that we interpret to somehow be "religious"?

Cosmopolitanism, it seems to me, is largely a moralistic claim, a type of ethical coexistence in a world reduced by the potentially hostile and generic forces of globalization. In this sense, Appiah's work represents an articulate plea for human diversity. However, it is uncertain as to how we could employ his notion of cosmopolitanism as a critical method in the academic study of religion. I assume that to study religious forms using a "cosmopolitan" hermeneutic means that we would have to take these forms seriously and at face value. We would have to accept them as is; to describe them using terms to which those of the religion in question would assent; and not attempt to undermine them using hermeneutics of suspicion, reductionism, or the like. In short, we would have to accord the other, as Morny Joy claims, "the integrity that is their due." Rather than function as a new hermeneutic as the editors would have us believe, "cosmopolitanism" is, if anything, little more than a rearticulation of the status quo.

Framed in this manner, it should now be clear why the editors of *Rethinking Religious Studies* are so quick to dismiss Orientalism, which engages in the *critical* study of Islamic texts.[33] It appears that their goal in mapping the "new" Islamic Studies is neither to be critical nor offensive to Muslim sensibilities. The goal, in short, is more of what we have already encountered in the previous examples: a theological presentation of Islam that refuses to ask hard questions or engage the *critical* discourses associated with certain subfields within the larger field of religious studies.

It gets worse, however. In an attempt to assert their authority and presumably to widen their privileged sphere, the editors of *Rethinking Islam* assembled a workshop with the same name at the 2010 annual meeting of the American Academy of Religion (AAR) in Atlanta. They write that "participants will receive a copy of *Rethinking Islamic Studies: From Orientalism to Cosmopolitanism,* edited by Carl W. Ernst and Richard C. Martin, in which fourteen scholars write on specific problems, methods, and theories in Islamic studies today. Within this framework . . . participants [will] meet in broad thematic breakout groups, to present current research projects for review, and to offer constructive analysis by the members of the group. Each group will be led by two scholars experienced in research, publication, and grant funding [who also wrote chapters in the book]"[34] Participants, in other words, received a copy of the book and were led in a series of breakout "discussions," wherein chapter authors examined and commented upon participants' research topics. The workshop had sixty spaces, which were quickly "sold out," and therein sixty young scholars and their research projects were presumably brought in line with the general apologetical "methodological" tenor of the volume. To me, this reeks of patrolling disciplinary borders. For example, what would the organizers do with someone like myself who wants to get at and interrogate the discipline's first principles? Would a project such as mine be eligible for the "new Islamic studies"? The workshop seems to have met with success because the organizers convened another workshop at the 2011 AAR annual meeting in San Francisco with the title of "Rethinking Islamic Studies: Gender, Sexuality, and Bodies in the Text."

II

Having showcased these six examples, numerous questions begin to emerge. Are these examples isolated incidents or are they six iterations of a much larger problem plaguing Islamic religious studies? What common set of assumptions or values strings these examples together? In the present section, I move to an analysis of these discourses and argue that, far from isolated examples, they represent categorical mistakes that are endemic to the subfield of Islamic religious studies.

All the aforementioned examples emerge, I want to suggest, out of a "theoretical framework" (if we can call it that) which scholars of Islamic religious studies have developed to create, imagine, or manufacture a particular version of Islam that conforms to their own liberal and apologetical agenda. The institutionalization of this consensus, moreover, has led to the existence of an increasingly authorized space from which scholars of Islam defend their data (i.e., "Islam") and the models used to bring it into existence.

The reasons for this are simple enough: *Islamic religious studies has become the platform of liberal Muslim theologizing.* Its practitioners—be they scholars who are Muslims, who are converts to Islam, or who are non-Muslims—all desire to create a progressive Islam that intersects with liberal democratic values, one wherein idiosyncratic voices are swept under the hermeneutical carpet. Evidence of the latter may be conveniently witnessed in the AAR workshops put on by those associated with the *Rethinking Islamic Studies* volume that I discussed earlier. Such workshops, I argue, are a way to impose a uniform vision on why and how Islam should be studied within Departments of Religious Studies throughout the North American academy.

Many associated with Islamic religious studies have subsequently disseminated this version of a liberal Islam that neatly coincides with Western democratic values in their academic writings, in the classroom, and in the media. My goal here is not to deny the existence of such an Islam, only to argue that it is but one version of the tradition and one that is largely the product of these scholars in their own interfaith work to make Islam not appear so other in the aftermath of events such as the attacks in the United States on September 11, 2001, or the attacks in London on July 7, 2005.[35] However, if we simply hold this version of Islam up—or historical versions that are made to coincide with it, such as the so-called egalitarian nature of Muhammad's Arabia[36] or the perceived gender justice found in Sufi sources[37]—as the paradigm with which to adjudicate other Islams, we miss out on the historical complexity of the tradition.

My worry is that soon we will have a generation of religious studies undergraduates, the graduate students and professors of tomorrow, who will agree with Ramadan and argue that the best way to understand Islam academically, and especially its prophet, is through "love" and who regard critical, unapologetic scholarship in the way that Ernst does: as Orientalist and Islamophobic with the result that it should be ignored or safely "buried" from sight. In fact, my concern is that we have already reached this stage.

We certainly have to factor into these apologetics the need to counter negative portrayals of Islam and Muslims after the events of 9/11 and the highly politicized environment on campuses when it comes to the Palestinian-Israeli conflict.[38] However, we must be on guard against mistaking the desire to nuance Islam, to engage in critical scholarship, or to examine the unchecked assumptions among those who study Islam with Orientalism, Zionism, Islamophobia, or some sort of other vaguely constructed right-wing agenda. The desire to nuance the tradition in its historical and geographic diversity—including its interactions with other social formations—is not tantamount to undermining the tradition.

In like manner, we cannot engage in apologetics and then call these discourses "critical theory," something that many of the scholars in the field do.[39] I worry that the field of Islamic religious studies has taken Edward Said's fascinating *literary* argument in *Orientalism* and turned it into a *historiographic* one, a call to arms to keep the barbarians at the gate, to make sure that the academic study of Islam conforms to an insider and largely apologetic agenda. My argument, here and elsewhere, is simple enough: we have to maintain a critical stance as a necessary corrective to what Islamic religious studies purveys so that we do not get lost in the slippery rhetoric of political correctness.

Unless we do this, we risk taking the rich complexities and competing histories of the many Islams that have existed both synchronically and diachronically and flattening them into a stereotype. Stereotypes, we would do well to remember, operate through an intricate system of generic terms that emphasize certain chosen characteristics (and marginalize others) as if they were eternal truths.[40] Islam is accordingly "peaceful," "liberal," based on "gender justice," and inherently "egalitarian." Such adjectives, with sufficient repetition, risk becoming mistaken for essential traits, ones that become immune from both history and disinterested scrutiny. The categories that flow from such language both manufacture knowledge of Islam and also, in many ways, create Islam—an Islam that Muslim intellectuals and their non-Muslim supporters (read: professors of Islamic religious studies) in the West have come to appropriate and deploy for their own ideological purposes and agendas.

My own working assumption is that if we simply stand aside and allow this essentialized and reified Islam (note the singular and not the plural) that is produced through this elaborate system of privilege and denial, then ultimately we deny these manifold Islams their histories. If we sugarcoat the tradition or treat it with kid gloves, we cease to take the manifold traditions that sit under the larger canopy of "Islam" seriously. This risks denying Muslims their agency as they contest the various tropes and symbols bequeathed to them and around which they contest and conflict with one another.

Islamic religious studies has become far too apologetic and there is a real danger that the study of Islam as carried out in Departments of Religious Studies will morph completely into a pulpit for liberal Muslim theologizing. I certainly have nothing against liberal Muslim theology (indeed I much prefer it to nonliberal Muslim theology); however, my concern is that theologizing of any variety carried out in Departments of Religious Studies is far too exclusive and largely uninterested in any sort of criticism of its primary object of study. There is a tendency to write off such critical voices as somehow passé or, even worse, as "Orientalist" or "Islamophobic." For Islamic studies, and *not* Islamic religious studies, to flourish, it must permit a plethora of different approaches and methodologies. If a discipline loses its critical edge, it risks installing half-truths as first principles, eventually leading to intellectual ossification.

III

Although I may not have smashed the regnant discourses of Islamic religious studies with a hammer, I trust I have at least articulated just how problematic they are, why we ought to avoid them and, where possible, expose them for what they are. In the third part of this chapter, I would like to begin the process of charting what a new Islamic studies might look like. Again, my concern is with the study of Islam as carried out within Departments of Religious Studies, what I pejoratively call Islamic religious studies—I will leave it up to those working in cognate departments to ascertain if there are the same problems and decide if my theoretical and conceptual modeling will be useful. In stating my program of reconstruction I follow in the footsteps of a previous Aronov lecturer, Bruce Lincoln, who published in 1996 his well-known thirteen "Theses on Method" to clarify what it is that historians of religions do (e.g., "history is the method and religion the object of study"). These theses, as Lincoln himself notes, are pithy comments aimed directly at the apologetic discourses that define the academic study of religion.

Within this context it is probably worth noting that the larger discipline of religious studies, of which the study of Islam forms but a part, is itself marred by a confusion of aims and methods.[41] As Lincoln himself notes in his twelfth thesis: "Although critical inquiry has become commonplace in other disciplines, it still offends many students of religion, who denounce it as 'reductionism.' This charge is meant to silence critique."[42] Although Lincoln's comments are directed primarily at scholars of religion, they would seem to be particularly relevant to scholars of Islamic religious studies.

In the spirit of Lincoln, I herewith present my own set of ten theses.[43] Their aim is to remove the largely apologetical scaffolding that currently surrounds Islamic religious studies. If we are to dismantle this scaffolding we must clearly isolate the discourses that both support it and that it supports. We must point out the apologetical and nonscholarly dimensions of existing discourses and, in the process, relegate their future deployment to a clearly defined or articulated realm of liberal Muslim theological apologetics. This, ideally, will prevent the slippage that currently goes on within Islamic religious studies, where we have theologians presenting their progressive Islam, in secular universities no less, proffering a version of the religion that they have largely created in their own image.[44]

Only by destroying what passes for existing methodological impulses in Islamic religious studies, as exemplified by the scholars and their work examined earlier, will it be possible for the study of Islam to enter the mainstream of informed study and criticism, two of the hallmarks of academic scholarship. I present these theses as an initial step on the lengthy and labyrinth-like path that will hopefully shift the direction of Islamic religious studies from the opaque to the transparent, from the essential to the historical, from the uncontested to the contested, and finally, from the apologetic to the critical. The result of this shift will hopefully be, what I here call, the "new Islamic studies."

Let me say a word about their structure. Theses 1–5 are largely destructive, a way of toppling the regnant discourses. Following this, as the dust settles, I present theses 6–10 as a form of reconstruction, highlighting a series of themes and issues that should be of importance to scholars of Islamic data. So without further ado, I hereby nail these to the office doorpost of all those engaged in the academic study of Islam within Departments of Religious Studies. May their bluntness and, I hope, acuity inspire further discussion as a way to move the conversation along.

Thesis 1

We must cease treating Islam, Muslims, and Islamic data as if they are somehow special or privileged objects of study. "Reverence," to quote from Lincoln's fifth thesis, "is a religious, and not a scholarly virtue."[45] This lack of reverence must be the bedrock for the creation of the new Islamic studies. Too many "scholarly" treatments of Islam, as we have seen, are completely unwilling to engage in critical analyses. The origins of the Quran and the problematic features of Muhammad's biography, for example, are rarely if ever entertained. Instead we are presented, staying with these examples, with a summary of Muslim accounts of the former (e.g., that the Quran is a product of divine revelation) and, as for the latter, with an assumption that later accounts are faithful historical documents and, even worse, with poetic descriptions of what Muhammad means to contemporary scholars.

A case in point comes from the highly apologetical 2012 president of the AAR, John Esposito, who actually complains that we tend to use a double standard because we "approach Islam differently than we [do] Judaism or Christianity."[46] Maybe political commentators and average citizens do this, but the case in Islamic religious studies is the exact opposite. These scholars, I have argued, get away with things that those dealing with other religions could and should never get away with. Recall, in this regard, Tariq Ramadan's hermeneutic of love. Another example comes from Omid Safi's *Memories of Muhammad* when he recounts Muhammad's harsh (but probably fair) treatment of a Jewish tribe that had conspired with his Meccan enemies. Safi writes that "it is hard to speak with certainty about this issue, so perhaps the best we can do . . . is to say alongside premodern Muslims: God knows better than we do (*Allah a'lam*). *There are simply situations whose historical veracity we cannot ascertain*, but God knows what truly happened."[47] Note the irony in this last statement: Safi is content to use later materials when it suits his story—to create, in his words, "*the authentic, real, and recognizable* Muhammad"[48]—but when history or sources threatens his portrayal of Muhammad it becomes something whose "veracity we cannot ascertain." This is not so much a hermeneutic as it is stacking the deck in one's favor.

These approaches are not scholarly, I submit, yet they are produced and indeed continue to be produced by scholars of Islam and derive their legitimacy from this. The new Islamic studies has no place for such hermeneutics.

Thesis 2

It is time to call all those approaches that masquerade as critical scholarship for what they are. Islamic identity formations, quite simply, are to be studied and analyzed, not defended. We have to admit to ourselves, to our students, and to the larger public that there are things that we know about the historical record and things that we do not.

There is, for example, no way to get around the aporia associated with the early centuries of Islam. Scholars like Safi, Afsaruddin, Ramadan, and many others try to do this naively by reading "as many sources as possible" or by claiming to read them "faithfully." But neither of these approaches, despite the fact that they may well inspire confidence in the nonspecialist or the student who is unfamiliar with the historical record, can get around the fact that even if we read as many of them as possible or as faithfully as possible, they are still later sources composed by subsequent generations for a variety of ideological purposes. Juxtaposed against such an approach, it is necessary to be honest about what we know and what we do not, what we can do and what we cannot do, when it comes to dealing with our sources.

Thesis 3

We cannot make claims about the tradition that are false or distorted because we believe that this is what others want to hear. The work of John Esposito and his clever use of statistics come to mind here. Recall in this connection, his ridiculous claim that the majority of those who commit honor killings in Jordan are not *real* Muslims because they do not pray five times a day or fast during the month of Ramadan. Rather than make such claims, predicated as they are on a neat bifurcation between religion and culture (i.e., culture kills, religion spiritualizes), Esposito overlooks a wonderful opportunity to engage seriously with their intersection. How, for example, does Islamic teaching or perceived Islamic teaching enter into the worldview of someone who commits an honor killing (or any other type of killing)? How is Islam used to legitimate patriarchy in places such as rural Jordan? But, of course, given Esposito's apologetic hermeneutic this is not something that he would ever entertain.

Thesis 4

Scholars of Islam must not bring the interfaith work they do in their private lives into the classroom. Certainly we have an obligation to defend the tradition from malicious slandering and to go to local churches and synagogues to explain Islam. But this must not go on in the classroom! Slogans such as "Islam is peace," "Islam preaches gender justice," or "terrorists have hijacked the tradition" are precisely that: slogans, not facts or truths. Repeating them time and again does not make them true. In this regard Afsaruddin and another contributor to the *Rethinking Islamic Studies* volume, Vincent Cornell, are regular participants in the Building Bridges seminars hosted by the archbishop of Canterbury. Cornell is currently the project director of something he calls "Toward a Muslim Theology of World Religions"—whatever that might mean. And then there is Omid Safi who claims in his contribution to the *Rethinking Islamic Studies* volume that he writes as "a participant-observer in the [Islamic Reform] movement."[49]

Thesis 5

We can be critical of Islam and Islamic identity formations without somehow undermining Islam, having an "ax to grind," or being a neoconservative. Although there are certainly a lot of ill-informed critiques of Islam out there, legitimate historical and scholarly criticism must occur. This is and has to be one of the defining elements of scholarship.

Thesis 6

Islams and the Muslim sources that produce them are our data, not our faith commitments. As such, we must situate this data within their historical social, ideological, and material contexts, even though the sources themselves tend to represent themselves as timeless and as ahistorical. This means that texts such as the Quran and individuals such as Muhammad must be studied in the same manner that other texts and other individuals are. Rather than talk about the "memories" or "footsteps" of Muhammad, why not examine the manifold ways that memories vector Muhammad for later generations or examine the changing sandal size of his footprints as later generations imagine him in their own image.

Thesis 7

We must ask of Islamic data what we would of any data. Or, to quote from Lincoln's fourth thesis, "The same destabilizing and irreverent questions one might ask of any speech act ought be posed of religious discourse."[50] We must accordingly analyze Islamic discourses and not simply transcribe or describe them using the terms and categories of insiders.

Thesis 8

As a social formation, Islam—like any such formation—is not a stable entity defined by readily ascertainable or accessible boundaries that effortlessly move throughout history. As social formations, these various Islams, or Muslim identities, are constantly cobbled together as opposed to simply being inherited—both synchronically and diachronically—in manifold ways.

Thesis 9

Islamic studies must appeal to the theoretical frameworks of other disciplines. History, for example, is a perfect antidote to the essentializing that passes for so much of what goes by the name of "critical" scholarship in the field. It is perhaps no coincidence that one of the hallmarks of Islamic religious studies is its presentism. Largely unconcerned with historical questions, the emphasis seems to be on thick descriptions of the manifold intersections between "Islam" and the "West," with very little analysis.

Thesis 10

Islamic studies must integrate itself with those critical discourses within the academic study of religion that are nonphenomenological. It cannot, as the essays collected in *Rethinking Islamic Studies* do, simply use theorists selectively and only when it suits them. The editors, Ernst and Martin, for example, invoke Talal Asad and reduce his complex work to the pithy statement: "He argued forcefully that Muslim societies must be understood on their own terms and not a superimposed model."[51] In this regard it is important to open the study of Islam up to other *critical* methodologies, not isolate it by gravitating to softer ones (e.g., cosmopolitanism, postcolonialism).

IV

The pithiness of these theses certainly demands further articulation and nuance, but neither time nor space permit me to do either here. Instead I have presented them as an initial step in the formation of what I hope will become the "new Islamic studies." This new study, as I move to conclude now, must be based on a new set of principles. Apologetical and theological study that passes for historical or critical scholarship confuses methods and, as a result, does no one any good. Instead, we need to sort out this confusion of method. This returns us to the axiom that all those who work with Islamic data (or any other data set, for that matter) must be self-reflexive about what they are doing, why they are doing it, and for whom they are doing it.

In this essay, as in my other recent work, I have attempted to call attention to, undermine from a theoretical perspective, and ultimately dismantle some of the regnant discourse associated with Islamic religious studies. Only once we do this can we begin the process of instigating a collective rethinking of the discipline. This rethinking, I submit, must go on at every level of our discipline: from the introductory textbook that introduces undergraduates to the field of Islam[52] to grad schools where the future generation of scholars of Islam can be exposed to critical discourses within the academic study of religion (and in such a manner that they are not afraid to apply them to their own data) to trade paperbacks that pronounce more "truthful" or, at least, nuanced accounts of the tradition.

The development of this "new Islamic studies" cannot take place in isolation, but must be part of the new conceptual modeling that is currently going on in religious studies. Scholars of Islam, students (both Muslim and non-Muslim), and general audiences (both Muslim and non-Muslim) must be exposed to a more nuanced version of the manifold traditions, practices, rites, and ideologies that we often conveniently label using the moniker "Islam."

As I conclude, let me reiterate the main point of this chapter. We need to replace much of the liberal theologizing that currently passes for scholarship with sober and disinterested analysis. We need to move, in short, from "Islamic religious studies" to the "new Islamic studies" that I have tried to chart in the third section of my chapter. Too often in the study of Islam—and, I think it is fair to say, the academic study of religion more generally—we reproduce the narratives that the people we study want us to tell about them. We take the rich complexities and complex richness of the many Islams that have existed historically and in the present and we flatten them into a set of stereotypes that reveal more about those who purport to study Islam than it does about actual Muslim identity formations.

Notes

A portion of this chapter appeared in chapter 6 of Aaron Hughes, *Theorizing Islam: Disciplinary Deconstruction and Reconstruction*. London: Acumen, 2012.

1. Friedrich Nietzsche, *Twilight of the Idols*.

2. Joy, "Postcolonial Reflections." Although a non-Islamicist, I here use Joy as an example of this larger apologetical postcolonialism that threatens the viability of the discipline. Overlooking or unaware of virtually all of the critical category analysis produced in religious studies at least since as early as Smith's *Map Is Not Territory*, Joy concludes that it "is time to accord the 'other'—be it a person or a religion—the integrity that is their due in an age when it is becoming increasingly difficult to do so" (192).

3. See, for example, Hughes, *Situating Islam*, and *Theorizing Islam*.

4. I am sure that many would point out that we do not present other religions any less apologetically. See, for example Lopez's study of Tibetan Buddhism in *Prisoners of Shangri-La*. And for an analysis of the general apologetic state of religious studies, see McCutcheon, *Manufacturing Religion*.

5. See the introduction to Hughes, *Theorizing Islam*.

6. McCutcheon, *Manufacturing Religion*, 3–26. For a similar critique, see Fitzgerald, *Ideology of Religious Studies*, 3–32. The classic study on how these assumptions enter the so-called comparative enterprise remains Smith, "In Comparison a Magic Dwells," in his *Imagining Religion*, 19–35; see also Smith, *Drudgery Divine*.

7. I first encountered the term in Ernst and Martin, eds., *Rethinking Islamic Studies*. Less cumbersome than "scholars of Islam working in departments of Religious Studies," I have opted to appropriate this term and use it pejoratively (though this is certainly not the manner in which Ernst and Martin use the term) in what follows to signify, both precisely and concisely, the set of largely apologetical discourses that currently characterize the field and against which I set up my own mode of analysis.

8. As of 2011, the major center for graduate training in Islamic religious stud-

ies is in North Carolina, particularly Duke and UNC–Chapel Hill, and at Emory University in Atlanta.

9. This desire to perpetuate the status quo of Islamic religious studies is clearly on display in the aforementioned book edited by Richard Martin (Emory) and Carl Ernst (UNC–Chapel Hill), *Rethinking Islamic Studies*, about which I shall have more to say below.

10. Parts of this section draw on and rework "The Scholarly Dream of Following Muhammad's Footsteps," which appears as chapter 1 in Hughes, *Theorizing Islam*.

11. Safi, *Memories of Muhammad*.

12. Ibid., 307.

13. Ibid., 32.

14. Ibid., 36–37.

15. Ibid., 14.

16. Ibid., 17.

17. Afsaruddin, *First Muslims*, xx.

18. Ramadan, *In the Footsteps of Muhammad*, xi.

19. "Recommended Reading."

20. Perhaps not coincidentally Omid Safi is also the cochair of this unit at the time of writing.

21. Afsaruddin, *First Muslims*, xx.

22. Ibid., 18.

23. Ibid., 160.

24. On the AAR and Tariq Ramadan, see Hughes, "Study of Islam before and after September 11." Tariq Ramadan is a Swiss scholar whom the AAR invited to present a plenary address on Islam in 2004, but the US government denied a visa to Ramadan, leading to a long legal battle over his exclusion from the US.

25. Ramadan, *In the Footsteps of Muhammad*, xi.

26. See, for example, Hughes, "Study of Islam before and after September 11."

27. The book was the winner of the inaugural Shaykh Muhammad Salih Bashrahil Prize for Cultural Achievement (Cairo) in 2004.

28. Ernst, *Following Muhammad*, 97.

29. Esposito and Mogahed, *Who Speaks for Islam?*, 123.

30. Ernst and Martin, "Introduction," 4.

31. Several excellent examples that come to mind are Powers, *Muhammad Is Not the Father*; and Shoemaker, *Death of Muhammad*.

32. Appiah, *Cosmopolitanism*, xv.

33. I am well aware of the closet assumption of Orientalism, so well-articulated in Said's work of the same name. For a good examination of Said's assumptions, see Varisco, *Reading Orientalism*.

34. "Islam Workshop."

35. I provide a genealogy of this version of Islam in Hughes, *Situating Islam*, 49–71.

36. Omid Safi, for example, opines that the marriage between Muhammad and Khadija, his first wife, "embodied a nurturing and loving relationship that lasted for twenty-five years" and that "this support and affection between Muhammad and his wife Khadija, *even their erotic relation*, would undoubtedly shape many of his views toward women." See Safi, *Memories of Muhammad*, 109 (italics added).

In like manner, Tariq Ramadan can write that "inside the mosque, the women would line up behind the men's ranks, as the postures of prayer, in its various stages, require an arrangement that preserves modesty, decency, and respect. Women prayed, studied, and expressed themselves in that space. Moreover, they found in the Prophet's attitude the epitome of courtesy and regard: he demanded that men remain seated in order to let women leave first and without inconvenience, there was always gentleness and dignity in his behavior toward women, whom he listened to, and whose right to express themselves and set forth their opinions and arguments he acknowledged, protected, and promoted." See Ramadan, *In the Footsteps of Muhammad*, 148.

37. But one example of this may be found in the work of Scott Siraj al-Haqq Kugle, who writes that

> the reformist or progressive approach must take into account new possibilities for human fulfillment in increasingly non-patriarchal societies like those evolving under democratic constitutions, where Muslims are living as minority communities and fellow citizens. In these new environments, it is possible for homosexual relationships to be based on ethical reciprocity, trust, justice, and love, just as heterosexual relationships ought to be based on these values in the ethical vision of the Qur'an. What matters is not the sex of the partner with whom one forms a partnership, as long as that partnership is contractual and on par with legal custom. Rather, what matters is the ethical nature of the relationship one has within the constraints of one's internal disposition, which includes sexual orientation and gender identity. (Kugle, *Homosexuality in Islam*, 3)

38. I have written about the impact of global events on the academic study of Islam in Hughes, "Failure of Islamic Studies Post–9/11".

39. In Ernst and Martin, "Introduction," for example, Ernst and Martin mention Asad and his *Genealogies of Religion* but reduce his complex work to the following utterance: "He argued forcefully that Muslim societies must be understood on their own terms and not a superimposed model" (9)! There is no engagement, for example, with Asad's critique of the political implications of the use and abuse of the very term "religion." Rather than simply state, as Ernst and Martin would imply, that Islam must be "understood on its own terms," Asad's claim is much more bold, implying that scholars of Islam should unpack generic and essential terms such as "Islam" into a variety of heterogeneous and historically specific elements, each one of which both embodies and reflects a variety of power relations

in local situations. This imbroglio of power relations, moreover, is something in which we as scholars are also invested, whether we know it or not or acknowledge it or not.

40. This is well articulated in Lopez, *Prisoners of Shangri-La*, 10–11.

41. On this more generally, see Wiebe, "Failure of Nerve." I reply to Wiebe's essay in Hughes, "Failure of Islamic Studies Post–9/11".

42. Lincoln, "Theses on Method." For a critique of the format of theses, see Fitzgerald, "Bruce Lincoln's Theses on Method"; and for Lincoln's response, see Lincoln, "Concessions, Confessions, Clarifications, Ripostes."

43. These theses, and much of this final section, originally appeared in Hughes, *Theorizing Islam*, chapter 6, "From Islamic Religious Studies to the 'New Islamic Studies.'"

44. A perfect example of this is Safi, *Progressive Muslims*. Incidentally, and again returning to the book recommendations of the unit chairs of the AAR, this book appears on the top five list of the "Contemporary Islam Group." See "Recommended Reading."

45. Lincoln, "Theses on Method," 225–26.

46. Esposito, *Unholy War*, xv.

47. Safi, *Memories of Muhammad*, 139 (italics added).

48. Ibid., 32 (italics added).

49. Omid Safi, "Between '*Ijtihad* of the Presupposition and Gender Equality," 73.

50. Lincoln, "Theses on Method," 226.

51. Ernst and Martin, "Introduction," 9.

52. This is something that I attempt to do in my textbook, Hughes, *Muslim Identities*.

10

Personal Self-Disclosure, Religious Studies Pedagogy, and the Skeptical Mission of the Public University

Martin S. Jaffee

Martin S. Jaffee visited the University of Alabama as the first Aronov lecturer in November 2002. The following essay is a revised version of the lecture that he presented.

In the public university, as a matter of legal principle, the study of religion is a historical and comparative enterprise. It is carefully distinguished from what is commonly still called the "seminary" model of religious study, one that can be found as well in private institutions historically linked to institutional churches. To oversimplify the contrast for the sake of moving along, we might put it this way: in the seminary model, the study of religion is motivated by the concern to present a particular faith tradition as a model for personal reflection and systematic embodiment; by contrast, the exponents of religious studies in the public university study religion in order to better understand human culture and history. The latter do not hope to convince their students that religion itself is necessarily a good thing, or that some religions—or a single religion—are better or truer than others. Professors of religious studies in public universities may be committed to teaching the truth *about* religion, but they are not in the business of professing the truth of religion or in the marketing of religious truths.

Now that I have oversimplified, let me recomplicate. As my colleagues in most academic Departments of Religious Studies well know, there are historically important and still-influential models of religious studies that have often been charged with concealing confessional commitments to religion in the language of academic interpretive discourse.[1] In such models, emerging in the late eighteenth century at the latest, the truth about religion is that it is, in some inchoate sense, "true"—or at least religion offers an angle of vision upon the world that discloses something we ignore to our own impoverishment. The "sacred" or the "holy" is really *THERE*, beckoning to us in the pluriform symbolic systems of the historical forms of religion. Our task as interpreters of these systems is to permit the sacred core to present itself to us and our students and, presumably, to humble or uplift us. Without such intuitive understanding of the sacred it is impossible to grasp what is involved in religion at all.

There are other models of religious studies, also deeply rooted in the history of Western Enlightenment traditions, which move in a different direction. These presuppose the illusory, delusional, or vicious nature of religion. They are usually styled as "empiricist" or "explanatory" models of religion. According to these models, the religious studies classroom is a place to expose and unmask religious error, to reduce religious ideas and beliefs to the economic, social, or psychological conditions that produce them in the first place. In these models, the truth about religion is that it is, in all senses that matter, "false." Or, at least, its claims about the world require reinterpretation in terms offered by one or another of the social sciences.

Most academic Departments of Religious Studies in public universities reflect the tensions between these two contrasting models. Many departments are tacitly or explicitly constructed to pursue one or the other point of view. In others, faculty hiring seeks to strike a balance between scholars sympathetic to religion and those hostile or, as they tend to put it, "neutral." In many settings, there appears to be a kind of polemical standoff. "Empiricists" charge their "hermeneutical" colleagues with smuggling sentimental religiosity into the classroom in the guise of secularist interpretation. "Hermeneutes," for their part, point out that empiricist explanations of religion are themselves grounded in a priori commitments that are embraced no less passionately than religious convictions—and are no more demonstrable or disinterested than those of the convictions they seek to displace.

My own graduate education at Brown University in the late 1970s was rigorously devoted to the "explanatory" models of religious studies. The department in those days contained a few faculty who were said to be "soft" on theological matters; but most of the big guns in graduate education were explicit that "serious" religious studies was a matter of reducing the data of religion to their social and cultural causes. I brought this attitude with me into my first academic job at the University of Virginia (UVA) in 1980. It was my practice, in those days, to inform my students about the "hermeneutical" model of religious studies; but my rhetoric and practice conveyed unmistakably that proponents of "hermeneutical" models should be suspected of committing covert theology until proven innocent. Having shown my students the errors introduced into the field by the excesses permitted under the "hermeneutical" orientation, in the first few years of my career, I spent most of my teaching time exploring the virtues of the "explanatory" models. But by 1987, when I left UVA for a position in Seattle, something most peculiar had begun to happen. A change had occurred in me that would continue to evolve through my first three or four years at the University of Washington.

To put it simply: I found myself increasingly distanced from the secular Jewish ethnicity in which I was raised from childhood and progressively drawn toward the religious practice of Jewish tradition in its more traditionalist forms. I will go into that story a bit more deeply in a moment. The main point of concern to me here is the impact of this personal change on the ways in which I pursued my profession as a teacher. My growth into what I suppose must be called an Orthodox Jewish religious identity did not at all inspire me to entirely abandon my commitment to a highly empiricist and rigorously reductionist model of religious studies pedagogy. Rather, without fully knowing where I was going with it, I began to develop a pedagogical style that foregrounded the apparent dissonance between the theory and practice of religion in my own life. I began to use my classroom as an opportunity to model a certain engagement with religion that combined rigorous theoretical critique of religion with an existential commitment to its practice. My method was to develop a controlled way of introducing my own experience with religion into the classroom discourse without turning the classroom into an autobiographical confessional.

Let me, then, take a few minutes to spell out in broad terms how I try to make this work. This will help me address three of the larger themes that I have attempted to explore. First, I will sketch out some ways in which I have found it helpful to turn myself into the object of my students' theoretical attention. Then I will indicate how the trust built through such self-reflection enables me to encourage students to engage in wide-ranging critiques of their own epistemological commitments—including commitments to the critical study of religion. Finally, I will spell out a few thoughts on how this type of religious studies pedagogy might contribute to and reflect the larger intellectual mission of the public university.

In my twenty-two years of experience as a professor of religious studies at public universities, I can probably count on two hands the number of students who have either been imaginatively daring in their religious faith or imaginatively daring in their rejection of religion for some other more compelling alternative. The overwhelming majority have been what I call conventionally pious or conventionally skeptical. That is to say, most have been thoroughly comfortable and secure in their inherited traditions of mind and sentiment. I have come to believe that the most valuable thing I can offer my students in their study of religion is to challenge their conventionalism. I have sought to do this not by overt confrontation but, rather, a more seductive approach—by inviting my students to consider my own situation.

In this enterprise I have an obvious advantage over colleagues whose outward appearances do not mark them so clearly as a member of a distinctive religious community. Most of my students, just by looking at me, assume they know where I stand. They assume at the outset that I will be a salesman for religion. My job as their teacher is to foil those assumptions as systematically as possible. I am, in fact, a salesman; but rather than selling religion in general or *my* religion in particular, I am a salesman for the study of religion. I represent a discipline that offers students the possibility of gaining—as an immediate return for their investment in efforts of understanding—critical interpretive distance from their own autobiographies. In my teaching I hope to enable students to reconsider the entire question of how the academy's mission of explaining and understanding religion might inform their own engagements *with* or disengagements *from* the religious opportunities they encounter in their own lives. The most direct way to encourage them in this project, it seems to me, is to show them how I do it myself. So in carefully constructed contexts, I make it clear that I am, for better or worse, a historian of religion who, in the full light of adulthood and a professional career in religious studies, chose to enter intensely into the life of the very religious community whose theology and historical memory I routinely subject to dissection and criticism in my teaching and research.

Accordingly, I find it very helpful from time to time to find ways of sharing myself as data for the study of religion and Judaism. I do so by filtering my personal experiences within Judaism through the prism of theoretical concepts in the study of religion or historical processes in the Judaic tradition. Let me offer here a couple of brief examples. The first comes from my introductory course on the study of religion, the second comes from an introduction to Judaism.

In the Universtiy of Washington program of comparative religion, all majors must take, among other things, a course on theoretical paradigms for the study of religion. One of the classical questions for such courses is the status of "religious experience." Students generally enter this course assuming that there is some sort of core experience that is uniquely religious and thus underlies all religions. Or they assume that each religion has at its foundation some sort of unique experience that is historically identical over time and distinguishes followers of one tradition from those of another. My own bias, as you may have anticipated, is that "religious experience" is a chimera and the search for such essential experiences is the ultimate quixotic enterprise. Good Durkheimian that I am, I feel bound to focus upon the role of social conditioning and peer groups in training members of religious communities in a certain vocabulary of symbolic expressions and in interpreting whatever inchoate personal experiences they may have in terms of the inherited symbolic vocabulary. I give my students an opportunity to read some sample discussions of the matter from the "explanatory" and "hermeneutical" schools and encourage them to consider the merits of each account. But in explaining my own preference for the social-conditioning paradigm of religious experience, I find it helpful to report upon my own migration into Orthodox Jewish life.

As I explain it to my students, mine was a Judaic migration utterly devoid of any blinding encounter with the God of Israel or his commanding presence. There was no single, life-transforming decision that turned me from one life path onto another, no primal experience of any particular kind. Rather, in my case, it all happened to sneak up on me. To be sure, the very decision to pursue the historical study of Judaism already suggested that I sought some clues to my own identification as a Jew. But this took no formally "religious" forms until my arrival in Charlottesville, Virginia, as an assistant professor in 1980. As the one Jewish studies professor in a small southern town with a tiny community of active Jews, my skills in Hebrew and knowledge of Judaism's history were of some value to a small prayer group that met on Sabbaths. Invited to participate, I felt an obligation to help them out. I had been trained, after all, to see myself as a resource for the Jewish community.

Over time, the pleasures of this group's company brought me more intimately into its processes. I began to knit myself into its way of life, particularly, its rhythms of Sabbaths, festivals, and days of mourning. I found an increasingly exciting set of connections between my own intellectual work at the university and my growing capacity to weave that work into my social experience in Jewish fellowship. Somehow I had become an observant Jew, a member of a Jewish community.

Eventually, I grew impatient with the group that had once taught me how to practice Judaism; I wanted a richer, more complex community within which to explore the growing connections between my professional Jewish persona and my internal Jewish landscape. I found such communities when I made my professional move to Seattle. I explored many of them until, much to my surprise, I found myself most at home in a Ha-

sidicly tinged Orthodoxy. It was in this group that I found a level of lit-
eracy in Jewish tradition that challenged me to grow in my own. It was
also here that I found compelling moral exemplars who taught me the
meaning of genuine devotion to values beyond self cast in a vocabulary
sanctified by millennia of continuous use. And it was here that I found
support and love when struck by poor health and other of life's great and
small tragedies.

To get to the point, my own story of Jewish conversion to Orthodoxy
can be told entirely without appeals to any single core experience or "moment" of conversion. It is rather a story of continual small tinkerings and
accommodations, unpremeditated choices, continuously revised through
social migration through a variety of different types of communities. This
way of telling my Jewish story, as it were, serves me well in my agenda with
my students. Why do I think that religious experience is a spurious explanation for religious behavior? Because my own religious behavior can be
explained in great detail without reference to it. Do I desire religious experience? You bet—I would welcome once and for all the voice of the living
God booming out of my Talmudic text. In this I am like the monk who
carefully walks the path of religious discipline in the hopes of receiving a
unio mystica that never arrives. But in the meantime, I will take my solace
in the perusal of the Talmudic text with my study partner over a glass of
seltzer and a piece of cake. And that is really just fine.

My second example of pedagogical autobiography is drawn from a variety of introductory courses in Judaism. One of the organizing themes
of these courses is the way in which Judaic representations of the past are
shaped and reshaped by the experience of the Jewish groups charged with
transmitting the meaning of Jewish tradition. Here the theoretical issue is
to illustrate, from the history of Judaism, how a culture's interpretations of
its past are continuously mobilized to address a current interest. To understand the meaning of representations of the past, that is, one must understand the historical conditions under which these representations are produced.

One way I illustrate this is to trace the history of the term "Holocaust"
as an interpretation of the catastrophe that befell European Jewry in the
Second World War. Most of my students do not know much about the
Holocaust, other than that it occurred and that it somehow is very important to contemporary Jewish communities. My own interest in it is not in
the mechanics of the genocide of Jewry but rather in how that genocide
has come to deliver diverse messages to the Jewish communities of North
America and Israel. A fundamental issue I want my students to consider

is the remarkable gap in time between the end of the genocide in 1945 and the emergence, in the late 1960s, of a consistent and cogent message about the meaning of the genocide that galvanized Jewish communities around the world.

As many sociologists and historians have observed, something barely acknowledged or discussed throughout the 1950s had become by the early 1970s a universal Jewish symbol. Here I find that a small detail of my childhood dramatically illustrates the degree to which the symbolism of the Holocaust has come to dominate the Jewish world in ways unimaginable soon after the war. Between 1960 and 1966 I attended a suburban New York public high school with a Jewish population of roughly 75 percent. Throughout these years I studied German. Of a class of thirty or so, probably twenty-seven were Jews. I do not know what brought all of us together into that class. But I do recall that as part of our education in German language and culture we learned to sing a series of Christmas carols in the original German. I can still sing "Stille Nacht, Heilige Nacht" if called upon in an emergency. The amazing thing about this from the perspective of contemporary Jewish culture in America is that we sang those songs year after year with not a single complaint from us or our parents about the incongruity of Jewish children, many of whom were children of death camp survivors, singing German Christmas carols not more than a generation after the German genocide of the Jews. Such a scenario could scarcely be imagined in American Jewish life after 1970, once the symbolic language of the Holocaust had finally emerged at the center of Jewish life. Yet I, born after the genocide, well remember a time before the meaning of the Holocaust was clear to me or my parents. After that time my singing of German carols would be a moral impossibility, but prior to that moment it barely drew comment. Jewish memory, structured around the symbol of Holocaust, now proscribes behaviors that only a short time ago were regarded as uncontroversial.

What do I gain from this strategy of selective, theory-driven self-disclosure in the classroom? Students see, first of all, that participation in a religious system need not entail blindness to its operative mechanisms or uncritical celebration of its results. Students also see the obvious point that there is no formal correlation between knowledge of critical approaches to the study of religion and dismissal of religion as a form of life capable of eliciting one's own deepest loyalties and commitments. My own example of culling my personal experience for illustrations of theoretical concepts in the study of religion encourages in my students a willingness to risk their own precommitments to explore with me the dimensions of an intellectual discipline into which I invite them. When I am successful, it is because my students perceive me as an honest broker who will not seduce them into an untenable personal position. Rather, they often find it encouraging to see, through my example, that one comes out on the other side of criticism a whole person.

I do not believe that this self-disclosive pedagogical style can be employed only by teachers who share with me an intense participation in a contemporary religious community. Indeed, I imagine that relatively few of my colleagues in religious studies have the sort of religious autobiography that I represent. Quite a few indeed grew up in intensely lived religious communities, only to leave them in young adulthood. For many of these colleagues, the critical perspectives of religious studies served as goads or guides in what must have been profound processes of self-criticism and self-discovery. Others, perhaps a majority, grew up at the edges of religious communities or out of all communion with them. But they found in religious studies a way of experiencing more richly the implications of their own continuously made choices to live in the light of explicitly humanistic, this-wordly frames of meaning. Teachers embodying each of these paths of experience—or others that we could imagine—present equally important testimony to the manifold ways in which the academic study of religion can serve as a loom on which teachers weave the meaning of their own life choices into the fabric of the discourse into which they induct their students.

As I pointed out earlier, the trust developed by selectively surrendering my experience to theoretical scrutiny earns me an important kind of credibility with my students. I have found that students are slower to act defensively to critical discourse once they have seen the teacher turned into the object of such discourse. The exploitation of my own experience as part of my pedagogy has enabled me to create in my students a certain receptivity to the various sorts of threatening lines of thought and their conclusions, which students must come to live with if they are to study religion with imagination and sensitivity. As I explain to them, there is a lot of bad news out there, if we follow theoretical models for the study of religion to their ultimate conclusions.

Sometimes, for my conventionally pious students, the bad news is rather self-evident, requiring only a moment of reflection to be appreciated. For example, it is bad news for some to discover that the religions of "primitives," "heathens," "pagans," and so forth penetrate deeply into the so-called advanced religions—the monotheistic religions practiced by my Jewish, Christian, and Muslim students in real life. Sometimes the bad news has to accumulate slowly in order for scattered insights to congeal into a troubling picture. It is bad news, for example, to learn, as we must, that the history recorded in sacred writings such as the Bible leads us to pasts that never existed as the creators and transmitters of such writings have imagined them. Similarly, it is bad news for many to discover that "revelation" in monotheistic religions is, among other things, a political rhetoric that privileges the authority of one textual community in its rivalries with others. And it is very troubling indeed to entertain the possibility that the savage hatreds unleashed in the history of monotheism may be essential to it rather than bizarre aberrations in religions that are all about love. All this is bad news indeed. But it is distributed equally among the Jews, Christians, and Muslims in my class.

Of course, since one man's ceiling is another man's floor, all this bad news for monotheists is really good news for my conventionally pious skeptics. It but confirms all they have suspected about the primitive, mindless, and superstitious foundations of religion from which they, in their courageous, unblinking secularism, are radically free. This is why they suffer most intensely from what is for them the worst, most vertiginous news of all. This news is that all the explanatory discourses of the modern university—the very theoretical paradigms that have helped us to discover and deliver all this bad news to religious folks—are themselves grounded in systems of power and authorization of which the appeal to universal reason is the fundamental mystification. To recognize this, of course, is to unmask all of our high-minded skeptical administration of bitter truths as yet another regime of reality construction that awaits its own dismemberment as truth. Yes, the most disorienting news of all is that skepticism is yet another program seeking to bring coherence to reality and to anchor the human project in a larger pattern of meaning—as defined by certain groups in positions of cultural and political authority.

Now, obviously, different sorts of courses and their student constituencies lend themselves more and less to different sorts of bad news. The sorts of messages I have just listed are germane in my little piece of the religious studies turf, where I offer courses on theoretical approaches to the study of religion, a general introduction to the monotheistic religions, and broad offerings in the history of Judaism. But I believe they are quite transportable to the study of other religious traditions with only a small bit of tinkering. The main thing is to construct courses that create an opportunity to see how the angles of vision enabled by critical discourses lead reflexively back to a critique of those very discourses. Criticism unmasks the rhetoric of religions, yet it also, when taken seriously, unmasks itself. Criticism has constructed the facts that we teach about religion and religions, yet criticism also discloses the ways in which facts are themselves manufactured to serve certain unquestioned programs of truth. Programs with different goals, therefore, or in pursuit of different agendas, might construct rather different constellations of facts.

To be entirely honest, I am rarely as successful as I would like to be in bringing my students to inhabit the self-reflexive critical space I seek to construct for them. Most of my students just want "the facts," thank you very much, and most basically want to know what I "really" believe so that they can say what they think I want to hear. And I do normally let them get away with that more or less. After all, I ask myself—am I really prepared in my role as a state employee to deal with the potential consequences of radical intellectual vertigo among students who can no longer live in their conventional religious or secularist pieties? Here and there, maybe yes—but hardly as a steady routine, day in and out.

That being said, I confess that I always walk into the first day of class harboring the fantasy that I am about to change lives in profound and constructive ways. And the power of this fantasy, I suppose, is driven by my desire to affect some of my students as deeply as I myself had been affected by my own education in an undergraduate Department of Religious Studies. When I think back on it, one of my most memorable and formative encounters with the general "bad news theory" of pedagogy came in spring 1970, when I was twenty-two. That spring I had interrupted my studies in the Religion Department of Syracuse University to engage in political action that, I had convinced myself, bore the promise of redemptive liberation for all humanity. Before leaving town, I dropped in on one of my professors who, it happens, actually taught in the Philosophy Department. His name was Theodore Denise. I decided to visit Prof. Denise because he taught a terrific course on epistemology. I had myself witnessed his ability to think out of existence the very lectern upon which his notes rested as he guided us through the idealism of Bishop Berkeley. This qualified him, in my view, to receive my own meditations on the meaning of existential political engagement.

So I sat in Prof. Denise's office—as I recall, my feet were bare and my upper body was clad only in a leather vest with a fleece lining—and explained how it was time to take the university's critical ideas and live them out in practice. That knowledge sundered from action rendered the knowledge itself valueless. I thought these allusions to the early Marx would impress him with the seriousness of my decisions. Prof. Denise listened very carefully, nodding frequently. I recall that he had a few things to say, most of them encouraging. But he closed with a comment that has stayed with me, and the meaning of which I am still progressively discovering. He said: "Yes, it's important to act on your knowledge. But it's also important to know how hard it is to know anything."

I am not entirely sure that Prof. Denise intended anything more profound than the simple reminder to be cautious. And he was surely not the first professor I had in college who pointed toward the difficulty of claiming knowledge. But without either of us knowing it at the time, what he said would become a theme to which I would return over and over in my development as a teacher. So let me now share with you how I see the implications of this theme for the ways in which Departments of Religious Studies may position themselves in the larger work of the public university.

It is precisely in this epistemological conundrum that I find the deepest connection between the work we do in the study and teaching of religion and the teaching mission of the public university. In my experience at two public universities, when tax-supported universities try to market themselves to state legislatures, the focus is on the role of the university as a site in which knowledge is stored and disseminated. I have always been uncomfortable with this. For my vision of the university has always been that it ought to be the place where what passes for knowledge is taken apart. What, after all, are our academic fields and disciplines but convenient conceptual and bureaucratic boxes within which to organize skepticism into programs of research and discovery? And in the humanities, generally speaking since the incorporation of the postmodern moment into our conceptual toolbox, we add to this the organized skepticism about the very methods we have devised to lead us beyond opinion to knowledge. That is, skepticism is itself a fitting subject of skeptical critique.

Many of my colleagues in other departments of the humanities and social sciences fully accept this understanding of the university's mission as a critic of what passes for knowledge. Yet they often still ask how the religious studies enterprise fits into this mission. They labor under the mistaken impression that the Department of Religious Studies is a kind of ecumenical seminary for the celebration of virtue and probity and the reinforcement of nurturing truths. In my discussions with them, I have to deliver yet more bad news. Those of us who are committed to the academic study of religion stand, in my view, at the center of the public university's exercise in organized skepticism.

The reason is simple. However we might wish to define that notoriously hopeless term "religion," we wish to claim that it provides one of the historically most ubiquitous models of a comprehensive, compelling, and utterly convincing body of knowledge that shaped human enterprises over centuries and even millennia of continuous tradition. And even after the collapse of religion's self-evidence in the face of the diverse modernist revolutions, it seems clear that whatever has replaced or shall replace religion must aspire in some sense to do the job of religion—to organize human sentiment, will, belief, and action into coherent patterns capable of sustaining meaningful life for billions of people. We live in an age, moreover, when it is increasingly obvious that the most compelling candidates to replace "religion" are the postmodern reinventions of the very religions that modernity was supposed to have deposed from authority. We are entitled, therefore, to entertain some skepticism about the cultural finality of the very skepticism upon which is grounded our entire enterprise.

In my view, the Religious Studies Department in the public university is one of those places in which skepticism about even skepticism is most productively explored. This is because, historically speaking, the field of religious studies has made its business to be the persistent critique of the most comprehensive systems of ideological construction human beings have produced. These systems number among them religions, most obviously. But we have come to recognize that they include as well cultural systems of all sorts that make claims to universal validity. And this includes the Cult of the Infinite Accumulation of Universal Knowledge of which the modern university serves as the principal sacrificial shrine, of which its faculty serves as the priesthood, and of which its students serve as proselytes. Our work—built upon the disciplines of linguistic study and the mastery of textual traditions in diverse oral, written, and figurative media—is rigorously historicizing, contextualizing, and comparative. Our range of interpretive material includes those provided by the entire recorded history of human cultures. And most importantly, it imposes upon us the obligation to historicize, contextualize, and compare, as cultural practices, the very systems of thought and disciplines of behavior that enable us to contextualize, and at least rhetorically disassemble, the worlds of our predecessors. If religion is subject to critical contextualization, so too is the critique of religion a candidate for historicization and deconstruction.

The seventeenth- and eighteenth-century Enlightenment cultures of criticism produced "religion" as the antitype of their own will to cultural power. Religion was constructed as an intellectual aberration that afflicted humanity in its childhood but which now, through the free exercise of reason, could be overcome. The idea of religion as a universal cultural force grounded elsewhere than in reason, in turn, generated the field of religious studies as an academic enterprise that would delimit the origins, nature, and functions of religion in a world growing beyond the power of religion to define or even to grasp. But now that we well know that religion continues to define the world for billions of our coinhabitants of the planet—even in the midst of the processes of secularization, industrialization, and globalization that were to spell its permanent demise—it is time to begin to grasp how our academic culture of criticism has failed to understand what has befallen us. To what degree did our critical constructions of "religion" themselves *create* the illusion that religious illusion could be thought out of existence? Is it possible, after all, that the culture of criticism is itself grounded in a kind of "faith"? Can we explore the proposition that differences between "religion" and the culture of academic criticism are differences of emphasis and degree rather than kind?

It is time to draw these ruminations to a close: as I reflect upon the teaching strategies I have adopted—particularly self-referential theorizing and the bending of theory back against itself—it seems to me that what I have been after is a way of enlisting my students as coconspirators against their own most intuitively obvious convictions. For what is the "intuitively obvious" other than an example of a belief held to be true simply because I live among others who do not question it? Well, as I have written elsewhere[2]—if there is some qualitative distinction between the thinking about religion that happens in a university and the thinking about religion that happens on a barstool, that difference has something to do with the university's commitment to counter the "intuitively obvious" with the impertinent "what's so obvious?" Here I will only add that among the "intuitively obvious" propositions subject to criticism is one that stands at the foundation of many of our critical enterprises—that academic criticism itself can proceed from an Archimedean point that is somehow beyond criticism.

This comforting naïveté of secularist faith is lost to us for the foreseeable future. It was founded, in no small measure, upon the successful critique of the comforting naïveté of traditionalist religious faith. But having succeeded in its work, it overtook and consumed itself. Our own cultural moment is epistemologically more humble than premodern religion or modern criticism could ever be. And the embodiment of that epistemological humility, I submit, is a professor of religious studies who is not ashamed to say, "This is what has happened to me," "this is how theory illumines what has happened to me," and, finally, "this is where theory itself begins to fall apart." Where this leaves us all epistemologically, I leave for philosophers to consider. But by illustrating in our own lives how the universalist claims of theory rub against the irreducible particularity of the personal, we teachers of religious studies offer our students at the public universities an opportunity to bring their whole educations and their whole selves into the drama of the examined life.

Notes

This essay, a revised version of the lecture that Jaffee presented in November 2002, was published, along with responses from faculty in the University of Alabama Department of Religious Studies, in the *Bulletin of the Council of Societies for the Study of Religion* 33, 2 (2004). It is published with permission of the copyright holder, Equinox Publishing.

   1. A particularly trenchant critique of such concealment is offered by McCutcheon in his fine book, *Critics Not Caretakers*.

   2. Jaffee, "Fessing Up in Theory."

Afterword

Reinventing the Study of Religion in Alabama

Russell T. McCutcheon

Preamble to Some Final Words

Given my own critique of the field, and, more specifically, my critique of how we, as scholars, often use the category of religion (i.e., to name an immaterial disposition that is supposedly pan-human), it may strike some readers familiar with my work as odd to find me writing this afterword or to learn that I chaired the department from 2001–2009, the period when we invented this lecture series, and, following my colleague Ted Trost's four years as chair, that I have just returned to the role. Prior to offering some concluding thoughts, I therefore think it useful to address some of these issues head on, hopefully in a way that links up with what I see to be important about this volume.

I remember hearing from a faculty member who worked with me when I was first hired to chair the Department of Religious Studies at the University of Alabama, back in 2001, that colleagues elsewhere in the country wanted to know what it was like to work with me since I was—in their opinions—intent on destroying the field. Such a judgment is sadly evidence of just how carefully we read each other (or, as the case may be, not read each other). Given how much I had written early on in my career concerning how I thought the study of religion ought to be organized and carried out, seeing a job announced (while I was working in southwest Missouri back in 2000) for the chair of a small BA- granting program in a major US state university that was, at the time, in need of reinvention, well, it seemed a good place to put my money where my mouth was, as we say. That we are still here hopefully indicates that destroying the field is not among my goals.

One of the curious things to me is that while many scholars critique "literature" or "culture," few if any of these critics think that Departments of English or Anthropology ought to cease to exist; instead, the argument is that a reconceptualized taxon will lead to a new way of talking about human behavior or the stuff that we seem to leave behind after we are gone (like those things we call texts, buildings, languages, or bureaucracies). So the rhetoric of "a threat to the field" is, I think, actually providing cover for another, unarticulated claim: *the field as it has come to be practiced by so-and-so or by those who think and act like so-and-so.* That is, my critique of the field is a critique of a certain way of approaching a subdomain of human practices, human *arts de faire* (to nod to the subtitle of Michel de Certeau's 1980 book, better known in English as *The Practice of Everyday Life*): a critique of assuming that some features of human beings somehow escapes the manner in which we study other mundane (but no less interesting because of it) things that people do. It is a terribly pompous position, if you think about it, for it dehistoricizes and depersonalizes the field as a domain of human practices, as if academia exists in some unchanging, Platonic realm, whereby any interloper who comes along and thinks that it is changeable, that it is contingent, and that it could be otherwise is, well, a threat. Of course, if this thing called the field or the discipline was as static and uniform as this position maintains then how could anyone be a threat to it? That is, built into the charge is the implicit acknowledgment that in fact things *could indeed* be different—perhaps radically different— and the wagons had better be circled against the incursion of novelty that is beholden to a different set of interests, seeking to achieve different goals.

So just because I am a critic of how many Departments of Religious Studies in North America or throughout the rest of the world are organized and the kind of work that takes place within them (whether they go by that name or the many others we group together in our field) does not mean that my goal is to destroy a unit within a university. Instead, the goal is to figure out how to rework it to accomplish something novel. For if we all know that "literature" is a convenient placeholder for a wide array of artifacts and that we use this word as a shorthand for complex debates among scholars or among the people they study, concerning what an author is, what a reader is, what a text is, and what they all accomplish, then why should the academic study of religion have to follow purer rules than Departments of English?

I'd like to think that I am pragmatic and that, while the people with whom I work have not had to reinvent themselves entirely, they have at least mulled over a few topics that do not just strike me alone as worth thinking through. After all, there is little, if anything, new in much of the work I have done—we stand on the shoulders of giants, after all. My own initial critique of the field, conceptualized and written in the late 1980s and early 1990s, was an attempt to apply in my own field the debates that had long been taking place in English literature—it is not a coincidence that, say, a literary critic like Terry Eagleton (at least his writings on literary criticism, as opposed to his more recent writings on theology) figures prominently in the citations of my early work. Although various rear guard actions resulted, some more successful than others, on the part of those trying to protect the aesthetic autonomy of what we might as well just call literariness, I'd like to think that, on the whole, English literature is healthier for confronting how its practitioners use such technical terms as text, author, writing, or meaning. Whether religious studies has equally benefitted from this type of critique has yet to be decided, I think, for despite the prominence now of the terms "method and theory," it is hardly common to come across scholars of religion who see their domain as but an ordinary subdomain of, say, culture—a domain that, for the sake of taxonomic convenience (i.e., there are only so many hours in the day and we cannot study "it all"), we further subdivide into something we call religion or economics. Instead, although they think they have shaken off a previous generation's theological motives, their work seems animated by the assumption that within this one domain, that which we call religion, we find the deepest and truest yearnings of this thing that we call the human.

But leaving the rest of the field behind for the moment, at least when it comes to the University of Alabama, I'd like to think that the strategies that we have adopted here (a reinvention from the top to the bottom, as I will discuss in a moment) to revitalize the study of religion have been pretty successful. We are still here, after all, people's careers are thriving and mortgages are being paid, many scholars whose careers started here have moved to wonderful jobs elsewhere, students are excited and using their degrees in innumerably inventive ways, and so that has to say something, no? We are small, yes, but I'd like to think that nimble, little programs can set national agendas as much as the ones that think they run the game (after all, we still judge ourselves based on how big our department is). For no one owns the game and, yes, things can be different. We are evidence of that. It does not come easy, but heck, what of worth does?

So in closing this preamble I recall the scholar at a much larger department in a state university, with masters and doctoral students, who, when I was visiting there to give a guest lecture some years ago, asked me somewhat incredulously, "What are *you* doing at a school like *that*?" (It reminded me, at the time, of the lamenting tone of some US friends when they responded to the news that I was moving to a job in Alabama—you could hear their old stereotypes of the South despite their congratulations and well wishes.) This was a tremendously impertinent question, if you think about it, though of course it was sugarcoated in collegial banter. But it was not disrespectful to me, for at this moment in higher education we all should be thankful to have a job; rather, it demeaned the program that hired me and invented this lecture series, the students who attend our classes and public lectures, the donors who made the endowment that funds the series possible, the preceding group of eminently qualified authors who came to Tuscaloosa to speak to us about their work, and the people who produced the book that you now hold in your hands. I hope readers are able to look at our situation rather more generously than that colleague and that they are willing to entertain that—yes, I will say it— size does not really matter.

*   *   *

At seven o'clock in the evening of Monday, November 4, 2002, Professor Martin Jaffee, of the University of Washington, delivered a public lecture at the University of Alabama. Hosted by the members of the Department of Religious Studies and funded by the department's Aaron Aronov Endowment for Judaic Studies, his lecture was the first in what has now become our annual Aronov Lecture. Next door to my office is the seminar room that the department uses and there hang the nicely framed flyers that advertised each of these events (a corresponding copy was presented to each lecturer so, hopefully, they still occupy places of pride in offices all over the country). Thinking back on that first evening, and now looking over this volume that collects a decade's worth of lectures, provides an opportunity to pause and consider from where we have come and how we got here.

Although we were an average-sized department when I arrived in 2001 from what was then known as Southwest Missouri State University to become the department chair, what sets us apart now—or, better put, what makes us an example worth considering—is that we have gone from only one of those faculty members (myself) being tenured back in 2001 to (at the time of my first writing this) having all but one faculty member tenured (at the time of publication we will have been joined by Eleanor Finnegan, a second tenure-track colleague). Due to the long predicted demographic shift among the professoriate, no one currently serving in this department as a faculty member has been here longer than our immediate past department chair, Ted Trost (who arrived as a tenure-track assistant professor, straight out of grad school at Harvard, in August 1998).[1] So, despite being of average size, we are rather different from the portrait found in the American Academy of Religion's *Census* from a few years back, in which the tenured to tenure-track ratio for the average department was about 3:1. For when I arrived in August 2001 our ratio was 0.2 tenured colleagues for every 1 tenure-track professor; but, with an anticipated tenure-track search in 2013–14 (to replace our deceased colleague Tim Murphy, who arrived in Tuscaloosa in 2002) along with our newly hired tenure-track colleague who began work in August 2013 (Eleanor Finnegan, mentioned above), the ratio is now 4:3, which is a rather far ways from 0.2:1 just over a decade ago.

With this dramatic change in faculty rank in mind, the question that lies in the background of our decade-old lecture series is: How does one reinvent a Department of Religious Studies in the early twenty-first century? For, although not stated explicitly, the establishment of this series, let alone the prominent place for its framed flyers (along with the forty-or-so framed flyers for our more informal "Religion *in* Culture"[2] lecture series that also line a wall in the seminar room, not to mention all those lunchtime discussions we have hosted where our students met visitors as well as professors from across our own campus), is evidence of a set of self-consciously developed strategies to revive a small department in a major public university—putting our own social theory to good use. But to know this story fully, we need a little more background: when I arrived twelve years ago, the unit had just been judged "nonviable" by the statewide accrediting body (more on that below), a new dean of the College of Arts and Sciences had just been hired, the previous year's search for a new chair had ended in a failed search, and the state of Alabama was in yet another "proration" year, in which various sectors of state government (such as education—including elementary, secondary, and higher education) were constitutionally mandated to return significant portions of their already committed operating budgets—conditions that might cause one to be somewhat pessimistic about the future of this small department filled with nontenured faculty. But the fact that our dean had, in his first year on the job (2000–2001), committed once again to search for an outside chair (the position into which I was then hired, as of August 2001) had already made clear that our challenge was to reinvent the study of religion—in the eyes of the accreditors, yes, but also in the eyes of university administrators, colleagues, as well as the students who might see majoring in the study of religion as something worth doing.

As with many North American programs in the academic study of re-

ligion, the University of Alabama's—by my accounting, still the only publicly funded Department of Religious Studies granting a BA major in the
state—dates to the mid- to late 1960s (it is tough to pin down an actual
date; only someone spinning an origins tales, such as this, could possibly
conjure up a definitive beginning, since the current department developed from various antecedents that do not much resemble what we today call comparative religion, the history of religions, or simply religious
studies). Prior to that, the university certainly offered courses on religious
topics, but—as with so many other programs in the US and Canada at
that time—they were indeed *religious* topics studied *religiously* and, what's
more, taught on a volunteer basis by a variety of religious functionaries
who were already involved in various forms of campus ministry. As described frankly in the university's 1965 proposal to the Danforth Foundation, requesting financial support to institute a new Department of Religious Studies: "These courses have been limited to two hours credit, and
students have been permitted to count no more than eight hours in the
department toward graduation. The ministers have received no pay for
their teaching. Courses have been devised and offered according to the
interests of the individual campus ministers with little thought given to
the general curriculum in religion or to its relation to the over-all University curriculum. As one might expect, the quality of the courses has been
mixed."[3] According to an October 1964 document that was included with
this proposal, between the fall 1960 and the fall 1964 semesters, a total of
81 courses were taught (with an average of 9 courses per semester), with a
total of 3,253 students attending these courses, averaging 40 students per
class and 365 students per semester—simply put, there was quite an operation up and running despite no department actually being present, at
least as we today understand the composition and mission of a Department of Religious Studies. Given the voluntary nature of the instructors
staffing these courses, these are truly impressive numbers; but, for such
reasons as early 1960s US Supreme Court judgments banning prayer in
public schools as unconstitutional, the increasing interest in "the East" that
was occasioned first by the war in Korea and then the "police action" in
Vietnam, as well as the counter-culture movement of this period, studying
religion as a religious vocation was, by the time of the mid-1960s, starting
to give way to a professionalization of the field.

Although the voluntary, "pot luck" nature of the curriculum at that time
was definitely a "good buy" for that day's administration (given that its
instructors were all voluntary), for a public university these classes were
rather troublesome, for their topics (let alone the manner in which they

were more than likely taught) were (as with much of the North American field back then) exclusively drawn from a Protestant seminary model, including such standards as: Old Testament, New Testament, Faith and Reason, Life and Teaching of Jesus, Christian Ethics, and the perennial Contemporary Religious Thought. Whatever the quality of these courses, the rationale that drove them was exploring the foundations of the faith, and that faith was a form of Protestant Christianity. Of course there were also those more specialized classes that simply narrowed the focus, such as individual courses on such figures from early Christian history as Peter, John, or Paul (as, lamentably, happens so often when one moves through a curriculum to this day—the exact same skills are taught at all levels and only the focus intensifies, from studying the meaning of the entire New Testament in a survey course to eventually writing a dissertation on the meaning of but one verse). Although likely not peculiar to our state, there was even an entire course, offered once every semester, on the Ten Commandments (as one of the department's standard classes it seated a total of 549 students in the early 1960s). What's more, I would hazard a guess that, much like the earlier course in archeology, its Hebrew language course (offered in the fall of 1960 and which attracted only five students), the course on the significantly titled Old Testament (offered every semester and seating 456 students in total—a course title finally changed to Hebrew Bible only during the time of our current Aronov chair, Steve Jacobs), along with the course on Judaism (offered only three times and seating a total of 38 students) were more than likely all efforts to find new significance in "other" people's textual artifacts—artifacts that, importantly, were assumed not just to predate but, as this old theological model presupposed, prepare the way for the eventual Good News (what was once, following a work by the fourth-century Christian apologist Eusebius, called in Latin *praeparatio evangelica*).

In the nearly forty years between the Danforth proposal and that first Aronov Lecture, a lot happened to ensure that the department moved away from its earlier overt theological motives and, instead, to work toward training students in an anthropocentric approach, studying religion cross-culturally and in a descriptive and comparative manner. Among the most evident of the changes was the arrival (and, eventually, the retirement) of faculty who had earned PhDs in what was then the newly forming field of religious studies. The first chair of the restructured department was Joseph Bettis, who stayed only several years after his arrival in 1964 and eventually retired an emeritus professor at Western Washington University; the late Leon Weinberger came to Tuscaloosa in 1964 as the director of the local chapter of the Hillel Foundation but was hired full-time by the department soon after (and then retired in 1999); Patrick Green, the long-time chair of the department and into whose faculty line I was hired, was first hired in 1970 and retired in 2000 (though we have seen him around teaching a course here and there since then); and William Doty first came to the department in 1981, retired in 2001, but, like Patrick, still teaches on campus for different units. Luckily, the College of Arts and Sciences had the foresight to fill these open lines (usually) with tenure-track hires; although it might be an error to suggest that the department thrived during the 1970s, 1980s, and 1990s, (for we must not forget that it is now not too much larger, in terms of faculty positions, than it had been in the 1970s), it did survive, which is no small feat, as already intimated, in the budgetary environment public education often experiences here in Alabama, where those institutions that are dependent on our largely sales-tax-driven state budget can sometimes be hit hard by economic slowdowns.

Most recently, however, I think that the word "thrive" aptly captures what has happened here, linked to such factors as: the department sharing two cross-appointments with New College as of 1998 (Catherine Roach and Ted Trost; Roach's position went exclusively to New College in 2006, and Trost, after completing his service as chair, returned to his 25 percent appointment to New College); the department gaining a targeted affirmative action hire in 2005 (when Maha Marouan was hired)—a line into which the department was later able to hire Merinda Simmons (a graduate of our own Department of English's doctoral program) when Marouan moved in 2010 to what was then called women's studies (but what is now known as gender and race studies); as of the fall 2013 semester, adding a new cross-appointment with the Department of History devoted to the study of Islam (75 percent Department of Religious Studies and 25 percent Department of History and held by our newest colleague, Eleanor Finnegan); the department's good fortune in being awarded a new line in Asian religions back in the late 1990s (first held by Reiko Ohnuma [now of Dartmouth], then by Kurtis Schaeffer [now department chair at the University of Virginia], and now by this volume's editor, Steven Ramey, who also directs the Asian studies minor on our campus); despite tight state budgets, receiving a replacement position when William Doty retired soon after my arrival on campus (Doty's line was then held by Tim Murphy, until his own retirement, and then untimely death, in March 2013); and, most importantly perhaps, the good fortune that comes with dedicated resources, such as a student scholarship fund kindly established by the late Dr. Joseph Silverstein, the Aaron Aronov Endowment in Ju-

daic Studies, which enabled Richard Cohen (now at the University of Buffalo) to be hired in 1989 as the first person to hold the department's endowed chair in the study of Judaism, along with two endowments that
honor the memory of two students whose lives ended far too early.[4] Since
2003, the Silverstein award has been given out nearly 150 times, helping
students to pay for their education, while, over the past twenty-five years,
the Aronov Endowed Chair has been held by several people (either as
professors, visiting professors, or postdoctoral fellows) and, since January
2001, it has been held by my colleague Steve Jacobs, a specialist in Holocaust and genocide studies.

And it was with funds from this endowment, and quite self-consciously
aiming to put ourselves on the map of our colleague's and students' collective mind's eye, that the department brought Professor Jaffee to campus, to
speak not specifically about the data that falls within the admittedly wide
area known as Judaic studies but, instead, to speak as a scholar of religion
involved in debates of relevance not just to our department but to all of
our peers in the university; for the department decided that what made us
unique was *not* that our object of study was special—as so many scholars
of religion yet presume—but that, although we studied an aspect of culture known as religion, it was simply a word we used to name a specific
subset of mundane but no less interesting human beliefs, behavior, and institutions, along with the various things that past actions left behind. (The
theme for our 2012–2013 public lectures, "The Relevance of the Humanities and Social Sciences in the 21st Century University," is but the latest
example of this attempt to persuade students and colleagues from across
the university that we are all in the same boat and can therefore benefit
from each other's insights; that our dean adopted this series and has kept
it going suggests we were, to whatever degree, successful in our efforts.)

But instituting a lecture series to feature national speakers able to translate their work for a wider audience was just a small part of our reinvention plan—an effort to ensure that people understood that, although we
were small, our reach through teaching, research, and service was surprisingly wide. For if a department such as ours was to reestablish itself successfully, it meant rebuilding from the ground up: designing a new curriculum driven not by personalities that happened to work here and the
data domains that come and go with every new hire or departure of a faculty member but by the common set of skills we hoped our students would
gain, regardless of the material on which they work (e.g., defining, describing, comparing, interpreting, explaining); a decade later, redesigning
it yet again, to try to make it more appealing to second majors; designing

new and engaging online courses to replace the sadly dated distance education booklets that, back in 2001, were still being mailed to a small number of distance learners taking courses in the department (though, now
that we have them, we work hard to ensure that the online classes do not
pull against our in-person lecture courses); creating a content-rich website
and then, when social media came around, devising ways to use Facebook
to help support our mission; rewriting long-outdated tenure and promotion documents (we have had two such revisions in the past decade); developing PR materials to distribute throughout the state's public and private secondary schools (at present we are debating beginning to develop
and offer professional development workshops for Alabama public school
teachers); contacting graduates and developing mailing lists, annual news-
letters, and surveys so we know more about who takes a course with us
and what our graduates do with themselves when they leave Tuscaloosa;
rewriting staff job descriptions and supporting long overdue staff promo-
tions, where needed; developing a host of procedures and routinizing the
ways in which student workers assisted the department in its work (hiring our own undergraduate students to work in the main office and assist in some of our classes has been one of our most successful, though
low-key, mentoring programs to date); setting up a rationale for awarding
student scholarships and a way to publicize it every year on what we call
Honors Day (large banners bearing every recipient's name now annually
fill our second floor balcony railings and, I would hazard a guess, populate
photo albums of quite a few families whose children passed through our
department); and investing energy in reinvigorating our student associations (something most recently accomplished by Merinda Simmons and
now taken over by Eleanor Finnegan); and tackling the work necessary to
give the department's physical space an overall face-lift—everything from
obtaining new classroom furniture to address the unfortunate "Welcome
Back Kotter" feel of the classrooms back in the late 1990s to creating a
student lounge; and even having a motto ("Studying Religion *in* Culture,"
as mentioned earlier) and a logo—our totem, if you will—designed by our
campus's University Relations office. Yes, we also have mugs and T-shirts.
The bottom line: it is tough to ignore us (literally, for a 150-foot-long
banner, three feet high, lines our building's New Orleans's styled wrought
iron railing balcony, declaring who we are and welcoming people to the
University of Alabama)—and that was the goal. We've even got a Vimeo
page for the movies that our graduate and recent staff member Andie
Alexander started making about the department (at http://vimeo.com
/uareligiousstudies).

But at the end of the day, all this effort was aimed not just at administrators but also at establishing rewarding work conditions for the faculty and staff with the hope that this too would bring students our way. For reinventing a department also meant meeting criteria established by the already mentioned Alabama Commission on Higher Education (ACHE). Comprised of commissioners appointed by the governor, ACHE long ago set the bar at 7.5 BA graduates per year (based on a rolling three-year average; MA- and PhD-awarding programs have their own, somewhat lower, minimum numbers, of course). Failing to meet this minimum meant that a degree program would be deemed "nonviable," a status that risks the loss of the major—a loss that would have turned our department into a "service unit" delivering only what we call core curriculum courses (i.e., general education classes) to students from other departments who were satisfying their breadth requirements. Our department's average, when I arrived back in 2001, was 6.6 graduating majors per year (up considerably from what it had been when ACHE first came knocking at our doors in the late 1990s), which meant that a detailed waiver application had to be submitted to the state commission as soon as I arrived that outlined the specific reasons why the status of "viable" ought to be granted, which it eventually was (in fall 2002; that our dean had invested in a new, outside department chair likely went some distance to help persuade ACHE that the University of Alabama was serious about this reinvention). Regardless of one's opinion of the role played by such state regulating bodies, the "bottom line" reality that such commissions and state legislatures inject into our lives provides a practical rationale for investing serious energy into reinventing the material conditions that make our own profession and careers possible. Since the department had most recently seen itself mainly as a service department (with students wishing to specialize in the study of religion often taking independent study courses to fulfill the requirements of the major) and with the department seemingly comfortable with a variety of other units offering courses in the study of religion, such as the Department of Philosophy owning the Philosophy of Religion, the Department of Anthropology owning the Anthropology of Religion, or the Department of History owning the History of Christianity), meeting the 7.5 bar required collective ingenuity and effort.

But of all these separate sites of social formation, the one that underlies them all involves constituting a shared imaginary among the faculty, staff, and our students. Despite their own individual accomplishments and expertise, it seemed to me back then that 2001's small group of energetic, tenure-track scholars had yet to figure out precisely how and why—apart from sheer happenstance—they comprised an academic collectivity. While we had adjacent offices and a classroom, it was not all that clear to me when I first arrived, and Ms. Betty Dickey handed me a master key, that there was actually a department here. For it surely takes more than just occupying adjacent space to form a department. To rephrase: the sort of intellectual and institutional space in which current faculty and students think and act themselves into an identity had, when the Aronov Lecture series began, yet to be formed, making the sort of introduction to this volume that my colleague has written, as well as the narrative web that holds its chapters together, not something we could have yet imagined. Inviting Professor Jaffee to set the table with his inaugural Aronov Lecture—an invitation extended because of the way in which he theorized his classroom experience and own sense of identity in his 1997 essay, "Fessing Up in Theory: On *Pro*fessing and *Con*fessing in the Religious Studies Classroom"—provided the faculty with a common starting point that allowed them to pursue a year-long meditation on issues of methodology, theory, the history of the field, the history and context of our particular department, the place of self-disclosure and identity in our work, the sorts of students we teach, the goal of our curriculum, and the rationale behind our own teaching styles—all topics at the heart of any active and engaged department's ongoing work. That this conversation now continues, despite the publication of a set of faculty responses to Jaffee's lecture (published in the *Bulletin of the Council of Societies for the Study of Religion* [2004]), is the evidence of just how fruitful our collective labors were; that a small BA-granting department previously off the radar of the self-designated important programs in the field has had a national effect constitutes a little more evidence, we'd like to think. A department blog now exists where the relevance of the humanities is discussed (as already mentioned, our department took the lead on a campus-wide conversation on this very topic), several of us work together on Culture on the Edge, a book series and blog initiative also involving scholars elsewhere, and devoted to redescribing identity studies, and over the past twelve years some thoughtful and motivated students have made us their home while figuring out what they wanted to do with their lives—today some of them are in grad school, but many more are teachers, small business owners, lawyers, and doctors. And then there is this very volume, of course, yet another collaborative effort that several of the faculty have tackled together.

We are indeed small when measured in some ways (though, if measured pound-for-pound, I'd hazard a guess that we are among the most productive units in the College of Arts and Sciences), but we are very ambitious and productive in yet other ways, making evident to anyone wishing to judge us that big ideas and impressive accomplishments come to fruition in all sorts of places. For I could not have imagined a collection of Aronov Lectures such as this back when I was listening to Professor Jaffee's talk that evening in Smith Hall's wonderful old, wood-lined lecture hall. It makes it rather exciting to wonder what the next decade holds for this department, its faculty, staff, and students. Of course many challenges have also come with the successes that resulted from all of this change—how to ensure that we maintain the sort of direct and personal contact with our students that they so value is one of them, despite inventing large enrollment lower-level classes (that seat from 120 to 150 people) and designing online courses that sometimes have on-campus students enrolled in them, all in an effort to help a growing university meet its enrollment needs (in 2001 we had about 18,000 students at the University of Alabama and now we have about 35,000—a systematic effort to disengage the university's budget from the vagaries of state funding). Our class sizes have grown and we often have a full-time instructor (or two) working in the department, as well as a couple of graduate teaching assistants, the former teaching rather more courses than the rest of us (but not more students, since the faculty recently agreed that instructors ought not to shoulder the work of large enrollment classes, thereby reserving their energies for smaller classes of honors students)—but how could these not be issues in our department, inasmuch as they are issues all across US higher education? But while not having control over the larger structural conditions that have led to such things as declining public financial support for higher education and thus increasing tuition, the department does control a number of factors that can make larger courses more engaging and intellectually provocative (a professor with a wireless mic and the confidence to walk the room while talking makes a surprising difference), strategies that can limit the footprint that the impersonal online environment has in the lives of local students eager for a face-to-face exchange with a passionate professor and that can ensure that early career people eager for tenure-track work can gain valuable experience in a supportive, small department. (In fact, we are understandably rather proud of the instructors who have worked with us and have gone on to interesting careers of their own. Thas was how I began my own career, in fact.) Like any department, our long-term well-being depends upon successfully managing all of this, along with making sure that we have a good supply of department mugs on hand, of course.

Although the preceding essays obviously do not start or end in the same place, their authors, like our faculty, all strike me as being involved in thinking through a common set of issues regarding the topics that have preoccupied me in this afterword: identity and scholarship. This commonality suggests that, at least when it comes to a university, every unit's shared identity is not to be found in the specificity of its members' separate data domains but, instead, in the shared set of problematics that they tackle and the tools that they use in going about that work. If this is the case, then my hope is that our labors in Tuscaloosa will be of some use to readers who are looking around for tools to use in doing some collective tinkering of their own. For, much like the student worker who, as I wrote an early draft of this, is going room to room to replace the old, faded black paper that lines the bulletin boards on the outside of each of our office doors, social groups require continual grooming so as to avoid the impression of fading away. If this work is successful, then you will never see it happening (which can make it appear to be a thankless task)—that is, not until ten years pass and we look back and decide to celebrate the work that might have once seemed invisible.[5]

Notes

1. Careful readers will ask how long the department's staff members have served. As is often the case, the institutional memory resides primarily among the staff, without whom the day-to-day running of the unit (everything from ordering supplies to putting together a class schedule, admitting students into courses, and bringing people onto the payroll) would be an utter impossibility. With that having been said, Ms. Betty Dickey, the office associate senior, has served the department for twenty-five years and is the soft-spoken rock to which our enterprise is tethered.

2. The italicized "in" is quite intentional. As stated on the page on our department's website (http://religion.ua.edu/motto.html) devoted to the motto that we came up with not long after I arrived:

> Basic to this [i.e., the dominant] way of approaching the field is the widely shared assumption that the area of human practice known as "religion" is somehow removed or set apart from those historical influences that go by the name of "culture" (which includes such things as language, art, types of social organization, and custom). Upon further examining this assumption it often becomes evident that an even more basic assumption concerns the popular belief that the area we identify as "religion" is in fact the public, and therefore observable, expression of what is believed to be a prior, inner experience, feeling, or sentiment. "Religion," then, is thought by many to name the public manifestations (such as texts, rituals, symbols, institutions, etc.) of an inner, personal experience. Because one cannot get inside other people's heads—or so the argument goes—scholars of religion are therefore left with studying these public expressions, comparing them across cultures in search

of the similarities and differences that may lead them to formulate a general theory of religion as a universal human phenomenon. "Religion and Culture," then, names the field which takes as its data the shape adopted by what is presumably the inner essence of religion—a shape taken when it is not just experienced but also expressed in such historical settings as art, architecture, writing, behavior, etc.

Contrary to this approach, to study religion *in* culture means one is not beginning with the assumption that these two distinct domains periodically bump into each other. Instead, the preposition "in" signifies that the area of human behavior known as "religion" is assumed, from the outset, to be an element within human cultural systems—systems which are themselves historical products. An assumption basic to this approach is that the objects of study for any scholar in any branch of the human sciences are assumed to be historical creations that had a beginning and that change over time. Whether these changes are random or governed by other factors—such as gender, economics, politics, cognition, or even geography and environmental features—is one of the areas that such scholars explore. To study religion *in* culture therefore means that [one's] object of study is a product of human belief, behavior and social systems.

3. "Proposal to Danforth Foundation," 1–2. During the mid- to late 1960s, it was common for the private Danforth Foundation to fund a department chair's salary for a newly instituted Department of Religious Studies, under the condition that the institution would continue to budget for the position after the foundation's initial three-year funding period ended. (My thanks to Charlie Reynolds, of the University of Tennessee [and my first department chair when I was an instructor there (1993–96)], for his anecdotal comments on the role played by the Danforth in helping to create our field.) The Alabama proposal requested funds for faculty salaries and library purchases, totaling between $17,124 and $28,750 between the years 1966–67 and 1969–70. According to a September 28, 2003, correspondence with Diane Moleski, the office manager for the Danforth Foundation, in 1966 a three-year program was indeed funded (for $16,500) "to aid in establishing a Department of Religion" at the University of Alabama.

4. The Amy Lynn Petersen Endowed Support fund allows the department to purchase a book for each student enrolled in our Capstone Senior Seminar each spring, in memory of a student minoring in religious studies, who tragically died in 2003. The Zachary Daniel Day Memorial Support Fund was established in the memory of a religious studies graduate who, in 2011, died quite unexpectedly. The inaugural annual Day lecture in religion *in* popular culture took place in fall 2013.

5. I hope that it is fitting that this volume ends with this substantial revision of what was originally the short introduction to the set of published faculty responses to Martin Jaffee's inaugural Aronov lecture; that introduction appeared in the *Bulletin of the Council of Societies for the Study of Religion* 33/2 (2004): 27–29.

Works Cited

Adler, Marcus Nathan, ed. *The Itinerary of Benjamin of Tudela. Critical Text, Translation and Commentary.* New York: Philipp Feldheim, 1907.

Adler, Rachel. "I've Had Nothing Yet So I Can't Tale More." *Moment* 8 (September 1983): 22–26.

Afsaruddin, Asma. *The First Muslims: History and Memory.* Oxford: Oneworld, 2008.

Allsen, Thomas T. *Mongol Imperialism: The Policies of the Grand Qan Mongke in China, Russia, and the Islamic Lands, 1251–1259.* Berkeley: University of California Press, 1987.

Almond, Philip C. *The British Discovery of Buddhism.* Cambridge: Cambridge University Press, 1988.

Appadurai, Arjun. *Fear of Small Numbers.* Durham, NC: Duke University Press, 2006.

———. "The Grounds of the Nation-State: Identity, Violence and Territory." In *Nationalism and Internationalism in the Post-Cold War Era*, edited by Kjell Goldmann, Ulf Hannerz, and Charles Westin, 129–42. London: Routledge, 2000.

Appiah, Kwame Anthony. *Cosmopolitanism: Ethics in a World of Strangers.* New York: Norton, 2006.

Arendt, Hannah. *Eichmann in Jerusalem: A Report on the Banality of Evil.* New York: Viking Press, 1963.

Arnal, William. *The Symbolic Jesus: Historical Scholarship, Judaism, and the Construction of Contemporary Identity.* Religion in Culture: Studies in Social Contest and Construction. London: Equinox, 2005.

Arnal, William, and Russell McCutcheon. *The Sacred Is the Profane: The Political Nature of "Religion."* Oxford: Oxford University Press, 2013.

Asad, Talal. *Genealogies of Religion: Disciplines and Reason of Power in Chrisitanity and Islam.* Baltimore, MD: Johns Hopkins University Press, 1993.

Ateek, Naim. "Pentecost and the Intifada." In *Reading from This Place.* Vol. 2, *Social Location and Biblical Interpretation in Global Perspective*, edited by Fernando F. Segovia and Mary Ann Tolbert, 69–81. Minneapolis: Augsburg Fortress, 1995.

Bailey, Kenneth. *Through Peasant Eyes: More Lucan Parables, Their Culture and Style.* Grand Rapids, MI: Eerdmans, 1980.

Barbieri, Alvaro, ed. *Marco Polo, Milione. Redazione Latina del Manoscritto Z.* Parma: Ugo Guanda Editore, 1998.

Bartlett, W. B. *The Assassins: The Story of Medieval Islam's Secret Sect.* London: Sutton, 2001.

Bastide, Roger. *African Religions of Brazil.* Baltimore, MD: Johns Hopkins University Press, 1978.

Basu, Amrita. "When Local Riots Are Not Merely Local: Bringing the State Back In, Bijnor 1988–92." *Economic and Political Weekly* (1994): 2605–21.

Bauer, W., et al. *A Greek-English Lexicon of the New Testament and Other Early Christian Literature: A Translation and Adaptation of the Fourth Revised and Augmented Edition of Walter Bauer's Griechisch-deutsches Wörterbuch zu den Schriften des Neuen Testaments und der übrigen urchristlichen Literatur,* trans. by William F. Arndt and Wilbur Gingrich. Chicago: University of Chicago Press, 1979.

Baum, Wilhelm. *Die Verwandlungen des Mythos vom Reich des Priesterkönigs Johannes: Rom, Byzanz und die Christen des Orients im Mittelalter.* Klagenfurt: Verlag Kitab, 1999.

Baumgarten, Albert I. "Josephus on Essene Sacrifice," *Journal of Jewish Studies* 45 (1994): 169–83.

Beech, Hannah. "The Face of Buddhist Terror." *Time,* July 1, 2013. http://content.time.com/time/magazine/article/0,9171,2146000,00.html (accessed December 19, 2013).

Belo, Fernando. *A Materialist Reading of the Gospel of Mark.* Translated by Matthew J. O'Connell. Maryknoll, NY: Orbis Books, 1981.

Benedetto, Luigi Foscolo, ed. *Il Milione, prima edizione integrale.* Florence: L. S. Olschki, 1928.

Borg, Marcus. *Conflict, Holiness and Politics in the Teachings of Jesus.* Studies in the Bible and Early Christianity, 5. New York: Edwin Mellen, 1984.

Boyle, John Andrew. "The Il-khans of Persia and the Princes of Europe." *Central Asiatic Journal* 20 (1976): 25–40.

Brooten, Bernadette. "Could Women Initiate Divorce in Ancient Judaism? The Implications for Mark 10:11–12 and I Corinthians 7:10–11." Ernest Cadwell Colman Lecture, School of Theology at Claremont, April 14, 1981.

de Brosses, Charles. *Du culte des dieux fétiches, ou parallèle l'ancienne religion de l'Egypte avec la religion actuelle de Nigritie.* Paris: n.p. Reprint, Paris: Fayard, 1988.

Bush, George W. "Presidential Address to the Nation" (October 7, 2001). In *We Will Prevail: President George W. Bush on War, Terrorism, and Freedom,* 2–3. New York: Continuum, 2003.

Canady, Chris. "Miriam." In *Women in the Bible,* edited by Marcia Cohn Spiegel, 41–43. New York: Women's League for Conservative Judaism, [1984].

Canizares, Raul. *Walking the Night: The Afro-Cuban World of Santeriá.* Rochester, VT: Destiny Books, 1993.

Caplow, Theodore, Howard M. Bahr, and Bruce A. Chadwick. *All Faithful People: Change and Continuity in Middletown's Religion.* Minneapolis: University of Minnesota Press, 1983.

Caplow, Theodore, and Margaret H. Williamson. "Decoding Middletown's Easter Bunny: A Study in American Iconography." *Semiotica* 32 (1980): 221–32.

Chancey, Mark. *Greco-Roman Culture and the Galilee of Jesus.* Society for New Testament Studies, Monograph Series 134. Cambridge: Cambridge University Press, 2005.

———. *The Myth of a Gentile Galilee.* Society for New Testament Studies, Monograph Series 118. Cambridge: Cambridge University Press, 2002.

———. "Review of *Herod Antipas in Galilee* by Morten Hørning Jensen." *Review of Biblical Literature* 4 (2007). http://www.bookreviews.org/pdf/5509_5804.pdf.

Chill, Abraham. *The Minhagim: The Customs and Ceremonies of Judaism.* New York: Sepher-Hermon Press, 1979.

Christ, Carol P. "Barth on Man-Woman Relation." Alverno Conference of Women Theologians, 1971. Alverno College Archives.

Cohen, Richard. "Faculty Profile." Appendix to "Annual Report from the Aronov Chair, September 1991." Photocopy, Department of Religious Studies, University of Alabama.

Cohen, Shaye J. D. "Judaism and Jewishness." In *The Jewish Annotated New Testament*, edited by Amy-Jill Levine and Marc Zvi Brettler, 513–15. New York: Oxford University Press, 2011.

Comte, Auguste. *Cours de philosophie positive.* Translated by Harriet Martineau, *The Positive Philosophy.* New York: C. Blanchard, 1955.

Cooley, Thomas M. *General Principles of Constitutional Law in the United States of America.* Boston: Little, Brown and Company, 1880.

Crimp, Douglas. *Melancholia and Moralism: Essays on AIDS and Queer Politics.* Cambridge, MA: MIT Press, 2002.

Critchley, John. *Marco Polo's Book.* Cambridge, UK: Variorum, 1992.

Curtin, Philip D. *Cross-Cultural Trade in World History.* Cambridge: Cambridge University Press, 1984.

Daftary, Farhad. *The Assassin Legends: Myths of the Isma'ilis.* London: I. B. Tauris and Co., 1994.

Daly, Mary. *Beyond God the Father: Toward a Philosophy of Women's Liberation.* Boston: Beacon Press, 1973.

———. *The Church and the Second Sex.* Boston: Beacon Press, 1968.

Danby, Herbert, trans. and ed. *The Mishnah. Translated from the Hebrew with Introduction and Brief Explanatory Notes by Herbert Danby.* Oxford: Oxford University Press, 1933.

Das, Veena. *Mirrors of Violence: Communities, Riots and Survivors in South Asia.* Delhi, India: Oxford University Press, 1990.

Descartes, René. *The Philosophical Works of Descartes.* 2 vols. Translated by Elizabeth S. Haldane and G. R. T. Ross. Cambridge: Cambridge University Press, 1911.

Deshen, Shlomo. *The Mellah Society: Jewish Community Life in Sherifian Morocco.* Chicago: University of Chicago Press, 1989.

Donahue, John R. *The Gospel as Parable: Metaphor, Narrative and Theology in the Synoptic Gospels.* Philadelphia: Fortress, 1988.

Draper, Jonathan. "Jesus and the Renewal of Local Community in Galilee." *Journal of Theology for Southern Africa* 87 (June 1994): 29–42.

Dubuisson, Daniel. *The Western Construction of Religion: Myths, Knowledge, and Ideology.* Translated by William Sayers. Baltimore, MD: Johns Hopkins University Press, 2003.

Dumont, Louis. *Homo Hierarchicus: The Caste System and Its Implications.* Chicago: University of Chicago Press, 1980.

Dunn, James D. G. *A New Perspective on Jesus: What the Quest for the Historical Jesus Missed.* Grand Rapids, MI: Baker Academic, 2005.

Durkheim, Emile. *The Elementary Forms of Religious Life.* Translated by Karen Fields. New York: Simon and Schuster, 1995.

Edwards, Douglas. "First Century Urban/Rural Relations in Lower Galilee: Exploring the Archaeological and Literary Evidence." *Society of Biblical Literature Seminar Papers* (1988): 169–82.

Eliade, Mircea. *The Myth of the Eternal Return.* Translated by Willard E. Trask. New York: Pantheon, 1954.

———. *The Quest: History and Meaning in Religion.* Chicago: University of Chicago Press, 1969.

Eliade, Mircea, and Charles J. Adams, eds. *The Encyclopedia of Religion.* 16 vols. New York: Macmillan, 1987.

Elliott, Andrea. "The Man behind the Anti-Shariah Movement." *New York Times,* July 30, 2011. http://www.nytimes.com/2011/07/31/us/31shariah.html?_r=1&ref=andreaelliott (accessed October 30, 2011).

Emswiler, Sharon Neufer. "How the New Woman Feels in the Old Worship." In *Women and Worship: A Guide to Nonsexist Hymns, Prayers, and Liturgies,* edited by Sharon Neufer Emswiler and Thomas Neufer Emswiler, 3–8. New York: Harper and Row, 1974.

Encyclopedia Judaica. 16 vols. Jerusalem: Keter, 1971.

Eng, David L. "The Value of Silence." *Theatre Journal* 54.1 (2002): 85–94.

Eng, David L., and Shinhee Han. "A Dialogue on Racial Melancholia." In *Loss: The Politics of Mourning,* edited by David L. Eng and David Kazanjian, 343–71. Berkeley: University of California Press, 2003.

Ernst, Carl. *Following Muhammad: Rethinking Islam in the Contemporary World.* Chapel Hill: University of North Carolina Press, 2003.

Ernst, Carl, and Richard Martin. "Introduction: Toward a Post-Orientalist Approach to Islamic Religious Studies." In *Rethinking Islamic Studies: From Orientalism to Cosmopolitanism,* edited by Carl Ernst and Richard Martin, 1–22. Columbia: University of South Carolina Press, 2010.

———, eds. *Rethinking Islamic Studies: From Orientalism to Cosmopolitanism.* Columbia: University of South Carolina Press, 2010.

Esposito, John L. *Unholy War: Terror in the Name of Islam.* New York: Oxford University Press, 2003.

Esposito, John L., and Dalia Mogahed. *Who Speaks for Islam? What a Billion Muslims Really Think.* New York: Gallup Press, 2007.

Evans, Bette Novit. *Interpreting the Free Exercise of Religion: The Constitution and American Pluralism*. Chapel Hill: University of North Carolina Press, 1997.

Feldman, Stephen M. "A Christian America and the Separation of Church and State." In *Law and Religion: A Critical Anthology*, edited by Stephen M. Feldman, 261–77. New York: New York University Press, 2000.

Feuerbach, Ludwig. *The Essence of Christianity*. Translated by George Eliot. New York: Harper and Row, 1957.

Fiensy, David. "Leaders of Mass Movements and the Leader of the Jesus Movement." *Journal for the Study of the New Testament* 74 (1999): 3–27.

Filippani-Ronconi, Pio. *Ismaeliti ed "Assassini."* Milan, Italy: Thoth, editions basilenses, 1973.

Fiorenza, Elisabeth Schüssler. "Word, Spirit, and Power: Women in Early Christian Communities." In *Women of Spirit: Female Leadership in the Jewish and Christian Traditions*, edited by Rosemary Ruether and Eleanor McLaughlin, 29–70. New York: Simon and Schuster, 1979.

First Church of Kopimism for the USA. "What Is Kopimism?" http://www.kopimistsamfundet.org/main/what-is-kopimism (accessed December 19, 2013).

Fitzgerald, Timothy. "Bruce Lincoln's Theses on Method: Anti-theses." *Method and Theory in the Study of Religion* 18.4 (2006): 392–423.

———. *Discourse on Civility and Barbarity: A Critical History of Religion and Related Categories*. Oxford: Oxford University Press, 2007.

———. *The Ideology of Religious Studies*. New York: Oxford University Press, 2000.

Foucault, Michel. "Nietzsche, Genealogy, History." In *Language, Counter-Memory, Practice: Selected Essays and Interviews*, translated by Donald F. Bouchard and Sherry Simon, 139–64. Ithaca, NY: Cornell University Press, 1977.

Frazer, James George. *The Golden Bough: A Study in Magic and Religion*. Abridged edition. New York: Macmillan, 1924.

Freud, Sigmund. "The Ego and the Id." In *The Standard Edition of the Complete Psychological Works of Sigmund Freud*, vol. 19, 19–27. Edited by James Strachey. London: Hogarth Press, 1961.

———. "Mourning and Melancholia." In *The Standard Edition of the Complete Psychological Works of Sigmund Freud*, vol. 14, 243–58. Edited by James Strachey. London: Hogarth Press, 1957.

———. *Totem and Taboo: Some Points of Agreement between the Mental Lives of Savages and Neurotics*. Translated and edited by James Strachey. New York: Routledge and Kegan Paul, 1950.

Freyne, Sean. "Bandits in Galilee: A Contribution to the Study of Social Conditions in First Century Palestine." In *The Social World of Formative Christianity and Judaism*, edited by Jacob Neusner, Peder Borgen, Ernest Frerichs and Richard Horsley, 50–68. Leiden: E. J. Brill, 1988.

———. "Galilean Questions to Crossan's Mediterranean Jesus." In *Whose Historical Jesus?*, edited by William E. Arnal and Michel Desjardins, 63–91. Studies in Christianity and Judaism/Études sur le christianisme et le judaïsme 7. Waterloo, Ontario: Wilfred Laurier University Press, 1997.

Gabriel, Alfons. *Marco Polo in Persien*. Vienna: Verlag Typographische Anstalt, 1962.

Garroway, Joshua. *"Ioudaios."* In *The Jewish Annotated New Testament*, edited by Amy-Jill Levine and Marc Zvi Brettler, 524–26. New York: Oxford University Press, 2011.

Gedicks, Frederick Mark. *The Rhetoric of Church and State: A Critical Analysis of Religion Clause Jurisprudence*. Durham, NC: Duke University Press, 1995.

Ginsberg, Louis. *The Legends of the Jews*. Vol. 1. Philadelphia: Jewish Publication Society, 1968.

Goldhagen, Daniel. *Hitler's Willing Executioners: Ordinary Germans and the Holocaust*. New York: Knopf, 1996.

del Guerra, Giorgio. *Rustichello da Pisa*. Pisa, Italy: Nistri Lischi, 1955.

Gumilev, L. N. *Searches for an Imaginary Kingdom: The Legend of the Kingdom of Prester John*. Translated by R. E. F. Smith. Cambridge: Cambridge University Press, 1987.

Gunn, Janet. *"'On Thursdays We Worship the Banana Plant': Encountering Lived Hinduism in a Canadian Suburb."* *Method and Theory in the Study of Religions* 21 (2009): 40–49.

Hallegua, S. H. "Simchat Torah in Cochin." *Kol Bina* 6:1 (1986).

Hamilton, Bernard, and Charles F. Beckingham, eds. *Prester John, the Mongols, and the Ten Lost Tribes*. Brookfield, VT: Variorum, 1996.

Harland, Philip A. "The Economy of First-Century Palestine: State of the Scholarly Discussion." In *Handbook of Early Christianity: Social Science Approaches*, edited by Anthony J. Blasi, Paul-André Turcotte, and Jean Duhaime, 511–28. Walnut Creek, CA: Alta Mira Press, 2002.

Hauptman, Judith. "Images of Women in the Talmud." In *Religion and Sexism: Images of Woman in the Jewish and Christian Traditions*, edited by Rosemary Radford Ruether, 184–212. New York: Simon and Schuster, 1974.

Hegel, G. W. F. *Lectures on the History of Philosophy*. 3 vols. Translated by Elizabeth S. Haldane and Frances H. Simson. London: Kegan Paul, 1892.

Herskovits, Melville. "African Gods and Catholic Saints in New World Belief." *American Anthropologist* 39:4 (1937): 635–43.

Herzog, William R., II. *Parables as Subversive Speech: Jesus as Pedagogue of the Oppressed*. Louisville, KY: Westminster John Knox Press, 1994.

———. *Prophet and Teacher: An Introduction to the Historical Jesus*. Louisville, KY: Westminster John Knox Press, 2005.

———. "Why Peasants Responded to Jesus." In *A People's History of Christian Origins*, edited by Richard A. Horsley, 47–70. Minneapolis, MN: Fortress Press, 2005.

Hinton, Alexander Laban, ed. *Annihilating Difference: The Anthropology of Genocide*. Berkeley: University of California Press, 2002.

Hodgson, Marshall G. S. *The Order of Assassins: The Struggle of the Early Nizari Isma'ilis against the Islamic World*. The Hague: Mouton, 1955.

Horsley, Richard. "Bandits, Messiahs and Longshoremen: Popular Unrest in Galilee around the Time of Jesus." *Society of Biblical Literature Seminar Papers* (1988): 183–99.

———. "Innovation in Search of Reorientation: New Testament Studies Rediscovering Its Subject Matter." *Journal of the American Academy of Religion* 62:4 (1994): 1127–66.

———. *Jesus and the Spiral of Violence: Popular Jewish Resistance in Roman Palestine.* San Francisco: Harper and Row, 1987. Reprint, Minneapolis, MN: Fortress Press, 1993.

Horsley, Richard, and John S. Hanson. *Bandits, Prophets and Messiahs: Popular Movements at the Time of Jesus.* Minneapolis, MN: Winston Press, 1985, Reprint, Harrisburg, PA: Trinity Press International, 1999.

Horsley, Richard, and James Tracy, eds. *Christmas Unwrapped: Consumerism, Christ, and Culture.* Harrisburg, PA: Trinity Press International, 2001.

Horton, Greg. "Hindu Group Wants a Monument on Oklahoma Capitol Grounds." *Religion News Service,* December 11, 2013. http://www.religionnews.com/2013 /12/11/hindu-group-wants-monument-oklahoma-capitol-grounds/ (accessed December 19, 2013).

Houlden, J. Leslie. *Jesus in Thought and History.* Santa Barbara, CA: Clio, 2003.

Hughes, Aaron. "The Failure of Islamic Studies Post–9/11: A Contextualization and Analysis." In *Failure and Nerve in the Academic Study of Religion: Essays in Honor of Donald Wiebe,* edited by William E. Arnal, Willi Braun, and Russell T. McCutcheon, 129–46. London: Equinox, 2012.

———. *Muslim Identities: An Introduction to Islam.* New York: Columbia University Press, 2012.

———. *Situating Islam: The Past and Future of an Academic Discipline.* London: Equinox, 2007.

———. "The Study of Islam before and after September 11: A Provocation." *Method and Theory in the Study of Religion* 24.4/5 (2012): 314–36.

———. *Theorizing Islam: Disciplinary Deconstruction and Reconstruction.* London: Equinox, 2012.

Hume, David. *Dialogues Concerning Natural Religion.* In *Writings on Religion,* edited by Antony Flew, 185–292. 1779. Reprint, La Salle, IL: Open Court, 1992.

———. *The Natural History of Religion.* In *Writings on Religion,* edited by Antony Flew, 107–82. 1757. La Salle, IL: Open Court, 1992.

Huq, Aziz. "Defend Muslims, Defend America." *New York Times,* June 20, 2011: A-27.

Huygens, R. B. C., ed. *Guillaume de Tyr, Chronique.* Turnholt: Brepols Editores Pontificii, 1986.

Ignatieff, Michael. *The Warrior's Honor: Ethnic War and the Modern Conscience.* New York: Hendry Holt, 1998.

Ilan, Tal. "Beruryah." *Jewish Women: A Comprehensive Encyclopedia.* http://jwa.org /encyclopedia/article/beruryah.

———. *Integrating Women into Second Temple History*. Tubingen: Mohr Siebeck, 1999.

Internal Revenue Service. "Social Security and Other Information for Members of the Clergy and Religious Orders." Publication 517.

"Islam Workshop on 'Rethinking Islamic Studies.'" *Religious Studies News*, October 2010. http://rsnonline.org/index8c49.html?option=com_content&view=article &id=188&Itemid=325 (accessed November 17, 2014).

Jaffee, Martin S. "Fessing Up in Theory: On *Pro*fessing and *Con*fessing in the Religious Studies Classroom." In *The Insider/Outsider Problem in the Study of Religion: A Reader*, edited by Russell T. McCutcheon, 274–84. London: Cassell, 1999.

Jaffrelot, Christophe. *India's Silent Revolution: The Rise of the Lower Castes in North India*. New York: Columbia University Press, 2003.

Jakobsen, Janet R., and Ann Pellegrini. *Love the Sin: Sexual Regulation and the Limits of Religious Tolerance*. Boston: Beacon Press, 2004.

Jensen, Morten Hørning. *Herod Antipas in Galilee: The Literary and Archaeological Sources on the Reign of Herod Antipas and Its Socio-economic Impact on Galilee*. WUNT II 215; Tübingen: Mohr Siebeck, 2006.

Johnson, Barbara C. "'Our Community' in Two Worlds: The Cochin Paradesi Jews in India and Israel." PhD diss, University of Massachusetts, 1985.

Josephus, Flavius. *The Genuine Works of Flavius Josephus*. Trans. by William Whiston. Edinburgh: William Coke Booksellers, 1777.

Joy, Morny. "Postcolonial Reflections: Challenges for Religious Studies." *Method and Theory in the Study of Religion* 13.2 (2001): 177–95.

Katz, Nathan. "How the Hindu-Jewish Encounter Reconfigures Interreligious Dialogue." *Shofar: An Interdisciplinary Journal of Jewish Studies* 16:1 (1997): 28–42.

———. "The Jewish Secret and the Dalai Lama: A Dharamsala Diary." *Conservative Judaism* 43:4 (1991): 33–46.

———. "The Judaisms of Kaifeng and Cochin: Parallel and Divergent Styles of Religious Acculturation." *Numen: International Review for the History of Religions* 2 (1995): 118–40.

Katz, Nathan, and Ellen S. Goldberg. "Asceticism and Caste in the Passover Observances of the Cochin Jews." *Journal of the American Academy of Religion* 57:1 (1989): 52–83.

———. "Jewish 'Apartheid' and a Jewish Gandhi." *Jewish Social Studies* 50:3–4 (1988/1993): 147–76.

———. *The Last Jews of Cochin: Jewish Identity in Hindu India*. Columbia: University of South Carolina Press, 1993.

Kaviraj, Sudipta. "The Imaginary Institution of India." In *Subaltern Studies*, vol. 7, edited by Partha Chatterjee and Gyanendra Pandey, 1–39. Delhi, India: Oxford University Press, 1992.

Kerby, Anthony Paul. "The Adequacy of Self-Narration: A Hermeneutical Approach." *Philosophy and Literature* 12:2 (1988): 232–34.

King, Richard. "The Copernican Turn in the Study of Religion." *Method and Theory in the Study of Religion* 25 (2013): 137–59.

Kintz, Linda. *Between Jesus and the Market: The Emotions That Matter in Right-Wing America*. Durham, NC: Duke University Press, 1997.

Klawans, Jonathan. "Methodology and Ideology in the Study of Priestly Ritual." In *Perspectives on Purity and Purification in the Bible*, edited by Baruch J. Schwartz, David P. Wright, Jeffrey Stackert, and Naphtali S. Meshel, 84–95. Library of Hebrew Bible/Old Testament Studies 474. New York: T & T Clark, 2008.

Knohl, Israel. *The Sanctuary of Silence: The Priestly Torah and the Holiness School*. Minneapolis, MN: Fortress, 1995.

Kugle, Scott Siraj al-Haqq. *Homosexuality in Islam: Critical Reflection on Gay, Lesbian, and Transgender Muslims*. Oxford, UK: Oneworld, 2010.

Lamer, John. *Marco Polo and the Discovery of the World*. New Haven, CT: Yale University Press, 1999.

Lévi-Strauss, Claude. "Le Pere Noël supplicié." *Les Temps modernes* 77 (1952): 1572–90.

Levine, Amy-Jill. *The Misunderstood Jew: The Church and the Scandal of the Jewish Jesus*. San Francisco: HarperSanFrancisco, 2006.

Lewis, Bernard. *The Assassins: A Radical Sect in Islam*. London: Weidenfeld and Nicolson, 1967.

Lincoln, Bruce. "Concessions, Confessions, Clarifications, Ripostes: By Way of Response to Tim Fitzgerald." *Method and Theory in the Study of Religion* 19 (2007): 163–68.

———. *Discourse and the Construction of Society: Comparative Studies of Myth, Ritual, and Classification*. New York: Oxford University Press, 1989.

———. *Gods and Demons, Priests and Scholars: Critical Explorations in the History of Religions*. Chicago: University of Chicago Press, 2012.

———. *Theorizing Myth: Narrative, Ideology, and Scholarship*. Chicago: University of Chicago Press, 1999.

———. "Theses on Method." *Method and Theory in the Study of Religion* 2.3 (1996): 225–27.

Lopez, Donald S., Jr. *The Prisoners of Shangri-La: Tibetan Buddhism and the West*. Chicago: University of Chicago Press, 1998.

Lopez, Roberto Sabatino. "Venezia e le grandi linee dell' espansione commerciale nel secolo XIII." In *La Civiltà Veneziana del secolo di Marco Polo*, 67–84. Venice, Italy: Sansoni, 1955.

Löseth, E., ed. *Le Roman en prose de Tristan, le roman de Palamède et la compilation de Rusticien de Pise, Analyse critique d'après les manuscrits de Paris*. Paris: Émile Bouillon, 1890.

Malina, Bruce. "Was Jesus a Jew? Was Aristotle a Greek? Translating 'Ioudaios.'" http://assemblyoftrueisrael.com/Documents/Yahshuawasnojew[1].htm (accessed November 18, 2014).

Malina, Bruce, and Richard Rohrbach. *Social-Science Commentary on the Gospel of John*. Minneapolis, MN: Augsburg/Fortress, 1998.

Marriott, McKim. "Interactional and Attributional Theories of Caste Ranking." *Man in India* 39:2 (1959): 92–107.

Masuzawa, Tomoko. *In Search of Dreamtime: The Quest for the Origin of Religion.* Chicago: University of Chicago Press, 1993.

———. "Our Master's Voice: Friedrich Max Müller after a Hundred Years of Solitude." *Method and Theory in the Study of Religion* 15: 4 (2003): 305–28.

McCarthy, Anna. *The Citizen Machine: Governing by Television in 1950s America.* New York: New Press, 2010.

McCutcheon, Russell T. *Critics Not Caretakers: Redescribing the Public Study of Religion.* Albany: State University of New York Press, 2001.

———. *Manufacturing Religion: The Discourse on Sui Generis Religions and the Politics of Nostalgia.* New York: Oxford University Press, 1997.

McGuire, Meredith B. *Lived Religion: Faith and Practice in Everyday Life.* Oxford: Oxford University Press, 2008.

McLaughlin, Eleanor. "Equality of Souls, Inequality of Sexes: Woman in Medieval Theology." In *Religion and Sexism: Images of Woman in the Jewish and Christian Traditions,* edited by Rosemary Radford Ruether, 213–66. New York: Simon and Schuster, 1974.

———. "Women, Power, and the Pursuit of Holiness in Medieval Christianity." In *Women of Spirit: Female Leadership in the Jewish and Christian Traditions,* edited by Rosemary Ruether and Eleanor McLaughlin, 99–130. New York: Simon and Schuster, 1979.

Meier, John P. *A Marginal Jew: Rethinking the Historical Jesus.* Vol. 1. Anchor Bible Reference Library. New York: Doubleday, 1991.

Ménard, Philippe, ed., *Le devisement du monde, edition critique.* Paris: Droz, 2001.

Merton, Robert King, and David L. Sills, eds. *Social Science Quotations: Who Said What, When, and Where.* New Brunswick: Transaction Publishers, 2001.

Meyvaert, Paul. "An Unknown Letter of Hulagu, Il-Khan of Persia, to King Louis IX of France." *Viator* 11 (1980): 245–59.

Morgan, David. *The Mongols.* Oxford: Basil Blackwell, 1986.

Most, Andrea. "'We Know We Belong to the Land': The Theatricality of Assimilation in *Oklahoma.*" In *Making Americans: Jews and the Broadway Musical,* 101–18. Cambridge, MA: Harvard University Press, 2004.

Mosstaert, A., and Fr. Woodman. *I tesori dell'Archivio segreto vaticano.* Florence, Italy, 1991.

———. "Trois documents Mongols des archives secretes Vaticans." *Harvard Journal of Asiatic Studies* 15 (1952): 419–506.

Moule, C., and Paul Pelliot. *Marco Polo, The Description of the World.* Vol. I. London: George Routledge and Sons, 1938.

Moxnes, Halvor. *Jesus and the Rise of Nationalism: A New Quest for the Nineteenth-Century Historical Jesus.* London: I. B. Tauris, 2012.

MSNBC.com. "School Pulls Musical 'Kismet' after 9/11 Complaints." MSNBC.com, September 20, 2011. http://www.msnbc.msn.com/id/44594371/ns/us_news-life/#.TupCIBzeMcN (accessed December 15, 2011).

Murphy, Joseph M. *Santeriá: An African Religion in America*. Boston: Beacon, 1988.

National Park Service. "Flight 93 National Memorial." http://www.nps.gov/flni /index.htm (accessed December 15, 2011).

Neusner, Jacob, and Bruce Chilton, eds. *In Quest of the Historical Pharisees*. Waco, TX: Baylor University Press, 2007.

Nickelsburg, George W. E. "Enoch, Levi, and Peter: Recipients of Revelation in Upper Galilee." *Journal of Biblical Literature* 100 (1981): 575–600.

Nietzsche, Friedrich. *Twilight of the Idols: Or, How to Philosophize with a Hammer*. Translated with an introduction and notes by Duncan Large. Oxford: Oxford University Press, 2008.

Nissenbaum, Stephen. *The Battle for Christmas*. New York: Alfred A. Knopf, 1996.

Nowell, Charles. "The Old Man of the Mountain." *Speculum* 22 (1947): 497–519.

Oakman, D. E. "Culture, Society, and Embedded Religion in Antiquity." *Biblical Theology Bulletin* 35: 1 (2005): 4–12.

Obeyesekere, Gananath. "Religious Symbolism and Political Change in Ceylon." In *The Two Wheels of Dhamma: Essays on the Theravada Tradition in India and Ceylon*, edited by Bardwell L. Smith, 58–78. Chambersburg, PA: American Academy of Religion, 1972.

Olschki, Leonardo. *L'Asia di Marco Polo. Introduzione alia lettura e alia studio del Milione*. Venice, Italy: Instituto per la collaborazione culturale, 1957.

Oppenheimer, Aharon. *The 'Am Ha-Aretz*. Leiden: E. J. Brill, 1977.

O'Reilly, Jane. "The Housewife's Moment of Truth," *Ms.* 12:2 (Spring 1972): 4–8.

Orsi, Robert A. *Between Heaven and Earth: The Religious Worlds People Make and the Scholars Who Study Them*. Princeton, NJ: Princeton University Press, 2005.

———. "Everyday Miracles: The Study of Lived Religion." In *Lived Religion in America: Toward a History of Practice*, edited by David Hall, 4–21. Princeton, NJ: Princeton University Press, 1997.

Pagels, Elaine. "What Became of God the Mother?" In *Womanspirit Rising: A Feminist Reader in Religion*, edited by Carol P. Christ and Judith Plaskow, 107–19. San Francisco: Harper and Row, 1979.

Paget, James Carlton. "Education: Was Jesus a Chartered Surveyor?" *Independent*, December 18, 1997. http://www.independent.co.uk/news/education/education -news/education-was-jesus-a-chartered-surveyor-1289324.html (accessed May 18, 2012).

Parvey, Constance. "The Theology and Leadership of Women in the New Testament." In *Religion and Sexism: Images of Woman in the Jewish and Christian Traditions*, edited by Rosemary Radford Ruether, 123–35. New York: Simon and Schuster, 1974.

Pellegrini, Ann. "Protesting Death: *Snyder v. Phelps* and the Space of Mourning." In *Law and Mourning*, edited by Austin Sarat and Martha Umphrey. Stanford: Stanford University Press, in press.

Penner, Hans H. *Impasse and Resolution: A Critique of the Study of Religion*. New York: Peter Lang, 1989.

Perkins, Pheme. *Hearing the Parables of Jesus*. Ramsey, NJ: Paulist Press, 1981.

Perlmann, S. M. "The History of the Jews in China." In *Jews in Old China: Some Western Views*, edited by Hyman Kublin, 119–?. 1843. Reprint, New York: Paragon Press Book Reprint Corp., 1971.

Perls, Frederick, Ralph F. Hefferline, and Paul Goodman. *Gestalt Therapy: Excitement and Growth in the Human Personality*. New York: Delta Books, 1951.

Perrin, Nicholas. *Jesus the Temple*. Grand Rapids, MI: Baker Academic, 2010.

Pertz, Georgias Heinricius, ed., *Arnoldi Chronica Slavorum ex recensione I. M. Lappenbergh*. Hannover: Impensis Bibliopolii Hahniani, 1868.

Pew Forum on Religion and Public Life. "Growing Number of Americans Say Obama Is a Muslim." August 18, 2010. http://pewresearch.org/pubs/1701/poll-obama-muslim-christian-church-out-of-politics-political-leaders-religious (accessed December 15, 2011).

Pietz, William. "The Problem of the Fetish, I." *RES: Anthropology and Aesthetics* 9 (1985): 5–17.

———. "The Problem of the Fetish, II: The Origin of the Fetish." *RES: Anthropology and Aesthetics* 13 (1987): 23–45.

———. "The Problem of the Fetish, IIIa: Bosman's New Guinea and the Enlightenment Theory of Fetishism." *RES: Anthropology and Aesthetics* 16 (1988): 105–23.

Plaskow, Judith. "Jewish Anti-Paganism." In *The Coming of Lilith: Essays on Feminism, Judaism, and Sexual Ethics, 1972–2003*, edited by Judith Plaskow with Donna Berman, 110–13. Boston: Beacon Press, 2005.

———. *Standing Again at Sinai: Judaism from a Feminist Perspective*. San Francisco: Harper San Francisco, 1990.

"A Portrait of Jesus: From Galilean Jew to the Face of God." http://www.aportraitofJesus.org/social.shtml (accessed May 18, 2012).

Powers, David S. *Muhammad Is Not the Father of Any of Your Men: The Making of the Last Prophet*. Philadelphia: University of Pennsylvania Press, 2009.

"A Proposal by the University of Alabama to the Danforth Foundation for a Grant to Assist in the Establishment of a Department of Religion, July 12, 1965." Photocopy, Department of Religious Studies, University of Alabama.

Puar, Jasbir, and Amit S. Rai. "Monster, Terrorist, Fag: The War on Terrorism and the Production of Docile Patriots." *Social Text* 72 20.3 (Fall 2002): 117–48.

Rabinowitz, Louis. *Far East Mission*. Johannesburg: Eagle Press, 1952.

de Rachewiltz, Igor. *Prester John and Europe's Discovery of East Asia*. Canberra: Australian National University Press, 1972.

Ramadan, Tariq. *In the Footsteps of Muhammad: Lessons from the Life of Muhammad*. New York: Oxford University Press, 2007.

Ramey, Steven. "When Acceptance Reflects Disrespect: The Methodological Contradictions of Accepting Participant Statements." *Method and Theory in the Study of Religion* 27:1 (2015): 59–81.

Rayfield, Jillian. "Oklahoma State Rep. Aims to Stop 'Liberal Judges' From Imposing Sharia Law." TPM LiveWire, June 11, 2010. http://tpmlivewire

.talkingpointsmemo.com/2010/06/oklahoma-state-senator-aims-to-stop -liberal-judges-from-imposing-sharia-law.php (accessed July 8, 2011).

"Recommended Reading." *Religious Studies News* (2011). http://rsnonline.org /index495e.html?option=com_content&view=article&id=1421:recommended -reading&catid=95:recommended-reading.

Reed, Jonathan. "Reappraising the Galilean Economy: The Limits of Models, Archaeology, and Analogy." Paper presented at the Westar (Jesus Seminar) spring meeting, March 2008.

Reichert, F. "Columbus und Marco Polo—Asien in Amerika." *Zeitschrift für historische Forschung* 15 (1988): 1–63.

Rennie, Bryan. *Changing Religious Worlds: The Meaning and End of Mircea Eliade.* Albany: State University of New York Press, 2001.

Renouard, Yves. "Mercati emercanti veneziani alia fine del Duecento." In *La Civiltà Veneziana del secolo di Marco Polo*, 83–108. Venice, Italy: Sansoni, 1955.

Richard, Jean. "Chretiens et Mongols au concile: la Papaute et les Mongols de Perse dans la seconde moitie du XIIIe siècle." In *Croises, missionaires et voyageurs*, edited by Jean Richard. London: Variorum, 1983.

Ringe, Sharon. *Luke.* Westminster Bible Companion. Louisville, KY: Westminster/ John Knox, 1995.

Rogow, Faith. "The Akedah: A Mother's Telling." *B'not Esh Newsletter*, Spring 1984.

Romm, Chava. "Miriam Argues for Her Place as Prophetess." In *A New Haggadah: A Jewish Lesbian Seder*, edited by Judith Stein, 11. Cambridge, MA: Bobbeh Meisehs Press, 1984.

Safi, Omid. "Between '*Ijtihad* of the Presupposition' and Gender Equality: Cross-Pollinations between Progressive Islam and Iranian Reform." In *Rethinking Islamic Studies: From Orientalism to Cosmopolitanism*, edited by Carl Ernst and Richard Martin, 72–96. Columbia: University of South Carolina Press, 2010.

———. *Memories of Muhammad: Why the Prophet Matters.* New York: HarperOne, 2009.

———, ed. *Progressive Muslims: On Justice, Gender, and Pluralism.* Oxford, UK: Oneworld, 2003.

Sanders, E. P. *Judaism: Practice and Belief 63* BCE*–66* CE. Philadelphia: Trinity Press International, 1992.

de Sandoli, Sabina. *Itinera Hierosolymitana Crucesignatorum (saec. XII-XIII).* Vol. 3. Jerusalem: Franciscan Printing Press, 1978.

Schein, Sylvia. "Gesta Dei per Mongolos, 1300." *English History Review* 94 (1979): 805–19.

Schilbrack, Kevin. "The Social Construction of 'Religion' and Its Limits: A Critical Reading of Timothy Fitzgerald." *Method and Theory in the Study of Religion* 24 (2012): 97–117.

Schmidt, Leigh E. *Consumer Rites: The Buying and Selling of American Holidays.* Princeton, NJ: Princeton University Press, 1995.

Scott, James C. "Protest and Profanation: Agrarian Revolt and the Little Tradition, Part I." *Theory and Society* 4.1 (Spring 1977): 1–38.

Scott, R. B. Y. *The Way of Wisdom in the Old Testament*. New York: Macmillan, 1971.

Seder Mincha Simhat Torah. Reprint, Cochin, India: Yaakob Daniel Cohen, [1877].

Shoemaker, Stephen J. *The Death of Muhammad: The End of Muhammad's Life and the Beginnings of Islam*. Philadelphia: University of Pennsylvania Press, 2012.

Siegel, Joel. "Islamic Sharia Law to Be Banned in, ah, Oklahoma." ABC News.com, June 14, 2010. http://abcnews.go.com/US/Media/oklahoma-pass-laws-prohibiting-islamic-sharia-laws-apply/story?id=10908521 (accessed July 8, 2011).

Sinha, Kounteya. "Irish Court Rules Sikhs Can't Wear Turban at Work." *Times of India*, May 31, 2013. http://articles.timesofindia.indiatimes.com/2013-05-31/uk/39654340_1_indian-sikhs-sikh-turban-kirpan (accessed December 19, 2013).

Sinon, D. "Les relations entre les Mongols et l'Europe jusqu'à la mort d'Arghoun et de Béla IV." *Journal of World History* (1957): 193–206.

Skerrett, K. Roberts. "Homosexuals, Heretics, and the Practice of Freedom; Commentary on *Love the Sin: Sexual Regulation and the Limits of Religious Tolerance*." *Studies in Gender and Sexuality* 6.4 (2005): 387–98.

Smart, Ninian. *The Religious Experience*. New York: Macmillan, 1991.

Smith, Jonathan Z. *Drudgery Divine: On the Comparison of Early Christianities and the Religions of Late Antiquity*. Chicago: University of Chicago Press, 1990.

———. *Imagining Religion*. Chicago: University of Chicago Press, 1982.

———. *Map Is Not Territory*. Chicago: University of Chicago Press, 1978.

———. *Relating Religion: Essays in the Study of Religion*. Chicago: University of Chicago Press, 2004.

———. "Religion, Religions, Religious." In *Critical Terms for Religious Studies*, edited by Mark C. Taylor, 269–84. Chicago: University of Chicago Press, 1998.

Snodgrass, Klyne R. *Stories with Intent: A Comprehensive Guide to the Parables of Jesus*. Grand Rapids, MI: Eerdmans, 2008.

Sohn, Ruth. "I Shall Sing to the Lord a New Song." In *Kol Haneshamah: Shabbat Vehagim*, 768–69. Wyncote, PA: Reconstructionist Press, 1994.

Sorensen, Adam. "Obama Breaks His Silence on Cordoba House." *Swampland* blog, August 13, 2010. http://swampland.time.com/2010/08/13/obama-breaks-his-silence-on-cordoba-house/ (accessed July 10, 2011).

Southern, R. W. *Western Views of Islam in the Middle Ages*. Cambridge, MA: Harvard University Press, 1962.

Sullivan, Winnifred F. "'The Church.'" *Immanent Frame*, January 31, 2012. http://blogs.ssrc.org/tif/2012/01/31/the-church/ (accessed April 20, 2014).

———. "Going to Law," *Immanent Frame*, October 13, 2011. http://blogs.ssrc.org/tif/2011/10/13/going-to-law/ (accessed April 20, 2014).

———. *Paying the Words Extra: Religious Discourse in the Supreme Court of the United States*. Cambridge, MA: Harvard University Press, 1994.

Sylvestre de Sacy, Antoine I. "Mémoire sur la dynastie des Assassins, et sur l'origine de leur nom." *Annales des Voyages* 8 (1809): 325–43.

———. "Mémoire sur la dynastie des Assassins, et sur l'origine de leur nom." *Mémoires de l'Institut Royal de France* 4 (1818): 1–84.

"The Theatre: Lavish Musical." *Wall Street Journal*, December 7, 1953, 12.

Theissen, Gerd, and Dagmar Winter. *The Quest for the Plausible Jesus: The Question of Criteria*. Translated by Eugene Boring. Louisville, KY: Westminster/John Knox, 2002.

Tiele, C. P. *Elements of the Science of Religion: Being Gifford Lectures Delivered before the University of Edinburgh in 1896 and 1898*. Edinburgh, UK: Blackwood, 1897, 1899.

Trawick, B. B. "Report of the College Committee on the Academic Study of Religion." Appendix 1 in "A Proposal by the University of Alabama to the Danforth Foundation for a Grant to Assist in the Establishment of a Department of Religion July 12, 1965," A1–A5. Photocopy, Department of Religious Studies, University of Alabama.

Tumulty, Karen, and Michael D. Shear, "Obama: Backing Muslims' Right to Build NYC Mosque Is Not an Endorsement." *Washington Post*, August 15, 2010. http://www.washingtonpost.com/wp-dyn/content/article/2010/08/14/AR2010081401796.html (accessed July 10, 2011).

Turner, Victor. *The Ritual Process: Structure and Anti-Structure*. Ithaca, NY: Cornell University Press, 1977.

Tyerman, C. J. "Marino Sanudo Torsello and the Lost Crusade: Lobbying in the Fourteen Century." *Transactions of the Royal Historical Society* 32 (1982): 57–73.

Umansky, Ellen. "Creating a Jewish Feminist Theology." In *Weaving the Visions: New Patterns in Feminist Spirituality*, edited by Judith Plaskow and Carol P. Christ, 187–98. San Francisco: Harper and Row, 1989.

Varisco, Daniel Martin. *Reading Orientalism: Said and the Unsaid*. Seattle: University of Washington Press, 2007.

Weissler, Chava. "Standing at Sinai." *Journal of Feminist Studies in Religion* 1 (Fall 1984): 91–92.

Whitney, William Dwight. "On the So-Called Science of Religion." *Princeton Review*, May 1881, 451–52.

Wiebe, Donald. "The Failure of Nerve in the Academic Study of Religion." *Studies in Religion* 13.4 (1984): 401–22.

Williams, Delores. *Sisters in the Wilderness: The Challenge of Womanist God-Talk*. Maryknoll, NY: Orbis Books, 1993.

Wilner, Eleanor. *Sarah's Choice*. Chicago: University of Chicago Press, 1990.

Winter, Dagmar. "Saving the Quest for Authenticity from the Criteria of Dissimilarity." In *Jesus, Criteria, and the Demise of Authenticity*, edited by Chris Keith and Anthony Le Donne, 137–61. London: T & T Clark, 2012.

Wordsworth, John. *The One Religion: Truth, Holiness, and Peace Desired by the Nations, and Revealed by Jesus Christ*. Oxford, UK: Parker, 1893.

Wyatt, Edward. "3 Republicans Criticize Obama's Endorsement of Mosque." *New York Times*, August 14, 2010. http://www.nytimes.com/2010/08/15/us/politics /15reaction.html (accessed July 11, 2011).

van den Wyngaert, Anastasius, ed. *Sinica Franciscana*. Vol. 1, *Itinera et Relationes Fratrum Minorum Saeculi XIII et XIV*. Florence, Italy: Collegium S. Bonaventurae, 1929.

Zalman, Schneur. *Shulchan 'Arukh Orech Chayyim*. 4 vols. Brooklyn, NY: Qehot, 1985.

Zeitlin, Solomon. "The Am Haarez: A Study in the Social and Economic Life of the Jews before and after the Destruction of the Second Temple." *Jewish Quarterly Review*, n.s. 23.1 (July 1932): 45–61.

Contributors

Aronov Lecturers

Arjun Appadurai has held professorial chairs at Yale University, the University of Chicago, and the University of Pennsylvania. He is currently Goddard Professor of Media, Culture, and Communication at New York University. His books and scholarly articles, including *Fear of Small Numbers: An Essay on the Geography of Anger* and *Modernity at Large: Cultural Dimensions of Globalization* address a range of topics from cuisine and agriculture to religion, social conflicts, and cricket. He is also one of the founding editors of the journal *Public Culture*.

Aaron W. Hughes is the Philip S. Bernstein Professor of Jewish Studies at the University of Rochester. His research and publications focus on both Jewish philosophy and Islamic studies. He has authored numerous books, including *Situating Islam: The Past and Future of an Academic Discipline, Theorizing Islam: Disciplinary Deconstruction and Reconstruction, Muslim Identities: An Introduction to Islam,* and *Abrahamic Religions: On the Uses and Abuses of History.* He currently serves as the editor of the journal *Method and Theory in the Study of Religion.*

Martin S. Jaffee is the Samuel and Althea Stroum Chair in Jewish Studies at the Jackson School of International Studies at the University of Washington, where he focuses on postbiblical and rabbinic Judaism. He is the author of various books, including *Early Judaism: Religious Worlds of the First Judaic Millennium, The End of Jewish Radar: Snapshots of a Post-Ethnic American Judaism, Mishnah's Theology of Tithing: A Study of Tractate Maaserot,* and *Torah in the Mouth: Writing and Oral Tradition in Palestinian Judaism, 200 BCE–400 CE.*

Nathan Katz is the Bhagwan Mahavir Professor of Jain Studies and professor of religious studies at Florida International University. He has contributed to the formation of Indo-Judaic studies, which highlights the interactions and affinities between Indic and Judaic civilizations. His publications address Jewish communities in India, comparative studies of Judaism, Hinduism, Buddhism, and Jainism, and historical links between India and Israel. His publications include *Who Are the Jews of India?*, the coauthored volume *Indo-Judaic Studies in the Twenty-First Century: A View from the Margin*, and *Buddhist Images of Human Perfection: The Arahant of the Sutta Pitaka Compared with the Bodhisattva and the Mahasiddha*.

Amy-Jill Levine, the E. Rhodes and Leona B. Carpenter Professor of New Testament Studies and professor of Jewish studies at Vanderbilt University, employs textual critical methods to analyze various sacred texts and community interpretations of them. She has been awarded grants from the Mellon Foundation, the National Endowment for the Humanities, and the American Council of Learned Societies. Her books include *The Misunderstood Jew: The Church and the Scandal of the Jewish Jesus*, the edited collection *The Historical Jesus in Context*, and the fourteen-volume edited series *Feminist Companions to the New Testament and Early Christian Writings*.

Bruce Lincoln is the Caroline E. Haskell Professor of the History of Religions at the University of Chicago. While his research often focuses on pre-Christian Europe and pre-Islamic Iran, he is particularly interested in issues of discourse, practice, power, conflict, and the violent reconstruction of social borders. His publications include *Theorizing Myth: Narrative, Ideology, and Scholarship*, which received the AAR Award for Excellence, *Religion, Empire, and Torture: The Case of Achaemenian Persia*, which received the Frank Moore Cross Award from the American Schools of Oriental Research (ASOR), and *Gods and Demons, Priests and Scholars: Critical Explorations in the History of Religions*.

Tomoko Masuzawa is a professor in comparative literature and history at the University of Michigan. Her work has highlighted the context and assumptions informing the creation of the field of religious studies and its dominant discursive structures. She is the author of *In Search of Dreamtime: Quest for the Origin of Religion* and *The Invention of World Religions: or How European Universalism Was Preserved in the Language of Pluralism*, among other works. She has received several fellowships, including through the Getty Research Institute Visiting Scholar (2008), Institute for Advanced Study (School of Social Science, 2010–11), and Guggenheim (2010).

Ann Pellegrini serves as an associate professor of performance studies and religious studies at New York University. She also has directed NYU's Center for the Study of Gender and Sexuality since 2008. She is the author of *Performance Anxieties: Staging Psychoanalysis, Staging Race*, coauthor, with Janet R. Jakobsen, of *Love the Sin: Sexual Regulation and the Limits of Religious Tolerance*, and coeditor, with Jakobsen, of *Secularisms*. Her essay "'Signaling through the Flames': Hell House Performance and Structures of Religious Feeling" won the 2008 Constance Rourke Prize from the American Studies Association.

Judith Plaskow is a professor emerita of religious studies at Manhattan College and a Jewish feminist theologian. She is a cofounder and coeditor of the *Journal of Feminist Studies in Religion* and is the author or editor of numerous works in feminist theology, including *Standing Again at Sinai: Judaism from a Feminist Perspective* and *The Coming of Lilith: Essays on Feminism, Judaism, and Sexual Ethics 1972–2003*.

Jonathan Z. Smith, a professor at the University of Chicago, has had significant influence on the critical study of religion. While his research addresses a wide variety of data from Hellenistic religions and nineteenth-century Maori cults to contemporary American debates, he has analyzed discourses surrounding the category of "religion," the dynamics of comparison, and the notion of canon, among other topics. Some of his books include *Map Is Not Territory: Studies in the History of Religions, Imagining Religion: From Babylon to Jonestown, Drudgery Divine: On the Comparison of Early Christianities and the Religions of Late Antiquity*, and *Relating Religion: Essays in the Study of Religion*.

Other Contributors

Steven Leonard Jacobs is the Aaron Aronov Chair of Judaic Studies at the University of Alabama, a chair he has held since January 1, 2001. His primary research foci are Holocaust and genocide studies as well as the translation and interpretation of early texts, including the Dead Sea Scrolls. Recent books include writing *The Jewish Experience: An Introduction to Jewish History and Jewish Life*, cowriting (with Carl Bartrop) *Fifty Key Thinkers on the Holocaust and Genocide*, and editing *Lemkin on Genocide*.

Russell T. McCutcheon is a professor in the Department of Religious Studies at the University of Alabama. He formally organized the Aronov Lecture series during his first term as department chair, a position he again holds. He teaches and writes on topics such as the rhetoric of religious experience and authenticity, the history of scholarship on myths and rituals, and the relations between the classification "religion" itself and the rise of the nation-state. He has published a range of books, including *Religion and the Domestication of Dissent: Or, How to Live in a Less than Perfect Na-*

tion, *Manufacturing Religion: The Discourse on Sui Generis Religion and the Politics of Nostalgia*, and *The Sacred is the Profane: The Political Nature of "Religion,"* which he coauthored with Willi Braun.

Steven W. Ramey is an associate professor in the Department of Religious Studies at the University of Alabama, where he also directs the Asian Studies Program. Drawing on his study of contemporary religions in India, he has critiqued the world religions paradigm and traditional understandings of religions as distinct entities and extended those insights to critique other contemporary religious labels, including the discourse of the "Nones." His first book, *Hindu, Sufi, or Sikh: Contested Practices and Identifications of Sindhi Hindus in India and Beyond*, illustrates the contested nature of the boundaries constructing Hinduism, Sikhism, and Islam.

Theodore Louis Trost is a professor in the Department of Religious Studies at the University of Alabama, where he recently served as chair. The longest-serving professor currently in the department, his teaching and research emphasize popular culture, New Testament, and American religions. For much of his time at Alabama, he has held a joint appointment with New College, an interdisciplinary program at Alabama. His publications include a monograph, *Douglas Horton and the Ecumenical Impulse in American Religion*, the edited volume *The African Diaspora and the Study of Religion*, and *Teaching African American Religions*, which he coedited with Carolyn M. Jones.

Index